Hang the DJ

HANG THE DJ

An Alternative Book of Music Lists

Edited by Angus Cargill

SOFT SKULL PRESS
NEW YORK

Copyright © Angus Cargill 2009

First published in Great Britain by Faber and Faber Limited.

Library of Congress Cataloging-in-Publication Data is available.

ISBN: 978-1-59376-259-9

Printed in the United States of America

Soft Skull Press
An Imprint of COUNTERPOINT
2117 Fourth Street
Suite D
Berkeley, CA 94710

www.softskull.com
www.counterpointpress.com

Distributed by Publishers Group West

10 9 8 7 6 5 4 3 2 1

Contents

Introduction

Pop music, in its many guises, is perhaps the great art form of our age, at once gloriously dumb and artistically valid. *Hang the DJ* is about being in love with this kind of music. It's for anyone who buys albums or goes to gigs; who has fallen in love to songs, albums or bands. The brief I sent out at the start of this was broad and open, I just asked people to write a list of ten songs or albums, bands or singers, movements or moments – anything that illustrated how and why music was important to them. My hope was that they would react to this as subjectively as possible, and produce lists that revealed things about them, through what they listened to and when. They wouldn't, in other words, be too like the kind of lists you might find in the music magazines or in critics' polls.

So who did I invite? Well, novelists, poets, journalists, musicians, bloggers, plus a couple of friends. I've tried, as much as possible, to present their lists as they were submitted. So from Simon Reynolds' brilliant, if numerically challenged, lists, to David Peace's gloriously grumpy spit and bile ('lists are for fascists and shoppers'), to Kathryn Williams' irreverent life soundtrack, no two are the same in tone or design. There is no theory or cultural criticism here, just a love for music and a celebration of it in all its weird glory.

I remember, in the early 1990s, one of my older sisters coming back from a Manic Street Preachers gig at Nottingham's Rock City, when they were still new and dangerous (and promising to split up after one album).

Aged about fourteen she had, hidden away in her bag, a black and white long sleeved t-shirt. Emblazoned across the back, when she proudly showed it to me in the safety of her room, was the slogan *Molotov Cocktails of Fantastic Destruction*, which was, to my young impressionable mind, inconceivably cool. When my mum finally laid eyes on this anarchic call to arms some days later, however, she wasn't quite sure what to make of it, and asked my sister if she knew what it meant. 'Of course,' she replied defensively, before crumpling into tears. Hardly a revolution. But after a childhood of Neil Diamond, Abba, and Billy Joel, music was starting to become a bit more interesting, and Way Ahead (now, sadly, no longer) suddenly rivalled the Baseball Ground as the most exciting place in Derby. Like the record store in *High Fidelity*, it was an indie store run by people who lived for music, with strange new sounds blaring out of its always open door.

So my teenage years ran through the grunge years and on into Britpop, two often maligned periods, but ones which were, for me, full of wonders. I remember first getting the four-track CD single of Oasis' 'Supersonic', and think it might still be the single most inspiring moment I've known in music. The tension of that opening scratch of the guitar string seemed to promise so much. And, as all good pop music does, this spun me off into broader and more diverse areas. Finding out what's influenced the people you look up to is surely the starting point for any good journey in music and art – and one that repeats itself across movements and decades – and for me there was the Stone Roses on the Byrds, Morrissey and Marr on sixties girl groups and Phil Spector, and Kurt Cobain on Teenage Fanclub and Daniel Johnston.

If you're reading this book then music probably means or has meant something like this to you, and in the lists that follow I hope you'll find stuff to recognise, to argue with and to see anew. From the mainstream to the alternative – by way of rock, pop, blues, country, soul, folk, jazz and even a little touch of classical – the music covered here is pretty eclectic, so, as Bob Dylan said on his very first *Theme Time Radio Hour*, 'We're like the New England weather – if you don't like what you're hearing, stick around, it'll change in a minute.'

Angus Cargill

PURE POP

From stuttered vocals to songs that should have hit the top spot

Owen King / Sam Delaney / Amanda
Petrusich / Simon Reynolds

Spit It Out! Ten Essential Stutter Songs

OWEN KING

Properly employed, there's nothing catchier, cooler, weirder, or funnier than a rock 'n' roll stutter. The sung stutter is a vocal expression of one's inner funkiness. It is the sound of a voice dancing. It's not always pretty, but you have to respect the effort. Singing like this isn't eh-eh-eh-easy!

10 'My Sharona' – The Knack

A quintessential one-hit wonder. All you need to gain rock 'n' roll immortality is a clattering lead-in, a very hungry bass line, and some jive about how her 'd-d-destiny' is to be getting it on with you.

9 'Movin' Out' – Billy Joel

While I'm not a huge fan, there's no denying the brilliance of Joel's delivery of 'heart attack-ack-ack-ack!' To me the 'ack-ack-ack' suggests a Gatling gun, and that naturally brings the end of *The Wild Bunch* to mind, and hey, you can't argue with the Wild Bunch.

8 'Fidelity' – Regina Spektor

This is one of the most recent additions to the stutter canon, a swelling pop song of unusual conviction, and a prime example of the stutter's romantic possibilities. When Ms Spektor says that her 'heart-ah-ah-ah-ha-heart' is breaking, it's impossible not to want to keep her from 'fa-ah-ah-ah-ah-falling'.

7 'You Ain't Seen Nothin' Yet' – Bachman-Turner Overdrive

Kind of cheesy, but kind of awesome. The message of this song is simple: Baby, I'm gonna make you come your brains out. Correction: that should be 'b-b-b-baby'.

6 'Changes' – David Bowie

What a lift this one gives me whenever I hear it. We all know that the last of our 'cha-cha-cha-changes' is going to be from sentience to absolute darkness, but for the three and a half minutes of this song it's hard not to feel an irrepressible hope. And how fun is it to say, 'cha-cha-cha-changes'?

5 'Welcome to the Jungle' – Guns N' Roses

Man, could Axl Rose screech the paint off a barn door, or what? I heard/saw the video for this song for the first time when I was eleven or twelve years old. I thought Axl was going to jump through the screen and bite my face off. So utterly terrifying, I was on my 'sha-nah-nah-nah-nah-nah-KNEES! KNEES!' begging for mercy.

4 'Lola' – The Kinks

That rarest of rock 'n' roll stutters: the lilting singalong stutter. La-la-la-la-Lola is the girl who has launched a thousand drunken karaoke choruses.

3 'My Generation' – The Who

A perfect blast of garage rock, where the stuttering can be heard as either barely contained spite, or jittery teenage energy. However you choose to hear it, there's no denying that Roger Daltrey is an elfin prince of rock 'n' roll poetry. If you're of the older 'g-g-generation' you obviously know that, but you young folks could do worse than to rediscover The Who.

2 'Psycho Killer' – Talking Heads

I'm aware that this could be a controversial choice. When David Byrne sings, 'Fa-fa-fa-fa-fah' does it blend into 'far'? That would make sense; one wants as much distance as possible between oneself and the psycho killer. But I've listened to the song repeatedly, and I can't be 100 per cent certain. He may just be fa-fa-ing, which would make 'Psycho Killer' better suited for the Top 10 Awesome Babble Songs. (By the way, No. 1 on that list is 'Hoodoo Voodoo', lyrics by Woody Guthrie, performance by Wilco and Billy Bragg.) Again, I'm just not sure. What is definite? This song is funky enough to squeeze into any list. Qu'est-ce que c'est? It's the No. 2 song.

1 'Peggy Sue' – Buddy Holly

The *Iliad* of stutter-songs. The instrumentation is muffled and rudimentary, the lyrics are mind-bendingly inane, and you can just smell the unplanned pregnancy waiting around the corner. And it's completely undeniable. 'Peggy Sue-uh-ew-uh-ew' is the girl that turns you to dumb lead. You see her and you can't play your guitar right. You can't think right. Your tongue won't even work.

Teenage Flicks, So Hard to Beat: Ten Songs from Eighties Teen Movies

SAM DELANEY

Those nostalgia shows tell us that the eighties were all about Thatcher, AIDS, Roland Rat and Smiths Square Crisps. But for those of us who grew up in dreary suburbs where seeing a yuppie riding to work on a Sinclair C5 while barking down a 14-stone mobile phone was about as likely as seeing a cat playing the harpsichord, the decade was quite different. It wasn't naff or grim or corny. It was fast paced and cool and sunkissed and fun. That was because we imbibed our sense of time and place through Friday-night video marathons involving movies about cool American kids who had much better lives than our own. They had rich parents, flawless skin and a swimming pool out back. Even the fifteen-year-olds drove to school in Porsches and the worst thing that ever happened to them was getting flicked with a wet towel by jocks in the locker room. Never mind that, back in England we were being mugged at knifepoint for our limited-edition Boba Fett figures at the school gates, then having to get three buses home in the pouring rain. We were living vicariously through those movies. We'd shuffle down to the local corner shop and survey their minuscule selection of dusty VHS tapes, picking out anything that featured Anthony Michael Hall, Molly Ringwald or Judd Nelson. Then we'd scuttle home and watch in awe as these supposedly angst-ridden American youths played out an impossibly glamorous high-school love affair to an exhilarating soundtrack of power pop and feelgood rock. Ah, those soundtracks. This was the birth

10

of the MTV era, when Hollywood studios wanted their movies to be like elongated music videos. Often, they were little more than ninety-minute montages in which kids would drive to school wearing Ray Ban Wayfarers, visit the mall, arrange a secret keg party while their folks were away, create a beautiful woman on their home computer or travel through time in a DeLorean sports car. The fast-cut sequences would all be set to music rich in lengthy sax breaks, ostentatious guitar licks, electro drum solos and indulgent use of the 'keytar'. The writers and directors might have thought they were making poignant meditations on adolescent frustration and insecurity but that kind of gloomy subtext was usually drowned out by the merry warbling of Kenny Loggins or Huey Lewis, who made teenage life seem so much easier to cope with. Mum and Dad don't understand you? Cheerleaders don't know you exist? Brother turning into a vampire? Who cares! Hire a hooker! Learn karate! Take some tanning pills and pretend to be black in order to get into Harvard! This is the eighties! It's hip to be square! Woo-hoo! Anyway, here are the cinematic musical moments that, back then, briefly helped me believe that I was in on the whole sexy world of teen misadventure in the suburbs of Illinois. Not stuck in Hammersmith waiting for the microwave to finish warming my Findus Crispy Pancakes.

10 'Oh Yeah' – Yello (from *Ferris Bueller's Day Off*)

Ferris Bueller is faking stomach cramps to get the day off school. It works, his parents leave for work and his day of freedom begins. You know it's going to be the most exciting day of his life because 'Oh Yeah' by Swiss electro-popsters Yello is creeping into your ears while Ferris delivers his opening monologue. This song contains every single noise you associate with eighties music – a heady concoction of bleeps, zings and squelches that sound like Metal Mickey puking all over a Yamaha Portasound. During the mid-eighties, it was as if the Directors Guild of America had enforced the use of this track on any movie of a jocular nature, with *Teen Wolf*, *The Secret of My Success*, *Planes, Trains and Automobiles*, *She's out of Control* and *K-9* also making use of its era-defining sound.

9 'Weird Science' – Oingo Boingo (from *Weird Science*)

When new wavers Oingo Boingo were hired by John Hughes to provide the title track for his 1985 film about two nerds who create a gorgeous girlfriend on their home computer, they took the literal route. 'She's alive!' it opens, over a pop-funk mix of meandering bass line and blasting horns. During the course of the opening credits, the song's lyrics almost blow the film's entire plot 'Plastic tubes and pots and pans / Bits and pieces and magic from the hand', snarls singer Danny Elfman, outlining the girl-friend-creation process. 'Not what teacher said to do / Living tissue, warm flesh'. All right already! We get the picture!

8 'You're the Best' – Joe Esposito (from *The Karate Kid*)

Director John G. Avildsen defined the sports-movie montage scene when he made *Rocky*. Here, he twinned inspirational rock music with scenes of athletic violence to similar effect, as Daniel LeRusso kicks and chops his way to the final of the All Valley Karate Tournament. 'Try to be the best / 'Cause you're only a man / And a man's gotta learn to take it', growls Esposito. I would play these lyrics through my mind prior to every PE lesson. Didn't make me any better at football, mind.

7 'People Are Strange' – Echo and the Bunnymen (from *The Lost Boys*)

There's not much room for subtlety and nuance in an eighties teen movie. Usually, they like to explain the premise within about the first thirty seconds and the right choice of song can play a crucial role in this. As the Emerson family (played by eighties cinema royalty Dianne Wiest, Jason Patric and Corey Haim) arrive in Santa Carla, Echo and the Bunnymen's spooky cover of the Doors' 'People Are Strange' plays over imagery of missing-person posters, teens wearing black lipstick and a suspiciously vampire-like Kiefer Sutherland skulking about in a fairground. Something tells you this film might be a bit edgier than *Pretty in Pink*.

6 'Soul Man' – Sam and Dave (from *Soul Man*)

C. Thomas Howell has pretended to be black in order to win a scholarship to Harvard. It's all going swimmingly until he tries out for the basketball team. He's rubbish! He keeps falling over and getting the ball in his face! This can't be right, he's black . . . aren't all black people good at . . . oh, hang on, this entire film is a bit racist, isn't it? Why didn't I realise this when I was eleven? Because Sam and Dave were distracting me with this sublime title track, that's why. This was just one example of how eighties film soundtracks reintroduced a post-punk generation to vintage soul (see also *Stand by Me*, *The Big*

Chill). Oh, and in case the basketball scene isn't quite rife enough with racial stereotypes for you, check out the movie's tagline: 'He didn't give up. He got down.'

5 'St Elmo's Fire (Man in Motion)' – John Parr (from *St Elmo's Fire*)

The definitive Brat Pack movie: 110 minutes of Estevez, Nelson, Sheedy, Moore, Lowe and McCarthy running around in sunglasses, smoking fags, dancing and shouting while this pumping soft-rock anthem bellows almost incessantly in the background. What the hell is going on? It's impossible to tell and John Parr's lyrics don't help much either: phrases like 'You're just a prisoner', 'Sometime if you feel the pain' and 'I'll be where the eagle's flyin'' lead you to suspect it was written by a special 'Random 1980s Rock Lyric Generator'. In fact, Parr wrote the track in tribute to a paralysed Canadian athlete called Rick Hansen.

4 'Old Time rock 'n' roll' – Bob Seger (from *Risky Business*)

Tom Cruise's Joel Goodsen is a high-school student who's been left alone in his palatial family home for the week. Endless possibilities stretch out before him. How does he embrace this thrilling opportunity? He gets a little bit drunk on his own and dances around the living room in his pants to some dad-rock. Yes, in retrospect he was a loser. But through my adolescent eyes, Cruise was the very definition of maverick cool. Even in those ill-advised white socks. Like every other teenager in the world, I made a ham-fisted attempt at imitating the scene the first time I was left home alone. It didn't quite feel the same with my mum's Elkie Brooks LP providing the soundtrack though.

3 'Never' – Moving Picture (from *Footloose*)

However, I can't say I ever tried to mimic Kevin Bacon's seminal 'angry barn dance' in *Footloose*. That was way beyond my athletic abilities. Frustrated by the blanket ban on rock music imposed by his hometown elders, Bacon's Ren McCormack takes refuge in a moodily lit barn. As the opening notes of Moving Picture's 'Never' begin pounding in the background, he angrily throws his beer bottle against the wall with almost balletic poise. Before you know it, the melodramatic power ballad is in full swing and Bacon has stripped down to his vest, pulling off all sorts of rage-infused somersaults and star jumps around the barn. It's spectacular. When a girl turns up applauding his performance, he acts all shy and says, 'What are you doing here? I thought I was alone?' Yeah, course you did, Bacon. That's how everyone dances when they think no one's looking. You big fat weird liar!

2 'Don't You Forget About Me' – Simple Minds (from *The Breakfast Club*)

It might be the most renowned movie of the genre but in many ways *The Breakfast Club* is an atypical teen flick. It succeeded in mustering the sort of pathos and poignancy that is drowned out by pranks and pop music in most other films of the era. Five high-school stereotypes form unlikely bonds during the course of a day-long detention. My adolescent soul was touched. And when the appropriately sombre yet uplifting Simple Minds anthem simmered in at the end, it was hard not to come over a bit dewy eyed. 'Jocks, nerds, cheerleaders . . . can't the grown-ups see we're all the same inside?' I muttered tearily to myself as Jim Kerr screamed the word 'don't' over and over again. All right, there were no jocks or cheerleaders at my school. But I still got the idea, okay?

1 'The Power of Love' – Huey Lewis and the News (from *Back to the Future*)

Here was a movie that shamelessly distilled everything that was exciting and cool about eighties teen epics, threw away the angst and navel-gazing bits and chucked a time-travelling sports car into the mix for good measure. It was a rip-roaring, spellbinding romp that created in Marty McFly the super-cool nerd we all wanted to be. Aged ten, it was the first time I got to go to the cinema without a parent; I sat next to my mate Shaun in Hammersmith ABC in awestruck, open-mouthed glee as Huey Lewis and the News blasted this exhilarating, pop-rock fanfare over the opening titles. Hearing it now still transports me back to that shabby, sticky floored, puke-smelling theatre where I spent two of the happiest hours of my entire youth.

'I'd Just Like to Take a Little of Your Time Here': Ten Spoken Interludes in Pop

AMANDA PETRUSICH

Sometimes, when plain old melisma is no longer satisfactory, and when singing alone fails to convey sufficient gravitas, pop vocalists may abruptly stop howling, lower their eyes, curl up to a microphone and launch into a spoken sermon. For the artist, it's an opportunity to inject a straightforward narrative into a story riddled with metaphor. For listeners, it's exceptionally weird – a dismantling of the fourth wall that's as unwelcome as it is disconcerting.

Spoken interludes are oddly common in classic country and R&B songs (see Elvis, the Shangi-Las, Clarence Carter, Baby Huey) and a handful of contemporary artists have maintained the practice – some earnestly appropriating the form (Boyz II Men, Michael Jackson, Britney), some snickering under their breath (Beck, the Velvet Underground). The best mid-song musing is usually spontaneous and strange, flanked by traditionally sung verses, and often only tangentially related to the rest of the track. Witness the Top 10 spoken interludes in the middle of otherwise unremarkable pop songs: all excellent fodder for karaoke.

10 'Give Him a Great Big Kiss' – The Shangri-Las

What colour are his eyes?

The opening line of 'Give Him a Great Big Kiss' – 'When I say I'm in love, you best believe I'm in love, L-U-V!' – is deeply revered, and has been referenced (in song) by

17

everyone from the New York Dolls to Ryan Adams. But it's the Shangri-Las' admission that the fellow in question is 'always wearing shades' that, perhaps, offers the deepest insight.

9 'Making Love (At the Dark End of the Street)' – Clarence Carter

I'd just like to take a little of your time here . . .

Clarence Carter's interpretation of James Carr's 'The Dark End of the Street' is, in all fairness, more a spoken-word piece than a proper song, although Carter does eventually begin singing – but not before explaining to 'children' how he likes to get himself fifty cents' worth of gas, drive way down a country road, and make love on the back seat of a car.

8 'Oops! I Did it Again' – Britney Spears

Britney, before you go, there's something I want you to have / Oh, it's beautiful, but wait a minute, isn't this . . .

Spears's homage to the interlude is particularly absurdist: aside from referencing *Titanic* apropos of nothing, it appears to have little or no relevance to the rest of the song.

7 'Hot for Teacher' – Van Halen

Whaddaya think the teacher's gonna look like this year? / My butt, man!

Van Halen insert a variety of hollered interludes into 'Hot for Teacher', and almost all are poorly rendered, if delightful, double-entendres.

6 'Debra' – Beck

Girl, I only wanna be down with you / 'Cause you got something that I just got to get with

It's hard to figure out how Beck maintains his falsetto with his tongue planted so firmly in his cheek. And yet: 'Debra' is an eerily accurate send-up of squealing soul smarm.

5 'End of the Road' – Boyz II Men

All those times of night when you just hurt me / And just run out with that other fella . . .

Boyz II Men managed to inject a spoken monologue into nearly all of their slow jams, thus making good, consistent use of Michael McCary's unnervingly deep voice.

4 'I Found a Reason' – The Velvet Underground

And I've walked down life's lonely highways / Hand in hand with myself . . .

It's likely that Lou Reed slipped this spoken verse into the middle of 'I Found a Reason' to spoof Elvis Presley, although (as with *Metal Machine Music*) Reed's true intentions remain largely unknown.

3 'Hard Times' – Baby Huey and the Babysitters

Eating Spam / And Oreos / And drinking Thunderbird, baby

Here, Baby Huey pauses to offer his audience a long, hard look at the ramifications 'hard times' may have on one's diet.

2 'Thriller' – Michael Jackson

Darkness falls across the land / The midnight hour is close at hand . . .

Vincent Price's mid-song exposition is useful in that it continues to give amateur dancers ample time to get into position before launching into the 'Thriller' video's famed zombie stomp.

1 'Are You Lonesome Tonight?' – Elvis Presley

Honey, you lied when you said you loved me / And I had no cause to doubt you . . .

Perhaps the best-known example of a spoken interlude, over one-third of Elvis Presley's 'Are You Lonesome Tonight?' is said rather than sung. The passage was loosely based on a monologue from *As You Like It*, and Presley had a tendency to spontaneously rework the lyrics, often to humorous effect – on 26 August 1969, while playing a show at the International Hotel in Las Vegas, Presley switched the line 'Do you gaze at your doorstep and wish I was there?' to 'Do you gaze at your bald head and wish you had hair?' before succumbing to a fit of giggles. A live recording of Presley's crack-up became a Top 10 hit in the UK in 1983 after it was released as a single.

Deserving but Denied: Thirty-three No. 2s That Should Have Been No. 1

SIMON REYNOLDS

It's obvious that you can't rely on the pop charts as a mechanism for tabulating the comparative excellence of hit records. But the charts are actually not much better at displaying how *popular* a pop single is. Because the volume of releases from the industry and the amount of purchasing power out there in Consumerland both fluctuate with the seasons, a No. 1 single in an off-peak period – like the post-Christmas lull of January – can have sold less than any Top 10 single during busier times of the year. The chart placing of a record is also affected by pure contingency – what releases by heavy-hitter groups just happen to go out at the same time. (Tough luck for all those sixties greats who happened to release a single the same week as The Beatles or The Stones.) This list honours those fantastically fine and/or epochal singles that were cheated by some historical quirk or other from fulfilling their true destiny: getting to No. 1. Upon investigation, these injustices turned out to be so numerous that the list-of-ten format overspilled thrice over, even after leaving out many fabulous No. 2 singles.

'My Generation' – The Who (November 1965)

It stands to reason that the sixties was a cruelly competitive decade. All the genius and creative energy around meant that many classic singles – the Dave Clark Five's 'Bits and Pieces', Petula Clark's 'Downtown', the Troggs' 'Wild Thing' – fell just short of the top spot. But it seems

21

particularly unjust that The Who's defining anthem of mod frustration and pride never went all the way. Indeed, a measure of The Who's distant third stature compared with The Beatles and The Stones was that they never would score a No. 1 at all.

'Penny Lane'/'Strawberry Fields Forever' – The Beatles (February 1967)

Arguably the Fab Four's greatest double A-side and conceivably the world's first concept single (both sides addressing the theme of nostalgia and helping to kick-start psychedelia's cult of childhood), this release none the less ended The Beatles' unbroken run of No. 1s (eleven in all) that went back to 1963's 'From Me to You'. Perhaps 'Strawberry Fields' was just too trippy for the general public, for a similar fate befell the equally out-there *Magical Mystery Tour* EP ('I Am the Walrus' etc.) at the other end of 1967.

'Waterloo Sunset' – The Kinks (May 1967)

One of a number of '67-defining singles – see also Traffic's 'Hole in My Shoe' – to stall at the runner-up spot, 'Waterloo Sunset's shortfall is particularly poignant because the song constitutes the summit of Ray Davies's achievement as a songwriter (give or take the Indian summer that was 1968's *The Kinks Are the Village Green Preservation Society*).

'I Want You Back' – The Jackson 5 (January 1970)

Anybody looking to prove that the universe is a botched creation ruled over by a callous, vindictive demiurge

22

need only point to the shocking not-actually-number-one-ness of this pop-soul cataclysm.

'American Pie' – Don McLean (January 1972)

As if somehow *always already* a 'golden oldie', this was a monstrously prolonged radio hit, and zeitgeist-wise it distilled the early-seventies mood of melancholy retrospection. But despite sixteen weeks on the chart it never actually topped it.

'Rock and Roll (Parts 1 & 2)' – Gary Glitter (June 1972)

Massive in discos, the almost-instrumental Part 2 was what drove Glitter's breakthrough single to the very edge of pop's peak. At once lumpen and avant-garde, the missing link between the Troggs and techno, this controlled stampede of caveman chants and dead-echoing guitar doesn't actually sound anything like the fifties rock 'n' roll it purports to resurrect. The following year's 'Do You Wanna Touch Me' and 'Hello! Hello! I'm Back Again' also stopped one place short, before 'I'm the Leader of the Gang (I Am)' finally put Glitter and genius producer Mike Leander where they belonged.

'Crazy Horses' – The Osmonds (November 1972)

Surprisingly hard-rockin' tune from the Mormon clan, with a whinnying synth-riff that winnowed its way into your brain and refused to budge. Kept off the top spot by Chuck Berry's execrable 'My Ding-a-Ling', but the Osmonds could take consolation from their own Little Jimmy's subsequent annexation of the Christmas No. 1 with the execrabler still 'Long Haired Lover from Liverpool'.

'Solid Gold Easy Action' – T. Rex (December 1972)

No. 1s galore under his belt, Marc Bolan can't complain about his treatment at the hands of the UK chart. That said, despite The Beatles-level fandemonium of T. Rextasy, several of his best tunes – 'Ride a White Swan', 'Jeepster' (held off by Benny Hill's 'Ernie (The Fastest Milkman in the West)'!), and 'Children of the Revolution' – swooped to No. 2 but never scaled pop's summit. Likewise 'Solid Gold Easy Action', Marc's strangest single of all, with its jolting beat, enigmatic title and the sculpted hysteria of its chorus.

'The Ballroom Blitz' – Sweet (September 1973)

From its deliciously campy intro patter ('Are you ready, boys?' etc.) to its frisky Bo Diddley beat, Blitz is the definitive Sweet monstertune, but – despite entering at No. 2 and hovering there for three weeks – it stayed *stuck*. Oddly, the same chart position was reached by its immediate predecessor 'Hell Raiser' *and* immediate successor 'Teenage Rampage' *and* the latter-day ultra-classic 'Fox on the Run'. Sole Sweetsingle to go all the way: 'Blockbuster'.

'This Town Ain't Big Enough for the Both of Us' – Sparks (May 1974)

Branded into the memory-flesh of anyone who saw the Mael brothers perform it on *Top of the Pops*, this torrid, swashbuckling fantasia was fended off the pole position by the Rubettes' sickly 'Sugar Baby Love'. Five years later Sparks tried to restore some cosmic balance with the would-be self-fulfilling prophecy of 'Number One

Song in Heaven' but, despite killer Eurodiscotronic production from Giorgio Moroder, to no avail.

'You Sexy Thing' – Hot Chocolate (November 1975)

As quintessentially seventies as Sparks or Sweet, these hardy hit-parade perennials paused poised at No. 2 for three weeks (thanks to the juggernaut that was Queen's 'Bohemian Rhapsody') with this risqué slice of Britfunk. Errol Brown's delivery of such explicit (for its time and context) adult content as 'Now you're lying next to me / Giving it to me' and 'Now you're lying close to me / Making love to me' flushed many a pre-teen cheek even though the song spoke of things beyond our ken. Touchingly, the 'miracle' Errol believed in was apparently his missus, Ginette. Consolation prize for not making it all the way: re-releases and remixes have made 'You Sexy Thing' the only song to be a UK Top 10 hit in the seventies, eighties *and* nineties.

'Silly Love Songs' and 'Let 'Em In' – Wings (summer 1976)

Culminating with bestselling-single-of-the-seventies 'Mull of Kintyre', 1976–7 was Macca's most successful post-Beatles phase (with the possible exception of 1983–4, but the latter period was non-stop dreck). This brace of winsome confections from *Wings at the Speed of Sound* confirmed everything the detractors (from Lennon on down) said about Paul's sweet tooth and miniaturist craftsmanship. But you'd have to be pretty hard-of-heart to resist their considerable charm, plus the metapop of 'Silly Love Songs' cannily deflects all critique in advance with its upfront and unashamed candour.

'Boogie Nights' – Heatwave (February 1977)

This sublime shimmer of discofunk hovered at No. 2 on both the UK chart (where it was eclipsed by Leo Sayer, God help us) and the *Billboard* Hot 100, appropriately enough given the group's transatlantic line-up. Heatwave's British keyboard player and 'Boogie Nights' songwriter Rod Temperton went on to pen 'Rock with You', 'Thriller' and other hits for Michael Jackson.

'God Save the Queen' – The Sex Pistols (June 1977)

Punk folklore maintains that conniving by the authorities kept this act of sonic sedition off the top spot to avoid the treasonous insult to Her Majesty during the Silver Jubilee. On one of the rival UK Top 40 charts, the No. 2 space was, in an Orwellian twist, blanked out altogether, turning the Pistols into an unband and 'God Save the Queen' into an unsingle, unrelease, unhit. Meanwhile Rod Stewart's 'I Don't Want to Talk About It'/ 'First Cut Is the Deepest' sealed over the cracks in the British polity by maintaining its emollient grip on No. 1 for a fourth week.

'Oliver's Army' – Elvis Costello and the Attractions (February 1979)

Costello's one true pop moment (his only other Top 10 hits were cover versions: 'I Can't Stand up for Falling Down' and 'A Good Year for the Roses'), so it's sad that this Abba-influenced piano-rippling number didn't climb to the highest height.

'Cool for Cats' and 'Up the Junction' – Squeeze (spring 1979)

More new wavers not getting their proper dues. Touted as heirs to Lennon–McCartney, choonsmith Chris Difford and wordsman Glenn Tilbrook narrowly missed No. 1 twice in the first half of 1979 with the cheeky disco-flavoured 'Cats' and the poignant sixties-evoking social realism of 'Junction'.

'Pop Muzik' – M (April 1979)

One of those hits so inescapably dominant that you have to rub your eyes in disbelief when checking the Guinness hit singles guide and discovering it never actually made it to No. 1. Robin Scott's proto-pomo metapop celebration was naturally a wow with radio DJs (as it was calculated to be), which doubtless explains the aura of ubiquitousness that clings to this tune. But Art Garfunkel's 'Bright Eyes' stopped its rise.

'Kings of the Wild Frontier' and 'Antmusic' – Adam and the Ants (summer/winter 1980)

Adam and his merry minions at their most witty ('Antmusic') and thrillingly tribal ('Kings' – ooh that double-drummer polyrhythmic intro). In consolation, the Antman would subsequently make it to No. 1 three times (most notably with the autumn-of-'81 dominating 'Prince Charming') before his star faded.

'Vienna' – Ultravox (January 1981)

Can't say I was ever a huge fan, but as a synthpop-era defining slice of pseudo-Mitteleuropa pomp, this deserved better than to hover beneath Joe Dolce's 'Shaddap You Face' for a full three weeks.

'O Superman' – Laurie Anderson (October 1981)

With Radio 1's evening DJs and then daytime jocks too falling into lockstep with John Peel, this vocodered oddity by downtown New York performance artist/ experimental composer Laurie Anderson joined the grand British tradition of novelty hits. But despite the cod-surrealist spectacle of an interpretative dance by the resident leggy troupe on *Top of the Pops* (there being no video and Anderson having declined to perform) 'Superman's climb was halted.

'Happy Birthday' – Altered Images (winter 1981/82)

Seventeen weeks on the charts and three of them at No. 2, this irresistible bounce 'n' shimmer of fizzy glee was a chart topper in all but hard unforgiving fact. With the gorgeous 'I Could Be Happy' they tried the classic trick of releasing a follow-up that contains the same keyword in its title (see Pete Frampton's 'Show Me the Way' and 'Baby I Love Your Way') but never hit as big again.

'Golden Brown' – The Stranglers (January 1982)

Only their second hit single about heroin (the first was 'Don't Bring Harry', their sick-and-twisted offering as Christmas single in 1979) but it sure would have been nice 'n' sleazy if they'd gone all the way with this beguiling waltz-time oddity. A fitting capper to the Stranglers' career as new wave's most prolific hit machine. Alas . . .

'Welcome to the Pleasuredome' – Frankie Goes to Hollywood (March 1985)

Not so much on its musical merits: a grand glistening Horn production of cinematic funk, it's a lot of record but not a lot of *song*. But getting a record-breaking four No. 1s with your first four singles would have been just reward for Frankie and ZTT Records having brought some tumultuous eventfulness to an otherwise fairly barren 1984.

'Push It' – Salt-N-Pepa (June 1988)

Golden age hip hop at its most hooky and instant, the electro-pulsating groove resembles a funked-up Devo (hark at the titular echo of 'Whip It'!) but the raunch of the vocals makes Salt-N-Pepa come over like the female equivalent/equal of Rick 'Superfreak' James.

'Groove Is in the Heart' – Deee-Lite (September 1990)

So omnipresent that its charm turned to irritant in record time, it's almost impossible to believe this wasn't a No. 1. Apparently, it *was*. Sales-wise 'Groove' tied with the reissue of Steve Miller Band's 'The Joker', so an arcane rule of chart tabulation was invoked and 'The Joker' was granted the supreme position because its sales had gone up more from the previous week.

'Justified and Ancient' – The KLF (December 1991)

Although Bill Drummond made it to No. 1 with the 'Timelords' (and then published a manual on how to have a No. 1 single) and then again with the KLF's '3 AM Eternal', it's still sad that his greatest feat as pop conceptualist and mischief-maker – getting Tammy Wynette to

29

sing 'They're justified and they're ancient / And they like to roam the land' over a house beat on *TOTP* – was not appropriately rewarded.

'Everybody in the Place' (EP) – The Prodigy (January 1992)

Hardcore rave classic thwarted by the *Wayne's World* spin-off re-release of 'Bohemian Rhapsody'. Gah!

'Raving I'm Raving' – Shut Up and Dance (May 1992)

What is it about ardkore rave and the number two? See also: SL2's marvellous 'On a Ragga Tip' the month before and Smart E's admittedly ridiculous 'Sesame's Treet' later that summer. 'Raving I'm Raving' went straight in the charts at No. 2 and might have gone higher if it hadn't had to be withdrawn on account of its hefty samples from Mark Cohn's AOR ballad 'Walking in Memphis'.

'Common People' – Pulp (June 1995)

Britpop's finest four minutes: Pulp's epic anthem brought class struggle back to the pop charts, the honed wit and keenly observed economy of the lyric confirming Jarvis Cocker to be the best wordsmith of his kind since Morrissey. It entered at No. 2 but was barred from full triumph by Robson and Jerome's 'Unchained Melody'.

'Heartbroken' – T2 feat. Jodie Aysha (December 2007)

The North rises again. Flagship tune of the vibrant 'bass-line house' scene (a UK garage offshoot based in Sheffield, Nottingham, Leeds, Huddersfield, and other

30

northern cities) the deliciously pop-frothy 'Heartbroken' crossed over big time, but in the end proved unable to breach the barricade of banality that was 'Bleeding Love' by *X-Factor* champion Leona Lewis.

HEARTBREAKERS

From Tom Waits to camping-trailer blues

Miriam Toews / Angus Cargill / Laura
Barton / Willy Vlautin

HEARTBREAKERS

From Tom Waits to camping-trailer blues

Miriam Toews / Angus Cargill / Laura
Barton / Willy Vlautin

How Not to Get Laid: The Ten Saddest Tom Waits Songs

MIRIAM TOEWS

When I saw Tom Waits perform live during his *Mule Variations* tour, he mentioned that he writes two types of songs – 'Grim Reapers and Grand Weepers'. This list is about the latter. The Waitsian pantheon is littered with sad songs like empty bottles and crushed cigarette packs – really, you could take half of *Blue Valentine* and half of *Mule Variations*, or *Small Change*, or – well, you name it – and you would have one seriously sad album.

But then what? What would that do for you? I remember reading an interview with Waits – and they were always so rare so it was really exciting when you could actually find one – where he said, 'No one ever got laid listening to my albums.' It's probably true. I've always been impressed by guys with good taste in music but I've personally never found sadness to be much of an aphrodisiac.

Tom at his saddest manages to merge the lowlife poeticism of Charles Bukowski with the sweetness of a baby's lullaby. He channels childhood innocence in a way that makes you long for that simplicity but still remember how much it hurt when your ten-year-old neighbour broke your tiny yearning heart. But what really, really takes it off the charts is when his characters become the broken and damaged ghosts of the streets – lurching from skid row to the charity ward and then reverting to the children they were before they became the damned.

I love Tom Waits. I've been listening to him since I was a kid, freak that I was. Every album from *Closing Time* all the way up to *Orphans*. This list, by the way, doesn't include any songs from *Orphans*' 'Bawlers' disc – that just wouldn't be fair. This list is about the truly, truly mournful sad songs. It's about the songs where at some point you just shake your head at the stereo and go 'Jesus, Tom – Man! Cheer the fuck up!'

But at the same time you don't want him to – you want him to put that universal sadness down, sing and scream from his spleen and give voice to your own sorrow in a way no one else ever could. You want a glass of whisky – probably need a smoke too – but there's comfort in knowing you're not alone in that melancholy, that all the creatures from this miserable tapestry are stoically raising a glass with you. Hell no, I'm not crying – just got some smoke in my eye, that's all. But I'm still going to keep my pants on.

10 'Christmas Card from a Hooker in Minneapolis' (*Blue Valentine*, 1978)

Well this one makes the cut first on title alone, though 'Misery Is the River of the World' was right behind it. As the title says, it's a Christmas card from a prostitute to an old friend – likely an old boyfriend named Charley – about other old boyfriends, family long gone, getting sober, getting off the dope, settling down with a decent husband who is going to raise the boy she imagines is in her pregnant belly '. . . like he was his own son'. All of it – as it turns out – a complete pack of desperate junkie lies.

9 'Innocent When You Dream, Barroom' (*Frank's Wild Years*, 1987)

Yes, it is such a sad old feeling when Tom mourns – in only three verses – lost love, childhood friendship, and then, well . . . lost love again. This is a true drunken weeper – best played loud. Drink far too much and sing along. Wake up alone – again.

8 'All the World Is Green' (*Blood Money*, 2002)

Most recently featured on the Julian Schnabel film *The Diving Bell & the Butterfly*, this has all the elements for Tom to ratchet up the sad quotient. A marriage gone wrong, a plea for forgiveness and a longing for the way things were. It has that sweet romanticism of looking back and remembering everything as being perfect – as the title says – but you just know something really, really bad happened to mess things up.

7 'Georgia Lee' (*Mule Variations*, 1999)

When it comes to dead young girls it's hard to pull any punches and Tom gets right down to it on this little feel-good number. First two lines – 'Cold was the night, and hard was the ground / They found her in a small grove of trees'. A short lament about lost youth and innocence that boldly chastises God for not being on the job and taking care of this kid – 'Why wasn't God watching?' You have to admit, it's a pretty sad song that takes God to task for being asleep at the switch instead of watching over a little girl being, quite likely, brutally murdered.

6 'Kentucky Avenue' (*Blue Valentine*, 1978)

A trip down memory lane, back to the old neighbour-hood and running wild with all the delinquent childhood friends who lived in it. Except this neighbourhood has a crazy old lady who'll 'stab you with steak knife if you step on her lawn' and a gal named 'Hilda' who not only plays strip poker, but Joey Navinsky swears 'she put her tongue in his mouth'. It's *West Side Story* without the dance-fighting – just inner-city kids being kids – except for the end, where the narrator professes his love or heart-wrenching pity for a handicapped girl: cripples AND bowery boys. Come on!

5 'Blue Valentines' (*Blue Valentine*, 1978)

A weeper made even weepier by jazz chords over a blues bass line – there is a howling desperation in every line Tom sings – he screams angrily, gets whispery soft – even throws in a little vulnerable falsetto for good measure. He sings the living shit out of this song – it's broken hearts on top of broken hearts.

4 'On the Nickel' (*Heartattack and Vine*, 1980)

A tune made sadder if you see the Ralph Waite film of the same name, a movie about 'The Nickel' – skid row in Los Angeles. The song, like the film, is less about the winos and bowery bums than it is about the little boys inside them – who they were and how they still have the same hopes and dreams – except now they're alkies on the bum.

3 'Tom Traubert's Blues' (*Small Change*, 1976)

Wasted and wounded indeed, from the full-on bawling and boozy Tom period, cribbing mournfully from the Australian anthem 'Waltzing Matilda', each and every verse is a drunkard's lament – bumming change, staggering skid-row city streets all melancholy and drunk on Bushmills and heartbreak – this is early Tom at his full-on saddest. Play it for your girl/boyfriend – watch them leave.

2 'The Day After Tomorrow' (*Real Gone*, 2004)

I played this song for a . . . well, very sensitive friend of mine – prefaced with 'Hey, listen to this – I think this might just be the saddest Tom Waits song ever.' When it was over, he screamed at me 'Don't you EVER – EVER play that song for me again!' It's not only an aching lament, it's quite likely the most political song Tom has ever done, written from the point of view of a twenty-one-year-old soldier questioning the whole concept of fighting anyone, or for any cause – other than to stay alive.

1 'The Train Song' (*Frank's Wild Years*, 1987)

Full disclosure – this is personal. I hadn't really paid much attention to this song – it was just part of the seemingly perpetual Tom Waits soundtrack in my house. Then, not too long after my father checked out of this world by laying down in front of a freight train on the most lonesome patch of prairie imaginable, my husband tactfully had this song playing at massive volume and I was truly shocked – it was as though Tom was describing my old man's sorrow and terrible tragic end completely personally. 'When the hell did he write that?' Thankfully, it turned out it pre-dated my dad's demise and Tom wasn't actually directly channelling my sorrow – where he found it makes no difference. Still, as a testament to its complete and overwhelming sadness, I haven't been able to listen to the whole thing since without losing my shit and breaking down. This song howls in desperation and bleeds a river of tears – it's freaking brilliant.

The Reverend Doctor William Grace: Ten Songs of Heartache, Misery and Woe

ANGUS CARGILL

Rock stars, and especially country and soul singers, aren't known for enjoying long, happy relationships. I guess you could say it's all part and parcel of the sex, drugs and rock 'n' roll lifestyle. And let's face it; security and happiness don't make for good material. So here – from the mournful to the devastated – are some of the great minor-chord songs.

10 'Let Me Down Easy' – Bettye LaVette

Along with Candi Staton, of her early FAME studios recordings, Bettye LaVette is the true queen of heartbroken soul. Released as a single in 1965 (inexplicably, no one would give her an album release for nearly twenty years) this is her signature tune. A truly great band performance and a lyric of horrible resignation, which hangs on the repetition of the word 'please', this is a staggering track of heartbreaking genius.

9 'The Dark End of the Street' – James Carr

This is a cheating song as opposed to a break-up song – sung by an adulterer to his secret lover – but it is no less heartbreaking for it. Written by Dan Penn and Chips Moman, it was first recorded by the undervalued James Carr, and it's his glorious, lamenting vocal 'they're going to find us someday' combined with the classic Southern soul sound that marks this as a great. It's been widely covered since, but the Flying Burrito

Brothers' version, led by 'Sneaky' Pete Kleinow's stunning pedal-steel guitar, is the other one well worth checking out.

8 'My Sweet Annette' – Drive-By Truckers

One of the great contemporary American bands, the DBTs combine country, blues, folk and heavy rock. Here, Patterson Hood – son of legendary Muscle Shoals session musician David Hood – narrates the story of a man who leaves his girl 'standing at the altar' as he elopes with her best friend Marilee, a classic example of a man realising his mistakes, but carrying through with them regardless. 'Lord have mercy for what we done' indeed.

7 'Last Goodbye' – Jeff Buckley

The cult of Jeff Buckley may have ballooned since his premature death, but this is one of the two or three self-penned numbers of his that really stands up. A brooding bass line, drums and acoustic guitar form the backdrop to Buckley's epic farewell. It peaks two-thirds of the way through, as the stunning Zeppelinesque eastern strings kick in, but the truly great line of the song comes earlier: 'Kiss me out of desire, babe, and not consolation', something we all know isn't going to happen.

6 'Jolene' – Dolly Parton

This may now be a staple of cheesy discos, but Dolly Parton's rhinestone classic actually tells the story of a wife confronting the red-headed temptress she believes is trying to steal away her husband. The narrator really lays herself on the line here, culminating with the bleakly brilliant penultimate line 'Please don't take him even though you can'. Gut-wrenchingly great.

5 'Let's Stay Together' – Al Green

With its echo of marriage vows 'Whether times are good or bad, happy or sad', Al Green's classic seems to be an ode to the joys of coupledom. But the more you listen to his achingly whispered vocals, the more the song's melancholy seeps through and the harder it is not to feel that there's something deeper going on. 'You'd never do that to me', he sings, but the tremble in his voice indicates he may know otherwise.

4 'Broken Heart' – Spiritualized

In 1997, when Britpop was sliding (away) into its most lazy and self-indulgent phase, Jason Pierce's Spiritualized fashioned *Ladies and Gentlemen We Are Floating in Space*. Featuring the London Community Gospel Choir along with New Orleans legend Dr John, it was totally out of step with the sound of the times, fusing soul, gospel and garage rock. Track nine, a gorgeous broken-hearted lament built around a repetitive, circular riff and sung in Pierce's high, hushed voice, tells the story of a man seeking oblivion as he fails to deal with the painful end of a relationship .'And I'm wasted all the time / I've got to drink you off of my mind'. Much was made at the time of the personal problems that lay behind this album – Pierce's break-up from his then girlfriend and the band's keyboard player Kate Radley; alleged heroin abuse – but over a decade later it stands up as one of the great albums of the period. Marrying melody and dissonance, its emotional core can perhaps be defined by this song, at once heartbroken and chemically benumbed.

3 'Back to Black' – Amy Winehouse

As with the above, an offshoot of this list could be the great break-up albums, with obvious entries like *Blood on the Tracks* and *Shoot out the Lights*, but the best recent example has to be Amy Winehouse's glorious second album. The title track, with its funeral video, is a stonewall classic, as she recounts the tale of her man leaving her to go back to his ex (ironically, the man she went on to marry after the album came out). The musical breakdown of the middle eight, and the singer's ever-deepening repetition of the word 'black' combine gloriously. Like all great soul songs, it is a cathartic outpouring of the singer's personal demons, and not surprisingly this one's in D minor, the saddest key of all.

2 'Waitin' Around to Die' – Townes Van Zandt

Allegedly the first song the late, great Townes ever wrote (for his wife no less), this tale of heartache and woe starts badly and just gets worse after his woman leaves him ('She cleaned me out and hit it on the sly'). Gorgeous guitar picking, a lonesome voice and those lyrics. The daddy of all misery songs.

1 '$1000 Wedding' – Gram Parsons

This takes the top spot, for many reasons, but chiefly because, as well as breaking the heart, it's weirdly enigmatic (and for once it's the groom left standing at the altar). Gram Parsons's privileged but troubled southern upbringing is well documented, and he mines it here to tell the story of 'the young bride that went away'. Has she eloped or even died? It's difficult to tell, but the possibility and small observations of Parsons' lyrics – as the groom sees people passing notes – are worthy of Flannery O'Connor or William Faulkner at his best. And the third verse, when we suddenly seem to be at a funeral, possibly hers, presided over by 'the Reverend Doctor William Grace' is pure storytelling genius. A great band performance and Emmylou Harris's lovely harmonies all combine to make this the most beautiful song ever about 'a bad, bad day'.

Anywhere, I Don't Care: Ten Songs for the Road

LAURA BARTON

'Some things', Prefab Sprout once noted, 'hurt more, much more, than cars and girls'. It was 1988, and the band was railing against the hot-rodded, cruisin'-with-the-cool-chick shtick of Bruce Springsteen and co., against the fact that much of rock 'n' roll could indeed be boiled down to those same two, seemingly vacuous, themes of cars and girls. Prefab Sprout's mistake, however, was to take the driving song at face value. These songs are frequently about more than just driving Chevys to levees, souping up their coupe, or heading out to the New Jersey Turnpike or Route 66: they are often about something else entirely – sex and freedom, loneliness and identity; about the things that hurt more, much more than cars and girls.

10 'Little Deuce Coupe' – The Beach Boys

We generally associate the Beach Boys with surfing, but in the early sixties, after the success of 'Surfin' Safari', 'Surfin' USA' and 'Surfer Girl', they strayed into other Californian teenage pastimes, namely hot-rodding and drag racing. Indeed, this song hails from their 1963 album *Surfer Girl*, which boasts almost an entire track-listing of car-related songs. It is an album of meticulous car geekery set to music, alive with lyrics such as 'My four-speed dual-quad posi-traction 409', and talk of 'Corvette mills, Naugahyde bucket seats' and a 'stereophonic speaker set with vibrasonic sound'. The musical

45

predecessor of *Pimp My Ride*, perhaps. Apparently much of this was due to the involvement of DJ Roger 'Hot Dog Rog' Christian, who co-wrote many of the songs with Brian Wilson and was something of an automotive obsessive. This particular number is a love-letter to the 1932 Ford Coupe, a car which proved itself perfect for hot-rodding. 'Just a little Deuce Coupe with a flat-head mill', he observes, 'But she'll walk a Thunderbird like it's standin' still'. It is a testament to the sheer talent of the Beach Boys that they somehow make these lyrics sound inviting.

9 'There Is a Light that Never Goes Out' – The Smiths

There is not a great road-song tradition in the UK. However, this 1986 work by the Smiths encapsulates the feeling of glorious teenage freedom provided by access to an automobile, and the simple joy of driving with someone you love. Driving at that age is an emblem of almost-adulthood, of disengaging oneself from home life and school life. It is a place where you are not a pupil or a child, a place where you are somehow weightless. In one's teenage years, a car offers many delights, among them an escape from sparring with one's parents, and the promise of sexual freedom ('And in the darkened underpass / I thought, oh God my chance has come at last'). There is also a delicious sense of danger to the aimless driving in the lyrics, and it has been mooted that the title may to be a reference to a line from Jack Kerouac's *On the Road*, in which he writes of his grandfather bawling at thunderstorms, how he would 'swing his kerosene lamp at the lightning and yell "Go ahead, go, if you're more powerful than I am strike me and put the light out!" . . . And the light never went out.' And there is, it seems, a certain Beatnik quality to 'There is a Light that Never Goes Out', in all its talk of driving 'anywhere'. Kerouac riding the grey, rainy streets of Manchester.

8 'America' – Simon & Garfunkel

Searching for America is one of the major themes of driving songs, a quest inherited perhaps from folk songs such as Woody Guthrie's 'This Land Is Your Land', from the hobos riding the railroads, and even from the Pilgrim Fathers. Here, the seeker is a passenger riding a Greyhound bus (though we learn, too, that he has hitch-hiked from Saginaw, Michigan, to Pittsburgh, Pennsylvania). It is a song that starts off, like all good journeys, with buoyant optimism: 'Let us be lovers . . .' it opens, the kitty of the singer and his 'bride' totalling a packet of cigarettes and some Mrs Wagner Pies. But the dream soon unravels, and by the closing verse the union itself has disappeared with Kathy asleep, and the protagonist staring out of the window, alone: 'Counting the cars on the New Jersey Turnpike / They've all come to look for America'. In song, cars and driving have always symbolised identity and freedom, but here Simon uses the cars on the freeway, rolling along as anonymously as the Ford plant conveyor belt, to communicate the sense of bewilderment and numbing conformity he feels. As that nice Mr Kerouac once put it: 'Whither goest thou, America, in thy shiny car in the night?'

7 'Route 66' – Nat 'King' Cole

This oft-covered song was composed by songwriter Bobby Troup as he drove from Pennsylvania to Los

Angeles, and first recorded and released in 1946 by Nat 'King' Cole. Its message is really rather simple: should you be contemplating making this journey, Route 66 is absolutely the best way to do so. More than anything, Route 66 reflects a new-found enchantment with driving, an activity to pursue just for 'kicks'; during the war years American car plants had ceased production, but when peace resumed in 1945, the car once again began to be viewed as a covetable item, with demand soon outstripping supply. By this time Route 66 was a well-worn road to drive: in the 1930s farming families heading west to look for work travelled this route (a journey recorded in John Steinbeck's *The Grapes of Wrath*, in which he refers to Route 66 as 'the Mother Road'), and again in the war years, lured by the promise of employment in California, many more Americans headed this way, choosing R66 because the road was fully paved. It held, in short, a warm familiarity in the minds of many Americans, and at times the song is little more than a series of crowd-pleasing call-outs to cities along the highway: St Louis, Missouri; Joplin, Missouri; Oklahoma City, Oklahoma; Amarillo, Texas; Gallup, New Mexico; Flagstaff, Arizona; Barstow, California and San Bernadino, California. In later years, the highway became something of a tourist route out to the west coast, and this, along with Chuck Berry's more up-tempo version, helped to bolster the continued success of the song.

6 'No Particular Place to Go' – Chuck Berry

Berry recorded quite a few songs about cars and driving ('Maybellene', 'Jaguar and Thunderbird' and 'I Want to Be Your Driver' among them); however, this offering from 1964 is a fine example of the joys of driving simply for the sake of driving – after all, he has 'no particular place to go'. The song also cements driving's relationship with music and sex: he is 'Crusin' and playin' the radio' and furthermore, he boasts, he has 'My baby beside me at the wheel'. Essentially this is the story of a date, two young lovers out driving and listening to rock 'n' roll, who park up for a little canoodling, but the date goes awry when he cannot unfasten her safety belt: 'Ridin' along in my calaboose / Still tryin' to get her belt a-loose', he notes of their journey home. There's probably some kind of metaphor in there. The words are set to precisely the same tune as one of Berry's earlier compositions, 'School Days', but here the faintly lurching rhythm perfectly reflects the stalled seduction.

5 'Mustang Sally' – Wilson Pickett

'Mustang Sally' is, of course, a thinly veiled reference to female sexuality; the Sally in question is 'running all over town', all she wants to do is 'ride', and our protagonist fears that she will end up crying. Prince employed a similar metaphor in his 1983 single 'Little Red Corvette', borrowing the suggestion that the woman ought to 'slow down' but cautioning that, rather than end in tears, her exploits would see her 'run your body right into the ground'. Indeed, there are very few driving songs that see a woman behind the wheel, and those that do tend to use driving as a metaphor for her promiscuity. The refrain 'ride, Sally, ride' is a nod to the skipping song 'Little Sally Walker', which instructs the skipper to 'put your hand on your hip, let your backbone slip' (a line Pickett would later filch for 'Land of 1000 Dances') and to 'shake it to the one that you love the best', bringing a strangely sexual air to a children's rhyme. The original 'Mustang Sally' was written and recorded in 1965 by Mack Rice, a native of Michigan, where the Ford Mustang had gone into production a year earlier. It was not only a period that offered increased mobility to the general American public, through high-performance yet affordable vehicles such as the Mustang, it was also a time of increasing freedom for women (the previous five years had witnessed the arrival of the pill, the Equal Pay Act, the Civil Rights Act, the establishment of the Equal Opportunities Commission and the publication of Betty Friedan's *The Feminine Mystique*), and Rice's song reflects both these cultural shifts. Pickett's version makes for a better driving song, however, spelling out the innuendo by slowing it down to a positively sultry pace, adding a more lugubrious brass section and replacing Rice's gaspier vocals with a series of guttural exclamations.

4 'Rocket 88' – Jackie Brenston and His Delta Cats

Proof that driving and rock 'n' roll have always lain a-bed, this track, often credited as the first rock 'n' roll record, is all about the joys of cruisin' along in a convertible. It was set down in March 1951 at Sam Phillips's recording studios in Memphis. The Delta Cats did not really exist – Brenston was Ike Turner's saxophonist and the song was written by Turner himself. It is a paean to the Oldsmobile 88, a vehicle first introduced in 1949 and a precursor to the muscle car, marketed with the slogan 'Make a Date with a Rocket 88'. The song owes much to Jimmy Liggins's 'Cadillac Boogie' and Pete Johnson's 'Rocket 88 Boogie', but is set apart by its rumpled piano and a kind of sprung-chassis rhythm. It also sets out the stall of the car as a seductive tool; 'the gals', Brenston states, will 'ride in style', while his lingering description of the 'V8 motor and modern design' borders on the sleazy. The car, henceforth, will not only be a pulling machine, it will itself become an object of lust.

3 'Born to Be Wild' – Steppenwolf

It would be easy to dismiss 'Born to Be Wild' as fuel-injected meat-headedry – its opening riff serves as cultural shorthand for a biker aesthetic (a connection largely forged by the song's inclusion on the soundtrack to *Easy Rider*) and the song provides the meat and two veg of most garage forecourt driving compilations. But in vocalist John Kay's thunderous insistence that 'Like a true nature's child / We were born, born to be wild' there is an unexpected, yet pleasing echo of Thoreau's words in *Walking*: 'The West of which I speak is but another name for the Wild; and what I have been preparing to say is, that in Wildness is the preservation of the World.' Though Thoreau and Steppenwolf (or Mars Bonfire, who wrote the song in question) may have chosen different methods of transportation, they share a common sense of liberation through the act of travelling (rather than departing or arriving) and a desire to flee the tame and conventional. For Thoreau, this was manifested in the pursuit of Naturalism and Transcendentalism, for Steppenwolf this was expressed in the desire to 'take the world in a love embrace'. In song, driving is frequently associated with wildness, be that the wildness of sexual promiscuity (Dion's 'The Wanderer', for example, Robert Johnson's 'Terraplane Blues', or 'Keep Away from the Fellow Who Owns an Automobile', written by Irving Berlin and recorded by Ada Jones) or the leather-jacketed rebel who chooses to live outside society (the Shangri-Las' 'Leader of the Pack', AC/DC's 'Highway to Hell').

2 'Stolen Car' – Bruce Springsteen

Much has been spoken on the subject of *Born to Run*: the strapping of hands across engines, the getting out while we're young, the runaway American dream. But this track from Springsteen's 1980 album *The River* is about a different kind of escape. It is about restlessness, about settling down with a little girl in a little house and then realising it isn't right, it isn't enough. It is a song about the need to get out. The protagonist goes out joyriding (be this the literal hot-wiring of cars, or screwing around) in an attempt to regain a youthful thrill, and to drive without the weight of owning things – a car, a house, a job, a family. But such is his suburban entrapment that he finds himself driving along not a road or a street or a highway, but an avenue, staid and planted and residential.

1 'Roadrunner (Thrice)' – Jonathan Richman and the Modern Lovers

Route 128 is a suburban ring road in Massachusetts. It runs from Gloucester on the north shore right down to Canton on the south. In 1976 Jonathan Richman wrote this extraordinary song about it (and its tributary roads), an homage to the neon lights, the pine trees, the Stop 'n' Shop supermarket and the Howard Johnson restaurants that line its route. It is a consummate example of what driving represents to the young, indeed it is a song brimming with youthful exhilaration, with the sheer delight to be found in roads and cars and music. The Plymouth Roadrunner was a muscle car, manufactured between 1968 and 1980, and during that period offered a cheap mode of freedom to many American teenagers. In this version of the song (one of many that Richman recorded) he drives all around Massachusetts, alone, at night. He is awed at the sight of the modern buildings and the industrial parks and the cold night air, he refers to the highway as his 'girlfriend', rejoices in the fact that driving with the radio on allows him to 'feel in touch with the modern world'. Joy and enthusiasm were characteristic traits of Richman's work, but here, with his gleeful exclamations of 'I got the power I got the magic! Radio on!' he excels himself to produce one of rock's most thrilling songs.

Riding with Lowell George: Music to Help You Try and Get Through

WILLY VLAUTIN

Ten songs/albums to listen to when you've just split up with your violent girlfriend and you're too broke to live anywhere but in a camping trailer in the backyard of your friend's house. These are to get you through a week-long bender without thinking about your life.

10 'Once Upon a Time in the West' – Ennio Morricone

The greatest desert music ever. This should be the first CD you put on when you wake in the morning. It's winter and cold and you've blacked out the windows in the trailer so the neighbours won't notice you living there. Things seem pretty bleak. You just lie in your sleeping bag and play Morricone over and over and wait until your friend and his girlfriend go to work. When you hear their car start wait ten minutes, then move into the house.

9 'Bad Man' – Juicy Bananas (from the *Repo Man* soundtrack)

This should be the first song you listen to when you go into their place. Open a can of beer, smoke weed and play the song over and over. This bad-man monologue is the best bad-man monologue around. Pretty soon you're in a bar full of repo men and they're giving you the worst advice you've ever heard. The repo wives are there too, and they're trying to molest you. If a guy just ran into a bus-load of kids you could still make him laugh with this one.

54

8 'Dim Lights' – The Flying Burrito Brothers

This is for when you start your second beer and you're getting a bit loaded. You might want to stay on the Flying Burrito Brothers for a while. *Sleepless Nights* is a great one. They can transport you like no other. Soon you'll forget you don't have a place to live, a girl, or a decent car. You'll just be surrounded by hippy/country girls at a party in the desert.

7 *Let It Be* – The Replacements (the whole record)

It's mid-morning and you call your boss to tell him that your sister, the one who you said just got beat up by her boyfriend and broke three ribs, has to be driven 800 miles back to your mom's house. The boss says, 'Don't worry, take the whole week off. And listen, we should kill that mother fucker.' You tell him you're trying, that you're really working on it. Afterwards you call your brother, 'cause you don't have a sister, and he tells you you're lucky as hell to have made it out alive with that 'crazy violent bitch' you were with.

6 'Christmas Card from a Hooker in Minneapolis' – Tom Waits

It's past noon and you're half drunk. You talk to your mom, who knows you're drunk and tells you that the break-up is a sign for you to make something of yourself. 'You got out of it without knocking her up. That's as lucky as you're going to get. Now don't fuck up again, and for God sakes I hate men who drink during the day so cut it out.' You hang up and start to spiral. How are you going to get your stuff out of your old place? Will she break your records? What about your dad's guitar and your framed picture of Carole Lombard? She's broken a lot of things so you start to worry. This is when you play the ballads. 'Alice', 'Rainbirds', 'Palookaville', 'Closing Time', 'Muriel', 'A Soldier's Things'. They help you start to pull out of it. Then you put on 'Christmas Card from a Hooker' in Minneapolis and suddenly you feel like you're going to make it.

5 *Willie Nelson's Greatest Hits (& Some that Will Be)* – Willie Nelson

You smoke more weed and put on this record to help build your confidence so you can leave the house. You try to read some of Willie Nelson's biography by Bud Shrake. You try to think like him, you try to convince yourself you're him and eventually it works well enough that you can go down to a local bar and get something to eat.

4 *Car Wash* – Rose Royce

The bar down the street isn't much, but their jukebox has the *Car Wash* soundtrack. You put on 'I Wanna Get Next to You', 'Daddy Rich', and the 'Richard Pryor Dialogue'. Then you order lunch and a couple drinks and go back to the jukebox and add 'I'm Going Down' and 'Crying'. Pretty soon you're in the movie. You're working at a car wash in LA and everything's all right and Richard Pryor is there and the sun's out and you work all day long with a guy who calls himself 'Super Fly'.

3 'Big City' – Merle Haggard

When you get back to the house you still have two hours before your friend gets off work. You open another beer and smoke more weed and listen to this song over and over. If you're lucky you'll make it to the middle of Montana without a job and you'll be hanging out with Merle Haggard and his third wife and her sisters in a hot springs.

2 *Sandinista!* – The Clash

Your friend gets off work early and you both leave the house before his girlfriend gets home and go driving around. You drink beer and listen to *Sandinista!* 'The Magnificient Seven', 'Somebody Got Murdered', 'Charlie Don't Surf' and 'The Equaliser'. You stop at the worst bars you can find and your friend tells you over and over how lucky you are. 'But the luckiest thing is she didn't stab you to death,' he says. 'She wouldn't have stabbed me,' you tell him. 'I'm too fast.' 'Jesus,' your friend says and starts laughing, 'you're as dumb as your brother says.'

1 'Willin'' – Little Feat (*Sailin' Shoes* version)

As pathetic as all this sounds, it gets worse. You have a small tape deck in the trailer and a tape that has Willin' playing over and over on a sixty-minute loop. You get in your sleeping bag and lie there and listen to the song and convince yourself you're riding with Lowell George through the desert of Arizona. And really all that works until you're almost asleep then you start thinking about the girl and the two years you spent together, and the decent times and even the good times. You spend all day trying not to think about the bad times but it's the good times that throw a wrench into everything. You end up telling yourself you'll get it together and quit drinking, get a better job, find a normal girl, and get a place to live. But really what you should do is repeat this day six more times first.

ROCK

From power ballads to the power of plaid

Richard T. Kelly / Will Hodgkinson /
David Peace / Nick Kent / Richard King

Big Hearts, Big Hair: Ten Rockin' Good Power Ballads

RICHARD T. KELLY

Power balladry is a disreputable genre widely thought to have reared its head in the late 1970s, alongside the growing readiness of rock fans to attend gigs in football stadiums and to hire guitar bands with poodle-hairdos to liven up their wedding parties. Soon, most ostensibly 'hard rock' albums would feature an Obligatory Slow One designed to get everybody's cigarette lighters aloft in the dark. Was it just a corporate hustle to sell more records to women? Or a genuine creative urge within the bands to tap the average head-banger's inner drama-queen? Maybe a bit of both.

One should say there is another (and possibly dominant) strain of power ballad, bigger on pianos than guitars, chiefly associated with Phil Collins, Céline Dion and Bryan Adams. But I have to say I'd sooner have my ears syringed than go there. No, this ten is chiefly about dedicated rockers trying to work in a more intimate register, with a deeper debt to emotional content, the music starting slow but building inexorably toward an excuse to turn the volume up to 11 and rip the knobs off.

10 'Total Eclipse of the Heart' (live) – The Dan Band

Jim Steinman is in the business of rock 'n' roll dreams made real, and in this line he certainly gave his all to the careers of Meat Loaf and Bonnie Tyler, who otherwise wouldn't have looked out of place running a pub together in Rhyl. For some listeners Steinman probably defines the power-ballad genre. He's not my cup of tea, but I can appreciate his gift when it's filtered through Dan Finnerty's faithful but foul-mouthed cover of Tyler's No. 1 smash, first showcased in the Will Ferrell movie *Old School*. The homeboy swearing ('I fucken *need* you more than ev-ah') actually relieves the song of its rock-god pomposity, bringing it back to the common-or-garden love pains that we mere mortals experience.

9 'Somebody to Love' (live) – George Michael & Queen

There are performers of such towering narcissism as to make any display of romantic yearning on their part ring utterly false – they might as well be singing into the mirror – and for this listener the late Freddie Mercury was one such. George Michael clearly adores himself too, and yet when it comes to grandstanding gay-rock cover versions the guy has always had something convincingly impassioned in his voice. I can recall the *Face* magazine rather smugly asking art-funk guru Don Was what he made of Michael's Wham!-era cover of Was (Not Was)'s 'Where Did Your Heart Go', clearly banking on some hipster put-down. 'He sang the shit out of that song, man' was Was's sagely approving response.

8 'Comfortably Numb' (live) – Roger Waters & Van Morrison

Over time I've learned to love a lot of music that I formerly hated, but I doubt even old age will endear me to the ponderously 'alienated' sixth-form doggerel of Roger Waters. And yet . . . this version of the heavily medicated Pink Floyd anthem, as performed at Waters's big Berlin concert of 1990, rolls out in familiar fashion – onstage Waters was pratting about in a doctor's coat before his

Deeply Symbolic Wall – until suddenly Van Morrison weighs in on the chorus, seeming to translate Waters's lyrics into a version of his own well-documented Belfast bluesman's quest for enlightenment. Martin Scorsese, famously unable to suppress his rock 'n' roll enthusiasms, wound up pouring the Morrison bits all over a love scene in *The Departed*.

7 'More than a Feeling' – Boston

This one ought to chart higher – I mean, it's godly stuff – but there's maybe just a tad too much sugared-and-decaffeinated mellowness to the rock stylings of Tom Scholz's Boston. That, and also the line 'I closed my eyes and she slipped away' has now been inducted into the celebrated Profanisaurus of *Viz* comic (as a euphemism for guess what?), so hilariously that I just can't hear the song in the same way any more . . .

6 'The Rain Song' – Led Zeppelin

Legend has it that George Harrison effectively goaded Plant/Page into writing this track by observing that the Zep didn't seem to 'do' ballads. The Zep then proceeded to 'do' a ballad in much the way as Cheops 'did' pyramids (man). The format is a classic slow build of Page fretwork towards a Bonzo-inspired eruption, whereupon Plant wails out one of the more emotive instances of his patented Tolkien-derived lyrical bent ('I cursed the gloom that set upon us . . . but I know I love you so').

5 'Alone' – Heart

Back in the 1970s Seattle sisters Ann and Nancy Wilson

fronted the most attractive of the many bands trying to base a career on the riff of the Zep's 'Immigrant Song'. Come the mid-eighties Nancy had perfected the high-kicking power chord and still looked fantastic despite a poodle hairdo; Ann had filled out a bit but swathed herself dramatically in black and still had a glorious voice. 'Alone' was Heart's biggest hit, an epic restatement of a glaring sentiment about thwarted desire. Even the po-faced indie-and-hip-hop purists of the *NME* c. 1987 found a way to say they liked it. It was playing in Woolworth's just the other day as I was buying my daughter some sweets, and I found myself loitering in the aisles long enough to hear Ann's unearthly howl of frustration that launches the second chorus.

4 'Estranged' – Guns N' Roses

The summer of 1991 – two albums hogging the top of the US charts, backed by a world tour, promo videos mounted on Hollywood budgets, even the theme tune to *Terminator 2* . . . not an unhappy run of events, but not enough to calm the neurotic beast within Axl W. Rose. A portrait of Rose's monstrous angst is presented in the triptych formed across the two *Use Your Illusion* albums by 'Don't Cry', 'November Rain', and 'Estranged'. And if some of Rose's 'issues' were to do with Erin Everly and/or Stephanie Seymour, these were clearly only the top items on a teetering pile. 'Estranged' is a break-up song but not as we know it, punctuated by Slash's superior soloing, but driven along its 9 minutes and 23 seconds by Rose's inimitably half-ranted, half-whispered, wholly self-excoriating vocals.

3 'Show Me Heaven' – Maria McKee

The magnificent Maria never quite became a star, despite great expectations from the minute she surfaced with Lone Justice during the Great American Country Rock Revival of 1985. The blessing is that she's had a far bolder and finer career instead. Her sole *Billboard* chart career move was this theme song for a typically rotten Tom Cruise movie. She co-wrote it and (per item 9 above) absolutely sang the shit out of it, a trademark honey-and-bourbon mix of sweetness and grain in her voice, with a Baptist purity on the soaring notes. Though at various times McKee has seemed to channel Van Morrison or John Cale or Stephen Sondheim, here in her phrasing of 'amazing grace' and the exultant rhyming of 'spine' and 'divine' she laid a fair claim to be reckoned as the white Aretha Franklin.

2 'The Unforgiven' – Metallica

Metal connoisseurs may bicker over whether Metallica's 'black album' of 1991 is their masterpiece or their sell-out to the mainstream, but for sure it's the one I'd want on a desert island. The rolling arpeggios of 'Nothing Else Matters' offer one power-ballad option, but I'll take 'The Unforgiven', a sort of existential Seven Ages invective against the Man and all his works. Its melodic elegance is matched by a new fineness in James Hetfield's singing voice, but he still sticks a ferocious bite on to half-lines like 'This whipping boy done wrong'. In a nice inversion of standard form the choruses are light and the verses heavy, though I have to say it's the latter that really get my blood going.

1 'Love Reign O'er Me' – The Who

As the trailblazers of 'rock opera' Pete Townshend and the 'Orrible 'Oo were always likely to top this division, and indeed Love Reign O'er Me seems to me the undisputed heavyweight champion – could, indeed, have been so on the strength of that brilliant title alone, were it not that the song itself is probably the perfect marriage of Townshend's ardent, roiling compositional dynamism and Roger Daltrey's chest-baring mike-tossing all-maleness. Of course, the piece properly belongs to the *Quadrophenia* album, its sentiments to the teenage mod protagonist Jimmy; and the 'Love' in question is not romantic/erotic but of the life-affirming pantheism that Townshend further explored in 'Blue, Red, and Grey' – a song that also tops my list of Ten Great Rock Tracks Played on Ukulele . . .

Born Losers: Ten Garage Cuts Lacking in Self-confidence

WILL HODGKINSON

Across America in the mid-sixties, some kind of a disease took hold. Seventy-three million people watched The Beatles make their US television debut on the *Ed Sullivan Show* on 9 February 1964. Once the rebellion of the Rolling Stones and the cynical wit of The Who and the Kinks was added to the mix, impressionable younger members of that huge audience knew what they had to do: rock 'n' roll.

A year later the country was awash with teenage bands, guitars bought using money saved up from paper rounds, practising in suburban garages and desperately trying to nail a decent version of 'Satisfaction' in time for the local High School Battle of the Bands. Before long many of these young rockers were straining their intellects and utilising all of their limited musical abilities to write songs of their own, but not everyone can be Lennon and McCartney. And most of the kids in garage bands were not captain-of-the-football-team material, either. What followed was the natural result of having frustrated, lonely teenagers who felt empowered every time they heard Mick Jagger's cocksure whine and humiliated when some kid half their age kicked sand in their acne-splattered face: garage punk.

A few garage bands made entire albums. Some, like the Standells and the 13th Floor Elevators, even had national hits. But most only managed to knock out one or two frantic singles, generally recorded at a cheap local studio over an afternoon, before slinking back into the shadows.

Knowing that this would probably be the only time any-one might actually hear what they had to say, a lot of the garage bands did what any unpopular, weedy teenage boy would do: voiced their sexual frustrations and self-pity on record. The results were nothing less than astounding.

Most of the tracks on this list were non-hits and the original singles are now impossibly rare. I'm not being obscure for the sake of it – the more successful garage bands could generally play their instruments, hold down a tune, and sound like they weren't just about to top themselves, so what follows is a list of whiny garage punk classics by forgotten losers who really did sound like they weren't going to get anywhere in life – and, sure enough, most of them didn't. The irony of it is that their suffering makes for our joy. The sheer honesty, emotion and downtrodden gallows humour in these songs is so powerful you cannot help but get excited by every single one of them. And they would have been lost for ever had not a handful of nerdy record-collector types rediscov-ered them in the seventies and eighties and stuck them on to compilations such as *Pebbles*, *Nuggets* and *Back from the Grave*. Now, some of the most pathetic moments in the history of music, created in a flash of misery and played with such urgency and an eye on the studio clock that there was rarely space for niggling issues like singing in tune or playing in time, will live for ever.

For anyone who has felt the misery of love's rejection, who knows what it's like not to be the big man on cam-pus, or who has shuddered at the sight of U2's Bono strutting about the world's stages singing 'Gloria' in bug shades and a cowboy hat, these songs are for you.

10 '(I Ain't No) Miracle Worker' – The Brogues

Featuring two future members of San Francisco psychedelic mainstays the Quicksilver Messenger Service, this
Modesto, California, band only hung around for nine
months in 1965 but managed to knock out two singles in
that time. Heavily into British-invasion groups like the
Animals and the Pretty Things, the five Brogues grew
their hair long, developed a sneering attitude and spat
out the British R&B hits of the day. Cut in Los Angeles,
'Miracle Worker', their second single, is actually a cover
version of a soul song but the Brogues managed to find
the hidden mix of defiance and misery in the chorus line
'I ain't no miracle worker . . . I do the best that I can'.
Then two of the band's members got drafted. And they
were really going places, too.

9 'Born Loser' – Murphy and the Mob

Don't let the title of this 1965 single put you off – Murphy
is a pretty hip cat. 'I sleep all day and I swing all night /
I'm so cool baby, I'm just outtasight!' he yelps to one of
the most primeval rock riffs ever laid down in a studio as
he tells his tale of the town squares shaking their heads
and calling him a born loser as he struts about by himself.
But this is a classic example of bravado masking a troubled mind: Murphy goes on to admit that he hasn't got
any friends. It's not easy being the coolest guy in town.

8 'I'm a Living Sickness' – The Calico Wall

What happens when you combine paranoid teenage
loserdom with LSD? Nothing less than a psychotic nightmare, as this brutal proto-psychedelic wailer attests. In

1967 this Minneapolis outfit released their one and only single, the bad-trip-inspired 'Flight Reaction', on Turtle Records, to deafening disinterest from the entire world. Recorded in the same session but unreleased at the time, this track took the drug-induced suffering one step further as the Calico Wall's singer screams 'I'm a living sickness . . . sick within my soul!' against a backdrop of angry fuzz guitar. When self-hatred reaches this level, it stops being funny and becomes disturbing.

7 'Can't Seem to Make You Mine' – The Seeds

Unlike most garage bands, Los Angeles' the Seeds were actually quite popular. Their leader Sky Saxon modelled himself on Mick Jagger, claimed that he was 200 years old and had once been 'a stand-in for Beethoven'. The truth came out in his songs, though; mostly snarling three-chord rants about being misunderstood. This 1965 hit is Sky's finest hour; a glorious whine in which he encapsulates the universal suffering of lusting after a girl who can't stand the sight of you. A decade later Sky was living in a free-love commune in Hawaii, presumably making up for lost time.

6 'That's the Bag I'm In' – The Fabs

These guys are truly hopeless. 'Every morning when I wake up / I burn my fingers on the coffee pot', claims the singer, clearly failing to learn by his mistakes. 'My toast is cold and my orange juice hot / I could start over but I'd really rather not / 'Cause it would only happen over again . . .' After listing these daily trials he descends into total despair, concluding: 'They'll probably drop the bomb the day my ship comes in'. This slice of sheer poetry from 1966 only made it on to wax because drummer Bob Ellis's mother paid for the recording with money made from the sales of her own make-up range.

5 'Iconoclastic Life' – The Beechnuts

This frantic garage-punk raver from 1966 features what sounds like a pretty tough guy having a nervous breakdown as he realises the girl he loves has left him for ever. 'My life is nil, I just take pills / I sit for hours, watching the flowers', he growls in desperation. But don't think he's on some kind of hippy trip – he's only watching the flowers because he's got nothing better to do. 'I spend my days, lost in a haze', he admits, before taunting the girl with the line 'You want to see me cry? I'll cry, I'll cry, I'll cry cry cry!' It collapses into meaningless howls of despair at that point.

4 'I'm a Nothing' – The Magic Plants

Believe it or not, this New York band featured members who went on to form the accomplished baroque pop group the Left Banke. Before they learned to play their instruments, though, they recorded this classic 1965 single for the Verve label. It is precocious in realising the emptiness of pop-star image: 'Take away my crazy long hair, wipe that silly make-up off my face . . . I'm a disgrace!' Unlike so many garage punkers, these dudes were hip – naming your band after marijuana was quite brave back in '65.

3 'No Reason to Complain' – The Alarm Clocks

Three terminal squares from Parma, Ohio, got together in the summer break of 1965 to play rock 'n' roll favourites like 'Money' and 'Louie, Louie' at legion halls and high-school hops, then saved up enough cash to lay down two tracks, 'Yeah' and 'No Reason to Complain', the following year. Released on the band's own Awake label, the ensuing single sunk without a trace and has since become the high-water mark of self-pitying garage punk. 'She's got another, bigger man / She doesn't know, doesn't understand', moans singer and bassist Mike Pierce over a sloppy beat, thereby distilling the essence of garage punk misery into one perfect line.

2 'I Can't Win' – The Monacles

The Monacles couldn't do anything right, least of all play in tune, keep in time, or even spell their own name correctly. It's pretty hard to make out the words through singer Marlowe Stewart's pathetic whine, but from what I can gather he stays up late to watch TV, goes to bed thinking of the girl he can't have, burns himself ironing his shirt the following day and ends up missing the school dance because he can't get out of the house in time. He simply can't win.

1 'I Never Loved Her' – The Starfires

From 1965, here is one of the greatest teenage rants ever written. 'Why are you guys always teasing me?' whines the lead singer of this LA-based band over a simple but ultra-tight and moody riff. 'Come on, fellas, just let me be'. What are they teasing him about? What else but the fact that he's in love with some girl who's dumped him? He denies his feelings throughout the verses with empty statements like 'Picked her up from school one day / Because her house was on the way', but the tender way

he sings 'You know I never did love her' in the chorus
reveals his pain. Every note is dripping with pathos, self-
pity, and teenage genius.

More Kicks than Pricks: Ten Japanese Bands I Love for No Good Reason Other than I Love Them

DAVID PEACE

Lists are for fascists and shoppers, not anarchists and rockers but, if you're reading this, you probably need all the help you can get. So here you go . . .

10 Mikami Kan

Not a band but a man and a voice and what a voice. Hardcore ultra-violent folk from 1970 to now, lyrically the missing link between Phil Ochs and Throbbing Gristle, or is that Jandek?

9 J. A. Caesar

Not a band either. But Terayama Shuji was the Pasolini of Japan – poet, playwright, film maker and agent provocateur – and Caesar was the man behind his soundtracks. Terayama is dead, but Caesar lives.

8 The Stalin

The Sex Pistols of Japan (to continue the Western references), but singer Endo Michiro will never appear on a reality/celebrity TV show. In other words, he still means it, man. Best album *Stop Jap* from 1982.

7 Inu

The yang to Endo and the Stalin's yin. One classic 1981 album, then split. Singer Machida Ko went on to win the Akutagawa Prize for his novel *Kiregire*.

6 Togawa Jun

As well as her solo work, she is also the operatic voice behind Yapoos and Guernica. Unique in every way. Try *Yapoos Keikaku*.

5 Kinniku Shojo Tai

Fronted by another genius, Otsuki Kenji. The only good news in 2007 was that Kinniku have re-formed. However, early stuff on Toy's Factory (as compiled on *Kinsho No Daisharin*) remains their best work.

4 Ningen Isu

The first Japanese band I ever saw and still the very best; Black Sabbath reborn in the Tohoku region of Japan. Fourteen albums to date and you need them all.

3 Sigh

The first ever Black Metal group in Japan. Probably more popular outside of Japan, so the one band on this list you can actually go out and buy.

2 Inugami Circus Dan

All of the above bands rock and rolled into one, fronted by the Dog God demon-ess Inugami Kyoko. They also play live regularly (and brilliantly) so, on the off-chance you find yourself in Tokyo, check out http://www.inugami.jp/.

1 Azarashi

The spiritual heirs of the Stalin; only one obscure CD and very few live shows – the way it ought to be – BUT check out vocalist Meguko's MySpace page – http://www.myspace.com/kusaremeguko – and hear what you're missing.

Also could have mentioned Asakawa Maki, Les Rallizes Dénudés, Kousokuya, Tetsuo Furudate, Ran Yoko, Inoue Yosui, YMO, Ruins, SS, Auto-Mod, the Comes, Gastunk, Gauze, Crow, Hi-Technology Suicide, Gargoyle, Kokeshi Doll, Boris, Gonin-Ish, Church of Misery, Green Machine, Corrupted, Nightmare, Swarmm, Envy, Muga, Abraham Cross, Gallhammer, Gyu-sha Ningen, Ha Ha Lemon, Ikochi, and Ningenkakuseiki. But that's the trouble with lists for you –

They're full of shit. Just like me.

The Walruses: The Ten Greatest Moustaches in Rock

NICK KENT

The early days of rock 'n' roll were exclusively populated by clean-shaven young men with curled sneers unencumbered by hair sprouting from their upper lips. Only folk singers dared to sport beards in the fifties and early sixties. But then in 1966 musicians started experimenting with strange drugs and even stranger facial foliage. It began with mutton-chop side whiskers but soon progressed to that region directly under the nostrils. When The Beatles welcomed in 1967 by all growing moustaches, they established a human walrus look that many musos since then have tried to duplicate. Occasionally they have succeeded but most of the time they've became something of a walking eyesore as a direct consequence. Here then is a salute to that rare breed, the ten most 'tache-tastic rock musicians of the past fifty years.

10 The Beatles

Technically speaking they weren't the first – Charlie Watts was already sporting a lounge-lizard 'tache in Stones promo shots as early as spring 1966 – but The Beatles' collective decision to sprout copious amounts of upper-lip hair at the dawning of the Summer of Love was a signal to male youth the world over to toss their razor blades into the garbage and follow suit.

9 David Crosby

No one took the psychedelic walrus look further than

sacked Byrd Crosby: the 'tache he cultivated in 1967 was so enormous it made the simple act of drinking soup with a spoon into a potentially messy and hazardous affair. 'The Cros' is universally recognised as a genius harmony singer and championship-level druggie but deserves further respect for the freak-flag-flying mega-'tache he's been stoically sprouting for over forty years now.

8 Jimi Hendrix

Arguably the classiest-looking 'tache-sporter of all late-twentieth-century music-makers, Hendrix kept his upper lip trim with two elegant pencil-thin lines of facial hair sloping down to join the svelte forest of stubble protruding from his ample chin. The press called him the Wild Man of Borneo at the time but he was only – as usual – being ahead of the pack, inventing the cool unshaven look two full decades before George Michael.

7 John Bonham

Birmingham was 'Tache Central in the late sixties, the place where all the meanest-looking and hairiest-lipped musos in Christendom seemed to hail from. Dig out an early shot of Black Sabbath and you'll instantly see what I'm talking about. But John Bonham dwarfed all his Black Country peers: not only was he the world's greatest drummer, he was also the region's most dedicated 'tache-head. True, he was sometimes sighted lurking ominously behind a full beard, but the man they called Bonzo would always return to his first love, the unreconstructed Brummie mega-'tache. Not unlike Samson, his lower nasal hair may well have been the source behind his supernatural drumming stamina.

6 The Band

Bob Dylan's former backing group raised the bar for facial hair growth in rock to a new high in 1968 with the release of their debut album *Music from Big Pink*. The quintet were all manly looking hombres who clearly had little use for shaving kits. Three of them were submerged behind copious beards but Robbie Robertson and Rick Danko were both die-hard moustache devotees whose ample outgrowths were duly copied by would-be roots rockers over the globe.

5 David Bowie

When androgynous glam-rock prevailed in the early seventies, the 'tache was suddenly out in the cold as a desirable male fashion accessory. And yet David Bowie – the genre's image kingpin – still briefly succumbed to sporting one in 1975 when he and Iggy Pop moved to Berlin together. A colour Polaroid taken at the time shows an uncertain-looking Bowie with what looks like a hairy caterpillar rimming his upper lip. Bowie promptly jettisoned the look before further photographs could be taken but still managed to grow an impressively walrus-like moustache in 2004 that even David Crosby might envy.

4 Freddie Mercury

When Freddie wasn't straining and soaring against the entire dark ages of music, he was straining and soaring against all conventional self-grooming wisdom by cultivating a look best described as 'gay Omar Sharif'. The mega-butch moustache he grew to achieve this style transformation has since become a much-revered iconic totem in both gay culture and rock history.

3 Shane MacGowan

Like glam, punk rock had little patience with the moustache. John Lydon and Joe Strummer wouldn't have been seen dead sporting one. But Shane MacGowan – their spiritual little brother from the Isle of Erin – went the whole hog in the nineties and harvested a full-on Genghis Khan-like hair sculpture around his snaggle-toothed mouth. Not a particularly pretty sight but still full marks for sheer audacity in facial hair growth.

2 Anton Newcombe

In the film *Dig!*, the Brian Jonestown Massacre's wacky leader grows a truly humongous moustache that seems to take on a life all of its own. The more it extends, the nuttier Newcombe becomes.

1 Nick Cave

With his fine head of ink-black hair now starting to recede and turn grey, Cave has lately opted to pep up his physical image by growing a big drooping moustache that makes him look like a cross between Marcel Proust and a corrupt Texas cattle-baron from the late nineteenth century. He and Will 'Bonnie Prince Billy' Oldham are currently the two most prominent unapologetic 'tache-sporters in the contemporary rock landscape, perpetuating a tradition that's as long-standing as it is often hard to look at.

The Mythology of Plaid: Ten Check-shirted Records

RICHARD KING

Just ask any recently laid off A&R executive – deportment and wardrobe are as integral to the delivery platform of any new act as the cabs 'n' flowers and mobile network co-op deal. And that's before we've even got on to social networking and viral media. The check shirt, however, is a *real* musician's staple. It asserts the artist's sense of independence by demonstrating a determination to bypass the stylists and photographers' assistants, and recklessly, romantically, focus on the material . . .

10 'Good Times' – New Kingdom (12" sleeve)

Nature Boy Jim Kelly in grunge-era soft red plaid, circular shades and peeked woolly hat gives a convincing representation of being, as the vernacular would then have had it, blunted, nicely making the case that the check shirt is really a security blanket for grown-ups.

9 *Quickness* – Bad Brains (LP sleeve)

Rescuing the brushed open weave from Ralph Lauren's weekend-in-the-Hamptons utopia, both Darryl and Dr Know evince the thrift-store restlessness of inner-DC youth in the grip of Reaganomics.

8 *77* – Talking Heads (LP inner sleeve)

The former art students' détournement of the honest-day's-work romanticism of plaid introduces check as a

81

signifier of the preppy tendency. David Byrne's quite hairy arms keep everything very real though.

7 *L'Amitié* – Françoise Hardy (LP sleeve)

Dusky blue in a light check signifies post-teenage Gallic ennui and combines bohemian Euro hauteur with chamber-pop sultriness. Basically, how to look like an auteur without the bother of writing your own songs.

6 *Marquee Moon* – Television (LP back cover)

Richard Lloyd nails the romance of the puckish floppy fringe/large check guitar antihero set piece, resulting in a shy-boy archetype.

5 *Trailer Park* – Beth Orton (LP sleeve)

Pink short-sleeved gingham appliqué offset with jeans, converse and a twilit backdrop. This forward thinking nod to Laura Ashley marks perfectly the point when festivals became family friendly and went all aspirational.

4 'Two Hearts Together' – Orange Juice (7" sleeve)

Hid behind a large orange lily (this was, after all, the early days of the art-direction industry) David McClymont's short-sleeved blue cheesecloth, in nice counterpart to Edwyn Collins's Scoutish neckerchief, feminises the check print and, like the band itself, lays the groundwork for the soon to be realised, if rather laboured, insouciance of indie, i.e. dressing yourself the way your mother did when you were seven. (See also Bobby Gillespie with added VU shades in chessboard check on the inner sleeve of *Psychocandy*.)

3 *Original Rockers* – Augustus Pablo (LP sleeve)

Clearly made out behind clouds of blue smoke and an industrial-scale chalice: a red western slim-fit cowboy shirt with popper fasteners. The shirt updates the Lee Perry Rasta-as-outlaw look circa *Return of Django* to the more existential plaid of the *Two-lane Blacktop* modern drifter.

2 *Everybody Knows This Is Nowhere* – Neil Young (LP sleeve)

Realising the full potential of the concept of the gatefold sleeve, Neil includes three shots of himself turned out in checked rural attire: two with dog, one with guitar. It's a nice move that, perhaps even consciously, juxtaposes his day-to-day realities with that of the conspicuous consumption of Crosby, Stills, Nash and their problematic yacht.

1 *Cosmo's Factory* – Creedence Clearwater Revival (LP sleeve)

The start of it all. John Fogerty's table-check blue plaid work shirt effortlessly gives warning of the band's no-nonsense chooglin' credentials and kills the debate that he's a Fortunate Son. Reckoned by no less an authority than Mike Watt to be the point when the relationship between rock and flannel got serious.

SONGS OF TERROR

From pixies to comas

Nev Bradford / Peter Murphy / Roger Armstrong / Cathi Unsworth / Gary Lightbody

Away with the Pixies: Ten Nightmarish Bedtime Stories with Black Francis

NEV BRADFORD

It was 3.45 in the morning. I was just a kid – suddenly awake, suddenly conscious of a recent nightmare of Biblical intensity. It had been a dreamscape of unprecedented mutilation and self-disgust set against the back-story of an alien abduction. I still had my headphones on – somehow I'd managed to fall asleep while listening to the Pixies' *Surfer Rosa*. My pride and joy – my red Sony Walkman – had been playing the tape on a loop for what must have been several hours. The AA batteries were now drained of juice, the half-speed tones of Black Francis low, drooling – part demented bluesman selling his soul at the crossroads, part Mexican bandit. But something was even more disturbing – this deranged Sandman had been inside of me, conducting my dreams.

I guess up until this point I had loved the Pixies on a purely instrumental basis. Their songs were sleek silver bullets that would slay you time and time again. What I didn't appreciate back then, though, was that Black Francis is, in fact, a master surrealist. As such, the stories and images – exposed and hidden – within the songs of the Pixies are purposely designed to gnaw on your subconscious. That's what makes them ripe for nightmares. If you're a big fan, you might have heard these songs a thousand times. But there'll only ever be one place where you truly confront the traumas you've subliminally ingested – your sleep.

10 'Debaser' (*Doolittle*, 1989)

This song scrapes in at No. 10 not merely for its

hallucinogenic properties and vivid imagery concerning eyeballs being sliced up. It's also a mission statement for all else to come. The whole track is, amazingly, an homage to Luis Buñuel and Salvador Dali's surrealist short *Un Chien Andalou* – a film which not only gives us two priests dragging a piano covered in dead donkeys but also an opening scene of an eyeball being sliced open. The chorus of 'Debaser' has Francis screaming out his declaration – 'I am a chien andalusia'. He's changed a word for poetic reasons, but it's clear what he means – he IS this weird, wonderful, nonsensical film, and now he's coming for your mind.

9 'Where Is My Mind?' (*Surfer Rosa*, 1988)

The sheer fact that this song is so hauntingly good is enough to give me nightmares. The out-take at the beginning sets this one up. As Kim Deal offers us a sweet but out-of-tune 'Ooooooh', angry Francis says, 'Stop,' like he really wants her to. It's classic Beauty-and-the-Beast stuff – a Siren lulls you in, then a body-builder rams a pistol into the back of your skull. The track itself has Black Francis asking a school of fish where his mind has gone, but it's the overall effect of this perfectly galvanised guitar song that leaves you searching for the location of your own.

8 'Wave of Mutilation' (*Doolittle*, 1989)

He kisses mermaids. He rides the El Niño. He walks upon golden sands with crustaceans. All this before saying his goodbyes and embarking on a killing spree of unfathomable despair. It's the most beautiful song ever to justify the use of extreme violence. Best in show within this particular genre of Pixies song.

7 'Cactus' (*Surfer Rosa*, 1988)

The sparse twelve-bar chug of this song provides the cement couch on which Francis reclines in order to confess his loneliness. It's basically a plea to an anonymous lover to bloody-up her hands on a cactus tree and wipe them all over her dress. He wants the dress sent to him – he's going to wear it when he gets lonely. The idea's not exactly traumatising, but it's got that kind of loving perversion that preys on your mind. On top of that, out of nowhere, there's a moment in the middle of the song where a barely audible half-gagged voice spells out the letters P-I-X-I-E-S. For a second it sounds like one of David Lynch's midgets cheerleading them from the touchline. Put that in your dream-pipe and smoke it!

6 'Hang Wire' (*Bossanova*, 1990)

Don't let the euphoric uplift of Joey Santiago's guitar layering on *Bossanova* fool you – this is still an LP containing moments all dreams should steer clear of. 'Hang Wire' is a minimal piece, but it's one of them. The sleeve artwork accompanying the vinyl manages to sum it up – there's a picture of a piece of barbed wire twisted into the shape of a noose. Just what will happen when Black Francis gets to 'meet you at the hang wire' is anyone's guess.

5 'Motorway to Roswell' (*Trompe Le Monde*, 1991)

It's got something to do with an alien abduction gone real bad.

4 'Something Against You' (*Surfer Rosa*, 1998)

Sub-two-minute demented festival of dirty noise and

retribution that would have most death-metal singers running for Mummy. It might be virtually impossible to hear what B.F. is screaming about behind all the loudhailer distortion – but you know he means it. There's no way I'd cross him, or want to be chased down a dark alley by him – especially when your legs have turned to dream-mush.

3 'Nimrod's Son' (*Come on Pilgrim*, 1987)

This is rock 'n' roll's greatest tribute to Oedipus. A motorcycle crash in the desert has left the singer with a bleeding head. Softly his sister whispers to him, 'You are the son of a mother fucker' – she means it quite literally. The rest of the song sees Francis coming to terms with the fact that the great 'joke' has come upon him. Be disturbed – be very disturbed.

2 'The Holiday Song' (*Come on Pilgrim*, 1987)

Just an everyday incest-driven confessional disguised as a 4/4 indie pop song. A brother gives birth to his sister – she seems to pop out of his head – then he 'paints her on the sheets'. Probably best to only scratch the surface of this one – just to know you've tapped your foot along to it is scary. As with most of these songs, the search for true meaning seems utterly pointless. At the end of the day they're just sparklingly dark glass marbles – cutting into them to understand the patterns within would be to destroy them.

1 'La La Love You' (*Doolittle*, 1989)

It's the drummer singing a love song – that's frightening enough.

Wails from the Crypt: Ten Songs to Make Your Skin Crawl

PETER MURPHY

The problem with any mix-tape is not what to include, but what to omit. Sure, you can let the theme be your oracle, but which theme, dammit?

I've decided to go with a list of songs that make the skin crawl. Songs that constrict my scalp and make my dangly bits want to crawl back up inside my belly.

Why?

Well, Doctor, let me tell you about my childhood. I grew up in Enniscorthy, Co. Wexford, the deep south-east of Ireland, a beautiful but also wonderfully eerie place, especially in winter, when it was already dark on the walk home from school, you could hear rats rustle in the gripe and the trees looked like famished ancestors trying to pull you into some awful brambled underworld.

No, I didn't spend too much time in front of the little black box watching *Twilight Zone* re-runs. My mother banished the television from our house in 1978, when I was nine years old, so the main forms of available entertainment were books and records, all of which aggravated rather than placated the imagination. *The Amityville Horror*, *The Omen*, *The Shining*, *The Dark* – I read 'em all through my fingers as the wind howled in the chimney flue and Bosch's most hellacious tableaux made themselves manifest in the fireplace.

Then my eldest brother went off to the air force, and when he returned on leave at weekends, he brought with him stacks of new LPs. Not the K-Tel or *Top of the Pops* compilations that had previously constituted the family

91

record collection, but albums by strangely named rock bands who never got played on the radio. My first impression of the weirdly bearded longhairs glaring out from those gatefold sleeves was that they were creeps of the lowest order. Perverts, deviants, degenerates, grave robbers and drug fiends.

Thus was I blooded. From that age I thought of all music as the Devil's music. I thought any song worth its salt should carry with it a whiff of rot or must or decay, that if music was any good it should sound ancient and uncanny.

And so, to this day, wholesome-sounding tunes don't do much for me. Sure, I can appreciate the genius of The Beatles and the Beach Boys, but if I'm being truthful, they don't carry the same mordant freight as the Stones or the Doors or the Jimi Hendrix Experience, bands that sounded like a force of nature – and not a benign one either.

So, friends, step into the murky shadows of my big brother's room and imagine yourself as a youngster, trembling and transfixed by the first shimmering fingers of Keith Richards's guitar as the blood-dimmed tides begin to rise . . .

Welcome to my nightmares.

10 'Gimme Shelter' – The Rolling Stones

Yep, like W. B. Yeats's 'The Second Coming', we've seen and heard it quoted from a hundred times, but the slow beast slouching towards Bethlehem that is 'Gimme Shelter' never seems to lose its fearful juju. For those of us among the Chicken Licken generation who grew up in the second (or was it the third?) age of nuclear paranoia, a period roughly bookended by Three Mile Island and Chernobyl, with *Threads* and *The Day After* providing the televisual dramaturgy, every day was the end of the world. And 'Gimme Shelter', the opening track on what is arguably the Stones' finest album, *Let It Bleed*, is an End Times war dance, carnal rite and bacchanal that throbs with the threat of violence and sexually charged dread (the sound of Merry Clayton's voice breaking on the line 'Rape, murder / It's just a shot away' tells us everything we need to know about la petite mort).

At one point during the Maysles Brothers' documentary *Gimme Shelter*, a lone black dog wanders across the stage, oblivious to or unbothered by the chaos, the noise, the marauding Hell's Angels. Robert Johnson's Hellhound gone astray, perhaps. Or maybe he's exactly where he wants to be.

9 'Blue Moon' – Elvis Presley

In which our clean-cut all-American hero takes his fuzzy-sweatered sweetheart to the high-school prom only to realise, just as a magnetic and weirdly hued moon emerges from behind a cloud, that those recurring lycanthropic dreams weren't dreams at all, but suppressed memories. A startling metamorphosis occurs: Presley's skinny body warp-spasms into a teenage werewolf intent on turning that pretty prom queen into beef chow mein. Of course, just as the sirens approach, the beast changes back into an innocent Elvis, standing shocked and lovelorn in the lunar light, his true love's viscera dripping from his fingers.

The beast in me, indeed.

8 'I See a Darkness' – Bonnie 'Prince' Billy

Here's the scene: an all-night lock-in in a country bar in the depths of December. You're having one of those never-ending bull sessions with your mate Alastair, a good guy but the kind of overly intense Yond-Cassius-thinks-too-much individual no girl will touch with a bargepole. Both of you drink and drink, but still you can't get drunk, until you reach some sort of alcoholic event horizon around four in the morning, the soul's midnight, when Alastair freezes, tankard stalled en route to his bloodless lips. 'There's a shadow over your shoulder,' he says. 'I think you'll die soon.'

7 'Bitches Brew' – Miles Davis

In 'How to Tell a True War Story' from Tim O'Brien's astonishing collection of Vietnam flashbacks *The Things They Carried*, the author relates a tale told to him by a soldier called Mitchell Sanders about a six-man squad dispatched on a seven-day listening-post mission in deep mountain jungle. The sortie requires strict field discipline, a total silence which can be broken only if the soldiers hear anything suspicious, in which case they are to radio for artillery or gunships.

After a day or two in full camouflage, shrouded in mountain fog vapours, the grunts begin to undergo a series of shared aural hallucinations, made all the more torturous by their being forbidden to speak. 'The sounds, man,' Mitchell says. 'The sounds carry forever. You hear stuff nobody should ever hear.'

He describes weird echoes, chimes and xylophones, 'this strange gook music that comes right out of the rocks. Faraway, sort of, but right up close, too . . . All kinds of weird chanting and Buddha-Buddha stuff.' One soldier sticks Juicy Fruit in his ears in an attempt to blot it out. Eventually, the patrol gets so spooked they call for an artillery strike that razes the entire mountainside.

'Bitches Brew', the title track from Miles's 1970 double set, is what I imagine that jungle music sounded like. More than even Hendrix's napalm paintings, the Doors, Creedence or Motown, it is the ultimate soundtrack to Vietnam as an *Apocalypse Now/Jacob's Ladder* allegorical bad trip. If not for Charles Mingus's *Let My Children Hear Music*, I'd have no hesitation in proclaiming it The Eeriest Jazz Album in the History of the World Ever.

6 'Into the Night' – Julee Cruise

Where we grew up, we thought David Lynch's *Twin Peaks* was a docudrama about our town, only with dubbed American accents. But even though the TV series was about fifteen years ahead of its time, the soundtrack was something else again, a nocturama of dusky, ghost jazz composed of promiscuous-sounding saxophone, foxy stand-up bass, fingerclicks, brushes like spiders' legs, and daubs of Link Wray's malevolent 'Rumble' guitar. Echoes of Mancini and Herrmann and Evans abound in this topiary of sound, the love theme is exquisite, and on torch songs like 'Into the Night' Julee Cruise sings in a sort of disembodied yet somehow carnal spirit-speak.

Incidentally, while you're in Lynchville, check out Angelo Badalamenti's 'The Pink Room' off the *Twin Peaks: Fire Walk with Me* soundtrack for the most ominous use of a bow since Lovecraft's story 'The Music of Erich Zann'. Not to mention Jimmy Scott's 'Sycamore Trees', which is like 'Strange Fruit' transposed to the Pacific north-west deforested stump country that also provided the backdrop to Nirvana's unplugged take on Leadbelly's 'Where Did You Sleep Last Night?'

5 'O Children' – Nick Cave and the Bad Seeds

Nick Cave has written more grimly fiendish tunes than even he can remember. There's the dribbling Dostoevsky-esque protagonist fingering his upstairs neighbour's stolen panties in the high-rise tower-block hell of 'From Her to Eternity'. Or in 'Red Right Hand' a plague harbinger and slumlord straight out of Poe's *Masque of the Red Death*. Or in 'Where the Wild Roses Grow' the ladykiller descendant of the bourgeois bludgeoner in the Blue Sky Boys' 'Banks of the Ohio'. But 'O Children', the closing track on *The Lyre of Orpheus*, is special because it dispenses with the archetypes and paints a scenario that is disturbing even by Nick's standards: a carriage-load of duped commuters on the Auschwitz Express, or maybe some Heaven's Gate type cargo cult with a one-way ticket to a mass-suicide-pact rapture, happy-clapping their way to the slaughter while the London Community Gospel Choir sings hallelujah in the background. We never find out exactly where the train is bound, but that's the song's genius.

4 'Ramblin' Man' – Hank Williams

Hank's vagrant anthem might on first listen sound like a simple dose of wanderlust, a travelling song that longs to go bar-hopping on some eternal Saturday-night honky-tonk odyssey. But don't be deceived. 'Ramblin' Man' is a long black train with a secret serial killer on board. And not just any serial killer, but a deathless badass who shapeshifts his way across continents and centuries. He could be Rafael Resendez Ramirez, the border-town midnight rambler suspected of multiple homicides who became the target of a massive FBI manhunt in the summer of 1999. He could be Anton Chigurh from Cormac McCarthy's *No Country for Old Men*. He could be the South African desert dervish in Richard Stanley's 1993 film *Dust Devil*. He could be Randall Flagg, the faceless, denim-clad, cowboy-booted Walkin' Dude from Stephen King's *The Stand*. Or the itinerant trickster musician in Horslips' 'Mad Pat'. Or the Irish hillbilly kiddie-fiddler in Pat McCabe's *Winterwood*. But maybe most of all, he's the evil twin of Hank's gospel proselytising alter ego Luke the Drifter . . .

3 'Black Wings' – Tom Waits

. . . Or then again, maybe he's related to this guy.

Uncle Tom has spun some unsavoury tales in his time (the ones on the *Black Rider* set being particularly macabre, closely followed by 'What's He Building?' from *Mule Variations*, where he recasts the Boo Radley next door as your friendly neighbourhood Unabomber), but I'd have to nominate *Bone Machine* as my favourite Waits album, not just because it sounds like hell on earth after the bomb, but also because 'Murder in the Red Barn' contains one of the great truisms: 'There's always some killin' / You got to do around the farm'.

'Black Wings', co-written with Waits' wife Kathleen Brennan (surely one of the most intriguing silent partners in any musical marriage), is a stoned and smoky fantasia located deep in side 2 that contains one of the most demented guitar breaks ever committed to tape, a sort of distorted Tex-Mex exercise in *Day of the Dead* necromancy.

The song's lyric conjures up the kind of mythical figure familiar to Appalachian, Ozarks, Black Forest and Blackstairs backwoods myths. Rumours and half-truths swirl around this shadowy traveller. Some say he once killed a man with a guitar string. Others say there are black wings sprouting from his back. All of which conspires to make him sound like the even creepier brother of Dylan's Man in the Long Black Coat. Oh, and here's the bad news: he's busted out of prison. His boots are mounting the staircase. And now the door is flung wide open. *He's not there for he has risen . . .*

2 'Waking the Witch' – Kate Bush

Side 1 of *Hounds of Love* is a suite of immaculately crafted experimental pop songs, but side 2 is a whole world unto itself, and one worthy of Guillermo del Toro or Terry Gilliam. Entitled 'The Ninth Wave', after Tennyson, this song cycle comes closer than any modern music to evoking the peculiar logic of dream and (with the possible exception of Ligeti) the terror of nightmare. And 'Dream of Sheep' lulls us into a hypnagogic spell before the horrors begin with 'Under Ice'. But the real bowel-loosener is 'Waking the Witch', an aural snuff movie with *Exorcist*-type voices (a bestial priest growls 'Confess to me, girl!') and bouts of convulsive glossolalia that make you visualise the singer's head doing the full 180, while the melodic hook is based on what sounds like a plague-rose nursery rhyme.

1 'In Dreams' – Roy Orbison

Sometimes the use of a song in a film for ever alters the way we hear it. Few of us who've seen *Boogie Nights* will ever clap ears on Night Ranger's 'Sister Christian' without visualising Alfred Molina's coke fiend in his underpants, as his catamite house boy lets off firecrackers in the living room. Or the episode of *My Name Is Earl* in which Giovanni Ribisi invites Jason Lee back to his strobe-lit abode to get skivvied off and boogie on down to Styx's 1983 concept synth-pop oddity 'Mr Roboto' (quite the bizarre little number itself – just what is it with soft-rock classics and crazed men in Y-fronts?).

But the use of Roy Orbison's 'In Dreams' in *Blue Velvet* is probably the premier example of how the meaning of a song can be irrevocably changed by the context it's placed in, one which shocked even its author.

Mind you, even before Dean Stockwell's freaky-deaky lip-sync job, there was always something a little off about this song. That candy-coloured clown they call the Sandman does not sound like the kind of creature you want tiptoeing into your room in the wee small hours to sprinkle stardust and whisper goodnight. And although 'In Dreams' is, to all intents and purposes, the true-hearted pledge of an estranged lover, sometimes I wonder if it isn't closer to the veiled threat of a jilted revenant. When Roy Orbison, chief tragedician and dark angel of pop opera, croons the refrain, 'In dreams I walk with you', it's less a promise of eternal devotion than a daemon lover's vow to haunt the bejesus out of his betrothed from beyond the grave if she ever dares shack up with another mortal.

Love, my friends, is far stranger than death.

What Is It Good For? Ten Songs Surrounding War

ROGER ARMSTRONG

Until the American war in Vietnam, popular song was mostly used to bolster the heroics and romanticism of war, but by the sixties, as live television beamed in the reality, the myth was finally blown and even the nostalgia for old wars dimmed as their mind-numbing horror was revealed.

10 'Goodbye Dolly Gray' – Big Four Quartet (Edison 7728, 1901)

What is it good for? Mindless promotion of heroism

The Boer War was one of those fought by bad comic-book generals in faraway places for very remote reasons. The Boers were, for reasons that became much clearer later, an enemy that was probably worth fighting, but that was not why they were taken on by the might of the British Empire 1899–1902. Lyricist Will D. Cobb seems to be wilfully vague as to the politics of the conflict but certainly knows how to tug at the heartstrings with his low expectation of the survival rates, and he wasn't far wrong.

9 'Butcher's Tale (Western Front 1914)' – The Zombies (CBS LPS63280, 1968)

What is it good for? First World War historians

Fifty years on and the Great War was finally being exposed in song for the sheer act of madness that it was. In stark contrast to the songs of the day about brave boys marching off to do heroic deeds, Chris White's chilling tale is particularly poignant given the protagonist's profession. His fragile vocal tells a tale of terror while listing many of the infamous battles, and is offset with a wheezing pedal organ that complements the despair of the lyrics.

8 'When the War Was On' – Blind Willie Johnson / 3 Mississippistaphas 3 (Columbia Co14545, 1929 / Deep Sea Records Sea D8002, 2003)

What is it good for? Enforced democracy

One song, two oddities share the No. 8 slot. Blind Willie Johnson's version was cut in 1929, five years after the death of President Woodrow Wilson, who took America into the First World War. Johnson's lyric harks back to the hard times created by the need to drive the Kaiser out of France, something Wilson saw as a crusade for democracy. Seventy-four years later and 3 Mississippistaphas 3 introduce a verse about the theft of America's democratic right by another president who launched his own crusade for democracy a few weeks after the release of their version.

7 'Lili Marlene' – Marlene Dietrich (Decca 23456, 1945)

What it is good for? International sheet-music sales

Though originating in Germany, this song was a huge hit with troops on both sides of the conflict in the Second World War. With its soft sop to the expectation of sex later, providing death didn't get in the way, it stands as a triumph of libido over naked fear. Marlene Dietrich had the prescience or good luck to depart Germany for the USA in 1930 after one hit movie, and it is ironic that this

101

song should have been instrumental in maintaining her cabaret career in both English and German.

6 'Korea Blues' – JB & His Bayou Boys (Chess 1449, 1951)

What is it good for? Not going

At the time of America's first great venture into South-East Asia, call-up papers were known as a Questionnaire and J. B. Lenoir was not that enthusiastic about getting one, fearing he would be shot down by the Chinese, whom he noticed had entered the war in Korea the previous year. But regardless, the general feeling was, 'Could you trust the girlfriend while you were away?' At the time this was known as 'looking out for Jody', a character probably derived from Joe the Grinder – the meaning of which is pretty obvious.

5 'Suicide Is Painless' (Theme from *M*A*S*H*) – The Mash (CBS SCBS8536, 1970)

What is it good for? Great TV

By 1972 the war in Vietnam was not going too well and there was a need for some nostalgia about wars past. So what better than a comedy TV soap about the recent 'forgotten war' fought in Korea between 1950 and 1953. Based on the 1970 movie and set in a field hospital, *M*A*S*H* was possibly the best TV show ever, acknowledging the pointlessness of it all while finding humanity in the camaraderie engendered. The theme song's airy optimistic view about the painlessness of suicide is undoubtedly incongruous, but like all great theme tunes still triggers great expectation.

102

4 'Feel Like I'm Fixing to Die Rag' – Country Joe & the Fish (Vanguard VSD 79206, 1967)

What is it good for? Irony in the USA

This jolly jug-band tune with lots of kazoos and whiz-bangs belies a bitter, sarcastic, irony-laden lyric. For the first time ever the gung-ho approach to war in music was overwhelmed by out-and-out revulsion, the soundtrack to the street protests. Even so, to include the line 'Be the first one on your block, to have your boy come home in a box' in a pop song was, and still is, very radical, particularly when the US body count from Vietnam was mounting daily, live on TV.

3 'Shipbuilding' – Robert Wyatt (Rough Trade RT115, 1983)

What is it good for? The pop charts

Thatcher's 'just' war in the Falklands lasted a mere couple of months in 1982, but by jingo did it work wonders for the jingoism count, propelling the Conservatives back into power in 1983 and provoking this subtle commentary by songwriter Elvis Costello. Wyatt's fragile vocal took a song about the complex contradictions in the financial benefits of war, via shipbuilding, with the deaths of many when those ships sunk, into the charts and on to the radio for six weeks.

2 'Masters of War' – Bob Dylan (Columbia CS8789, 1963)

What is it good for? The military-industrial complex

Bob Dylan is one of the great observers, though over the

years many took this to mean he was a 'protest' singer. This polemic from his second LP leaves no doubt as to his opinion of those who make fortunes from mass death and don't really mind who is killing whom. Regardless of the victor they'll always pop up on top of the financial shit heap, but in 'Masters of War', Bob Dylan rightly sees no hope of redemption.

1 'War' – Edwin Starr (Gordy 7101, 1970)

What is it good for? Absolutely nothing

This is the definitive anti-war song, lyrically the most straightforward and what is more it was a huge hit record back in 1970. Motown Records spent most of the sixties concerned with personal issues, but the civil-rights movement opened out black consciousness to take in broader social and political issues, but with the same direct, no-nonsense approach, to produce hits to dance and think to.

Music to Get Killed By: Ten Sonic Psychodramas

CATHI UNSWORTH

Long before I started writing crime novels, the music that I was obsessed by suggested to me the stories I would find when I did. Patient killers eking out a pot of tea in the far corner of a greasy spoon; a last resting place on the stained mattress on the floor of a lonely bedsit; a tuneless whistle echoing under a railway arch for a requiem. Crumpled papers bleed the details into the gutter of memory, the final witnesses an unshaded 100-watt bulb and an overflowing ashtray where one solitary butt bore the scarlet lipstick kiss of the victim. Lipstick that was the exact same shade as my own.

The compilation tapes I made back in the early nineties served me well as the soundtracks for the books I would begin writing ten years later. All of the songs on the list featured heavily. They would be arranged around music that belonged to real movie scores, like Bernard Herrmann's *Taxi Driver*, Elmer Bernstein's *The Man with the Golden Arm* and John Barry's *Beat Girl*. But the tracks that are on this list are perfect psychodramas in their own right, songs that suggest the whole plot to you in the space of a few minutes by either the brilliance of the lyrics or the threat of the music or, in some cases, both. Music that rises out of those basement clubs with their green doors and beckons you in; music that leads you to dance with a stranger; music that stalks you through the lonely streets of 4 a.m. while the houses all look the other way. Music to get killed by.

10 'Tyed' – Tindersticks

Tindersticks walked an unsteady line between melancholy and whimsy, putting Vera Duckworth's home furnishings on their front covers, writing about babies' teeth and doing drunken covers of sentimental songs such as Bowie's 'Kooks'. I found that quite rewardingly sinister, as if they were only trying to be nice to lure you into their world, to join all the other friends that could never leave. In the October of 1993, Tindersticks' eponymous first album was never off my stereo. It was perfectly autumnal with bassoon and clarinet, swirling keyboards and violin, and perfectly lonely, too. Suart Staples's hesitating vocals mentioned cold, empty rooms full of yellow lino, peeling wallpaper and cups of milky tea. Mad dreams he had about boats floating in harbours of sand. He sounded like a serial killer to me. The album gave me the title of my fist book – *The Not Knowing* – but it was this second track that really haunted me. Stuart haltingly and uncomfortably describes the history of a rug that once was a sheep that was cut open, bled, dried out and hung on his wall. See what I mean?

9 'For One Moment' – Lee Hazlewood

There are so many songs by Lee that I could have chosen, but this one fits into the world that Hazlewood aficionados Tindersticks, Gallon Drunk and the Earls of Suave had opened up for me in the early nineties. I was living in Ladbroke Grove, where suave killer Stuart Staples was still serving behind the counter in the Rough Trade Shop. Up the road was the Record and Tape Exchange, where in those days it was still possible to find Lee records for a couple of quid. This one is from the MGM album *These*

Boots Are Made for Walking, which also includes Lee's own version of his most famous song. But this track is a pure spooked-out chiller, in which Lee drinks deep from his bottle of Chivas Regal at the back of the bar and reflects mournfully upon the love he has just lost. The lady whom those *Psycho* strings that welled up around his deep, dark voice were suggesting to me might just have been buried out there in the desert.

8 'Ace of Spades' – Link Wray

I had the absolute pleasure of interviewing Link in 1993, when he told me about the time he played in bikers' clubs in Washington DC to the encouragement of the local longhairs shouting things like: 'Hey, Link! Play "Run Chicken Run" while I knife this guy!' They loved him because he had made a record that actually got banned without uttering a lyric, the seminal 'Rumble', which Link was promoting at the time I met him, for the Ace reissue of *The Original Rumble* CD. Link told me the track had come to him in a dream while he was lying on a gurney with one lung shot out, a result of his service in the Korean War. Once discharged, Link and his brothers holed up in a shack where they invented reverb and other types of fuzztoid effects by recording under stairwells and ripping up their amps. This is my favourite of his adventures in sound, managing to compress all the impending violence of a wrong turn down a 1950s Washington DC alley late at night into one utterly stylish, bristling swagger.

7 'Romeo Is Bleeding' – Tom Waits

Probably the most perfect juvenile-delinquent crime

story ever written is this tale of a handsome cop killer, who had probably just come back from watching Link on Bunker Hill when he had his fatal encounter with the law. Tom describes Romeo's peacock strut, his oiled hair and his swarm of acolytes all reaching to light his cigarette for him so vividly you can see the entire scene, lit in a pool of neon like a Hopper painting. Romeo's death, watching James Cagney's towering-inferno exit from *White Heat* up on the silver screen, is the final touch of genius. Never to be confused with the terrible Gary Oldman film of the same name, this highlight from the sublime *Blue Valentine* is a track to go back to and learn from every time a full moon waxes over Ladbroke Grove.

6 'No No Man' Parts 1 & 2 – Steven Jessie Bernstein

Sub Pop was the label that brought you the best guitar music of the 1990s and also *Prison*, the 1992 collaboration between Seattle poet Steven Jessie Bernstein and musician Steve Fisk, perhaps the greatest lost album of the decade. Bernstein used to open for Nirvana and Big Black, performing his pitch-black beat poetry with a voice that made William Burroughs seem hopeful and a rat hanging out of his mouth. The LP *Prison* was envisioned as spoken-word answer to Johnny Cash's San Quentin and Folsom albums, and Bernstein was recorded live at Washington State Penitentiary Special Offenders Institute. But shortly afterwards, just before his forty-first birthday in 1991, he killed himself by cutting three lines in his neck. Fisk rose to the unenviable task of building a score around Bernstein's last howl with visceral brilliance, creating dub, ambient and industrial settings throughout the album. But none are so perfect as the tracks that bookend *Prison*, the heart-rending night carnival of police and freaks intoned by the No No Man with a noir jazz that Steven Jesse's namesake Elmer would have been proud of. It's enough to make you weep.

5 'Son of Thumbs of a Murderer' – Shock Headed Peters

There is a brilliant Ruth Bayer photograph of SHP front-man Karl Blake on the inside sleeve of the *Several Headed Enemy* album that depicts him amid a swarm of locusts. With his wild mane of hair, pointed beard and jacket adorned with horse brasses, there has always been something about Karl and his music that recalls eerie childhood memories of dark British folk tales. This track, from 1993's *Fear Engine II: Almost as Though It Had Never Happened*, plugs straight into that memory hole. A duet with former Lemon Kittens collaborator Danielle Dax, it begins with a flourish of Spanish guitar before the dark intonations of a drum machine and Danielle singing in innocent tones about having the 'paddle-shaped' thumbs of a murderer. Then, wielding his mighty axe both literally and metaphorically, Karl delivers us straight into the killer's den, that workshop deep in the woods where you wander at your peril. There is something entirely satisfying about the timbre of Karl and Dave Knight's thunderous guitars and those vocals, curses couched in a beguiling, Scott Walkeresque beauty, that makes this the perfect record to nurture revenge by. Karl Blake is also one of the greatest gentlemen I have ever met.

4 'It'll Be Me' – Jerry Lee Lewis

The B-side to the original 7-inch of 'Whole Lotta Shakin' Goin' On', this song used to be on the jukebox of my favourite pub in Camden Town when it was a repository for rockers and the second front room of the inhabitants of Arlington House hostel. The memory of that, coupled with the truly terrifying nature of the lyrics, made it a natural for the soundtrack of *The Not Knowing*. My heroine-in-peril Diana woozes drunkenly around a thinly disguised version of said boozer while the original bad boy and now last man standing of the Billion Dollar Quartet raves a stalker's frenzy of threats around his demonic, pumping piano. Again, we are back in a landscape of myth, this time the haunted backwoods of Jerry Lee's Louisiana childhood where, caught between Haney's Big House juke joint and the Southwestern Assemblies of God University, he truly came to believe that he was making the Devil's music. In these three minutes of hell brew, Jerry Lee chases his girl up a telephone pole, down a crawdad hole and even jumps up in her sugar bowl. But perhaps none of these things is quite as chilling as his reference to himself as 'something crawling across the floor'. They don't call him the Killer for nothing.

3 'Knives in the Drain' – Lydia Lunch

An endless source of inspiration, femmes don't come any more fatale than Lydia, whose every release is a new revelation. You could get yourself killed to most of her back catalogue, on her travails of anonymous motel rooms from the backwoods to the Big Nowhere of LA and all the desert in between. But this track, from her genre-defying *Queen of Siam* album of 1980, is particularly special as it gets to the root of all noir – the gulf of empathy between a man and a woman. Lydia summons the ghosts of New York's past, with the twisted big-band arrangements of Billy Ver Planck and fretful guitar of Voidoid Robert Quine, to create an aural Weegee snapshot of a Lower East Side crime scene, comparing the blasted buildings to the wreckage of a female body: 'My windows are on the street and there is knives in my drain . . .' Though hardly out of her teens, the weariness in Lydia's young voice imparts a lifetime's experience of man's inhumanity to woman, boiled down to the bleak sexual metaphor of the title. She sounds as if both Hubert Selby Jr's Tralala and a dying Billie Holiday are inhabiting her simultaneously: 'I'm blackened and bleeding / I'm ripped to my youth / Every man's madness and I ask / What's the use?' This is hard-boiled non-fiction from the gutter of the naked city.

2 'Paying for Pleasure' – Gallon Drunk

No one does London like Gallon Drunk, whose multi-instrumentalist singer and main songwriter James Johnston literally plucks his songs from the air around him, travelling at all times with a Walkman to record the sounds of the streets and lugging in at bar-room conversations for authentic dialogue. Gallon Drunk fused the live power of the Pistols and Suicide with a connoisseur's knowledge of soundtracks and jazz and presented it looking like the last gang in town, all dressed like Al Pacino in *Scarface*. Unfortunately, everyone who copied them did a lot better commercially than they did, mainly by diffusing the rage and idiosyncrasy inherent in their

111

sound, or as one critic put it, 'this disgusting racket'. Their masterpiece 1993 album *From the Heart of Town* was a fevered trip around the boozers of Camden, over the concrete flyover of the Westway and culminating in this trip to the fleshpots of Soho that could easily have been entitled 'Once Upon a Time in the West End'. Beginning with a foreboding organ drone, James plucks out a banjo motif that emulates Morricone's classic spaghetti score, shot across with guitar slashes that reverberate like bullets and a howling harmonica refrain. You picture Charles Bronson slowly walking towards Walker's Court, his narrowing eyes drinking in the tacky strip of neon-lit cheap thrills, his finger itching on the trigger and revenge on his mind.

1 'The Big Bamboozle' – Barry Adamson

The man who invented the imaginary soundtrack on his 1988 solo debut album *Moss Side Story*, Barry Adamson is acutely sensitive to the sounds of danger and despair and the promise of redemption that is only a fleeting dream before dying. He had been exploring the themes of dual identity as an undercover musicologist spy through 1992's *Soul Murder* and 1993's *The Negro Inside Me*, using funk, jazz, blues, ska, dizzying Bernard Herrmann-style strings and big-band brass, inventing the persona of Harry Pendulum, the Swinging Detective, to carry out his investigations. During 1995–6 he hit a creative high, scoring tracks for David Lynch's *Lost Highway* and putting together the blockbuster album *Oedipus Schmoedipus*, whence this track, the greatest Bond theme that never was, comes. In part, this is a summation of his career to this point, tipping its hat to Elmer Bernstein's

The Man with the Golden Arm, his first-ever solo release, replaying memories of his favourite John Barry 007 soundtracks and harking back to cases opened at the beginning of *Soul Murder*. But this is also Barry telling you just how damn good he really is on a track so irresistible that since its release, it has accompanied a multitude of TV soundtracks, so that even if you think you don't know it, the chances are you do. Hats off then, to the master.

Twenty-five Years Later: Ten Unsettling Songs for a Middle-American White Guy to Awake to from a Coma

GARY LIGHTBODY

My time frame is 1983–2008 for convenience.

10 'Come to Daddy' – Aphex Twin

Well, any of his tracks really, but this is the only song with a sliver of a chance of being played within earshot of a hospital, perhaps from the open window of a car outside. Our recently awoken man (let's call him Patient X because it sounds cool, like a character from a Cold War thriller or a Kafka novel) might even assume robots had taken over the earth, or giant insects were climbing the outside of the hospital and he was to be eaten imminently by a gargantuan atomic spider.

9 'Nazi Punks Fuck Off' – Napalm Death

I picked this song of theirs in particular because I agree with the title. The lyrics are grunted and mostly unintelligible but even that seems apt for the subject matter. Most speed or death metal would run the risk of causing severe sickness in the recently thawed, most likely presenting itself as vomiting from the ears. Napalm Death are, however, at the top of a very spiky tree of music to wet the bed to. They are also awesome.

8 'A Joy' – Four Tet

If he slipped into a coma in 1983, even if Patient X was

hip enough to have 'Let's Dance' by Bowie spinning noiselessly on his turntable as he lay prostrate unwittingly awaiting discovery and rescue, waking up from his quarter-century of snoozing he'd still be hard pressed to comprehend the wild spasmodic drums and careening loops of Four Tet's *Everything Ecstatic* opener. Fear not though, Patient X, as the sweet embrace of madness will soon clutch you tight and all will be well.

7 'Fuck the Police' – NWA

Rap was pretty much in its infancy in 1983. It was still underground and it would be another six years before NWA would unleash their unstoppable polemic on to the world. A sorry state indeed though to fall asleep with Reagan in the White House and wake up to find Bush Jr in there. I would love to think that an album as visceral, antagonistic and vital as *Straight Outta Compton* (and a whole generation of life-changing rappers and rap crews in hip hop's golden age: Public Enemy, Pete Rock and CL Smooth, Eric B and Rakim, Run DMC, Ice T, etc.) would have had more effect on both electoral and social trends. Music, though, does not work miracles but it is a place you can escape to. But hold on a minute, I do share one thing in common with Patient X: I'm white, so what the fuck do I know?! The music I escaped to when I was a kid was rock and it wasn't until my early twenties that I discovered hip hop for myself.

Still, waking up to this NWA classic would be like sitting bolt upright in bed miraculously after twenty-five years only to be punched square in the face by a manic orderly. That's nearly what it felt like when I heard it first time, but then I like the rough stuff . . .

6 'Something in the Way' – Nirvana

Speaking of rock music that I escaped to. Into Nirvana's arms I ran without caution. For 'twas warm (and spiky too but, as I said, I like that) in their bosom. The song I've chosen may seem unusual as there are a hundred loud and more immediately frightening songs in their canon that would terrify time-travelling conservatives all the more readily. I've gone for the slow burn on this one. Of all his songs I find this the most disquieting. It is a desolate funeral procession through a tortured mind: 'I'm living off of grass and the drippings from the ceiling'. Wake up to that, Popsicle X!

5 'Clara' – Scott Walker

Perhaps the most unsettling song ever recorded, regardless of whether you've been awake the last twenty-odd years or not. It is about Mussolini's mistress Claretta Petacci, who insisted on being hanged with him when it all went tits up for Il Duce. They were then both hung upside-down in the Piazzale Loreto in Milan so that passing Italians (or tourists, not too many about in those days though) could punch and beat them. Walker symbolises this by getting his percussionist to punch repeatedly a slab of pork. This, combined with Walker's lyrics, delivery and general behaviour during the track, makes it stomach churning, angry, insane and thoroughly harrowing. It's also twelve minutes long and maintains a truly outrageous level of mania for the full dozen. Incredible, really. Brave, inventive, intelligent and utterly, utterly terrifying. This song could dissolve the sturdiest mind, so our coma-boy stands no chance.

4 'The Frog Chorus' – Paul McCartney

'Excuse me nurse? Nurse?'

'My God, you're awake!

(*Calls outside of room*) 'Patient X is awake! Get Doctor Happytennis!'

'Nurse?'

'Yes, Patient X, or may I call you Allan?'

'Patient X is fine. Nurse, that person singing sounds awfully familiar?!? I can't quite put my finger on it . . .'

'Oh yes, that's Paul McCartney.'

'Paul McCartney!? From The Beatles!?'

'Yes.'

Beeeeeeeeeeeeeeeeeeeeeeeeeeeeeeeeeeeeeeepppppppp.

'Damn it! We've lost him. Time of death seven forty-two.'

Okay, so this is a cheap shot as the man is a god. Even after The Beatles he wrote 'Maybe I'm Amazed', one of my favourite songs of all time, but as rude awakenings go 'The Frog Chorus' must rank among the rudest.

3 'The Real Slim Shady' – Eminem

Okay, so I'm thinking more the video for this than the song itself, as Patient X wouldn't have a clue what most of the pop culture references in the lyrics pertained to. Granted, he wouldn't have much of a clue of anything at all. Just when our thawing relic thought he might be getting a handle on the basics, his senses returning and the life whooshing back into him with every new second, his focus sharpens on the TV in the room (why it's on I don't know, one of his relatives was watching it maybe, feet up on the bed, maybe their fidgeting and farting is what finally woke him) only to reveal a masked white guy in a cape babbling freestyle word jazz and sitting on random people's faces with his giant fake baboon ass. It's a bastard mind-melt collage that'll spin him out of the bed, out of his pyjamas and out the window. Maybe.

2 'When the Levee Breaks' – Yat Kha

Nothing like a bit of Siberian folk punk to get you up and about after a long snooze. Led by the marvellous gravel-rasped throat singing of Albert Kuvezin. If Patient X was familiar with the Led Zeppelin original before his deep freeze, this version might feel like a disorientating and woozy continuation of the coma. Like a dream you're convinced you're awake in while you're in fact still asleep, but the opposite. It is an extraordinary discipline and talent Kuvezin possesses, I'm just not sure our man wouldn't be overwhelmed by its tantric power. That, coupled with the plink and plonk of the instrumentation (thumb pianos, Jew's harps and zithers all rising and falling inside of berating and incessant percussion), creates the oppressive atmosphere of a musical shark cage. Up and at 'em, Patient X!

1 Novelty Pop

I've tried to keep my list to songs that are genuinely upsetting by their subject matter, form or context and not their idiocy. In fact, every track on this list is close to my heart for one reason or another (I even recall loving 'The Frog Chorus' as a kid) and would only upset the test patient either because the song is so far ahead of its time or his, or because it is so visceral or explosive it can barely be contained. HOWEVER, it would be remiss of me to

118

scratch out a list such as this without making at least a passing reference to the most unsettling of all music: novelty/one-hit/shit pop. Pop has been beautiful, inventive and even breathtaking (Madonna, Girls Aloud, Sugababes, Boyz II Men, Ultravox, etc.) over the years. It can also make you want to rip your own ears off, eat them, then kill yourself. I'm thinking Aqua's 'Barbie Girl'; Whigfield's 'Saturday Night'; the Crazy Frog . . . Need I go on? Music without a single redeeming quality, made by idiots for idiots. Any of this would smash the poor guy back into his coma within the wink of a pantomime eye.

I would never, of course, deliberately torture someone. This is all hypothetical . . .

LO-FI

From English folk to pirate radio

John Williams / Rick Moody / Andrew
Benbow / Patrick McCabe

Sheepshearing: Ten Classics from the British and Irish Folk Revival

JOHN WILLIAMS

I first started listening to folk music in 1979 as an eighteen-year-old looking for a music with the same harshness and directness and sense of its own identity that punk had once promised to be. I wasn't expecting to find it in the folk clubs but, to my surprise, I did. Week after week, in places like the Moorlands folk club in Splott, Cardiff, I was able to listen to artists like Nic Jones, Dick Gaughan, and the Watersons, artists at the absolute peak of their powers playing music that was utterly strange to me – the traditional folk music of Britain, music as harsh and beautiful as I could have hoped for. This is a list of ten of the finest records I came across back then. So there's nothing very surprising here, I'm afraid, nothing super rare and re-released on fetish vinyl last year. If you know this stuff, you'll see it's pretty much a *Sgt Pepper*, *Pet Sounds* kind of list, full of the tried and tested and universally revered. If you don't know this stuff, though, you're in for a treat. These are still the records I love best.

10 *Both Sides Then* – Peter Bellamy

Peter Bellamy was peculiar: once the leader of the Young Tradition, the hippest of the sixties neo-folkies, by the time I came across him he used to perform in canary yellow jumpsuits (a Norwich City fan, apparently), which toned nicely with his long blond hair, and sing in a voice that sounded at first like a parody of an elderly folk singer. Only gradually did my ear attune to the art in it, finding my way in via his wonderful reading of 'The Trees They Do Grow High', a song little popularised by my punk-folk comrades the Janet & Johns. This is probably the most accessible of his albums.

9 *The Well Below the Valley* – Planxty

Folk supergroups – in which a bunch of solo folkies get together to try and up their booking fees – are generally to be avoided like the plague. The partial exception to the rule is Ireland's Planxty. They're a mite inconsistent, but when they're really firing, as on the version of 'Little Musgrave' here, with Christy Moore singing his heart out, they've a delicate power that's undeniable.

8 *False True Lovers* – Shirley Collins

It's very difficult picking out the plum from a recording carer as varied and brilliant as Shirley Collins's: *Love, Death and the Lady* is probably the best of the records from her seventies period, when she recorded with her sister Dolly's portative organ and elaborate arrangements. Before that, her duo with Davy Graham produced *Folk Roots, New Routes*, a wonderful record but one that still feels a little unfinished. So maybe it's perverse, but I'll go for her first record, *False True Lovers*, with her voice pure and young, and her own underrated banjo playing to the fore.

7 *There Was a Maid* – Dolores Keane

If you get seriously into the folk-music stuff you will be confronted by the question of what constitutes a real folk singer. Is it enough to sing folk songs you've learned from

124

recordings, or do you have to have learned them at your mother's knee, as part of a living tradition? The first kind of singer is often called a revival singer and the second a traditional singer, and folk snobs tend to favour the latter over the former, even though the latter are often unbearably harsh to listen to for the uninitiated. Anyway, in Ireland, where the tradition really is living, the lines between the two kinds of singer are often blurred, as in the case of the great Dolores Keane, born into a traditional singing family but with a career as a commercial musician. Whatever. All you need to know is that her later, singer-songwriter, records are dreadful, but this is the real deal. 'The Generous Lover' is particularly epic, wild and sexy.

6 *The Noah's Ark Trap* – Nic Jones

Nic Jones could have been the biggest star of all the seventies folkies, had his career not been cut short by a terrible car accident that left him unable to play the guitar or even remember his songs. A tragic loss, as Nic Jones combined the guitar-playing virtuosity of Martin Carthy with the sweetest voice of any English folkie. *Penguin Eggs*, his last album, has the most accomplished performances, but *Noah's Ark* gets the nod because of the quality of the material, including three enduring folk-club classics in 'Annachie Gordon', 'The Indian Lass' and 'Ten Thousand Miles'.

5 *Shearwater* – Martin Carthy

There are a great many more than half-decent Martin Carthy records, but if I'm going to be really harsh I'd say that the early records, from the sixties, are a little undercooked and the later records, from the eighties on, a trifle mannered. His seventies records, though, are in the very top drawer of guitar and vocal interpretations of traditional folk songs. And this is probably the best of them by dint of including his masterpiece, 'Famous Flower of Serving Men', which marries a jaw-dropping guitar riff to an epic murder ballad wonderfully reconstructed by Carthy from a few surviving fragments of text.

4 *Welcome Here Kind Stranger* – Paul Brady

Brady was the greatest of the Irish revival singers, and it's an absolute tragedy, artistically speaking, that he went into rock music in the 1980s (not a tragedy for him, obviously, as Tina Turner covered several of his songs and made him a packet). *Welcome Here Kind Stranger*, his one full solo album of traditional material, is a peerless work of consistent beauty, the most fully realised album – as opposed to collection of songs – of any listed here. Highlight is the definitive version of the much sung 'The Lakes of Pontchartrain'.

3 *For Pence and Spicy Ale* – The Watersons

First proper folk record I ever bought. Spectacularly horrible cover looks like a souvenir from a particularly twee rural tea shoppe. Nothing twee about the contents, though, featuring as they do the harsh and glorious harmonies of the three Waterson siblings and Norma's new husband, Martin Carthy. From the opening 'Country Life' to the magnificent closing hymn, 'The Good Old Way', this is English singing in excelsis. There was no greater noise for me than the Watersons in full flight.

2 *Handful of Earth* – Dick Gaughan

Scots guitar vocal legend Gaughan's finest album overall, edging out *Kist O' Gold*, *Gaughan* and *No More Forever* by a nose. The double whammy of 'Now Westlin' Winds' and 'Craigie Hill' provides ample proof that music is indeed the art closest to heaven.

1 *Anne Briggs* – Anne Briggs

Very likely the record I have played most often in my life. There are plenty of singers who are regularly described as free spirits but in practice this mostly translates as over-indulged kids. Anne Briggs was a thoroughgoing free spirit who refused to record an album at all during the sixties, preferring to hang out in rural Ireland and sing for the joy of it. Her first studio album, from 1971, translates that joy on to vinyl. The opening three songs – 'Blackwaterside', 'The Snows They Melt the Soonest' and 'Willie O'Winsbury' – are untouchable.

Got Rhythm: Ten Great Bands without Full-time Drummers

RICK MOODY

rock 'n' roll lives and dies based on the drum kit. That's how some people see it, anyway. Without that meathead behind the kit, twirling his sticks, performing his tedious solos, rock 'n' roll wouldn't be rock 'n' roll. Yes, there are certain drummers who must be admired. I concede the point. Keith Moon, for example, with the maniacal rolls and double-time passages. Maureen Tucker and her primitive toms. Grant Hart of Hüsker Dü, whose sound was all trebly with splashes like a jazz drummer's. Levon Helm, whose light touch in The Band gave the music its drive but in a subtle, unobtrusive way. By and large, however, rock drumming leaves me cold. As far as I'm concerned, the problem started in the eighties, back when 'Panama', by Van Halen, dominated the American airwaves. That Alex Van Halen snare sound – mixed up loud with a quantity of reverb meant to bludgeon you into submission – became de rigueur, giving way in the course of popular history to the pyrotechnical and ultimately tedious Lars Ulrich, who in turn spawned those forgettable new-metal drummers of the present century. Drums, in the military-industrial now, demonstrate the Wagnerian crypto-fascist quality in most rock 'n' roll. Rock 'n' roll, besides being multinational corporate pabulum, currently serves as an aid in extreme interrogation. See the reports on Abu Ghraib and Gitmo, if you don't believe me. As a balm for the weary, I have compiled this list of satisfying bands that have no drummer to speak of.

10 The Carter Family

It's the dread (and the almost offhanded way that dread is deployed) that makes the Carter Family among the greatest of all popular music acts. Since the dawn of the recording era! The Carter instrumentation, for the uninitiated, amounted to no more than solo guitar. Or perhaps guitar and autoharp. There were one or two voices. These days it would sound skeletal. But the Carter Family, in the early decades of the twentieth century, managed to have more drama and passion, more eccentric rhythms, more religious awe, than just about anybody else ever. Maybelle, the guitar player, tuned down to C sharp, like a death-metal guitarist, and her style, the celebrated 'Carter scratch', spawned a legion of bluegrass and country imitators, not one of them as good. AP and Sara sang above as though they never would be redeemed. The Carters' time together was dogged with interpersonal complications, but the songs were unforgettable, and the likes of this will never come again.

9 Young Marble Giants

They made only the one album. Among its ardent fans was Kurt Cobain (his wife also flattened 'Credit in the Straight World' in the period before her disfigurement by cosmetic surgeons). There was a synthesised rhythm generator that clacked along on the album occasionally, but it was nothing like a drum. The YMG sound also featured a really beautiful, melodic bass player in Phil Moxham. And yet it was the lyrics, by Stuart Moxham, and the subtle monotonal delivery of singer Alison Statton that made drums irrelevant (especially on one of my favourite short songs ever, 'Salad Days'). They broke up after the one album as though they had nothing more to say. As a result few albums have been as underappreciated, as seductive, as evanescent, as memorable.

8 Suicide

'Band' doesn't do them justice, the workers in this penumbral collaboration, whose synthetic/poetic vision was complete right from the outset. Even in the old punk-rock days, Suicide was a divisive entity. People loved them or hated them, the vast majority in the latter camp. Even when I was listening to Pere Ubu and the Residents and Glenn Branca, Suicide was an interest I kept to myself. My allegiance was fitful, uncomfortable, episodic. I got what Alan Vega, the singer, was all about. In retrospect, he's even better. He was a revolutionary. There was an improvised way he wrote and delivered his exhortations. He was better at this style than a lot of other such people. Better than Jim Carroll. Often better than Lou Reed. And Martin Rev's synthesisers were creepier and more industrial in the analogue prehistory of electronic music than what came later when there were racks and racks of keyboards all wired together – in Skinny Puppy or Ministry or Nine Inch Nails or Daft Punk. Suicide never disappointed, though listening to them was (and is) demanding. More than a person can take is often a good thing.

7 Simon and Garfunkel

The lyrics were pretentious, yes, and Paul Simon has never understood what he was really good at: pop songs in two-part harmony that owed a lot to the Everly Brothers. (But with more melancholy.) And Art

Garfunkel, though possessed of one of the best white soul voices ever, mystifies with his own strange post-Simon-and-Garfunkel journey, which prioritises walking. None the less, when I was a kid in the sixties, this was the sound of the times. I mean, we liked The Beatles and the Stones. I remember thinking 'Purple Haze' was strange and crazy. But what I listened to on my parents hi-fi when it was up to me was Simon and Garfunkel. Even now, *Bookends* and *Bridge Over Troubled Water* seem to me to be almost perfect, as good as commercial folk music got. And when they played live, they often played alone, just the two of them, with the single guitar.

6 Traveling Wilburys

One day we'll get to hear the demos. I bet the demos will be far, far better than the finished albums. Having said that, I still think the first official release (*Volume I*), is one of the great pop albums of the eighties, and this despite the fact that Jeff Lynne gave it the ELO sheen. Admittedly, there is a truly superb drummer on the Wilbury albums, Jim Keltner (he referred to himself as a 'Sidebury'), but the rhythm section was overdubbed, and when the demos get released, you'll get to hear what it was like for five of the greatest singer-songwriters of the rock 'n' roll era to sit around with acoustic guitars and play. George Harrison was an infrequently sublime lyricist, but I think the casual and confident shape of the Wilburys' material, largely his vision, is one of the misunderstood parts of his musical legacy. In fact, the Wilburys amount to some of the best post-Beatles material any of the Fab Four turned out. Certainly better than most of Paul McCartney's solo work. Runners up for all-star bands without full-time drummers: the Highwaymen.

5 Gastr del Sol

It's not fair to put this band on here, since I play with
David Grubbs myself, but I love Gastr del Sol (especially
Camoufleur). and they are a perfect example of the two-
man band as a composing entity. They demonstrate how
a really deep collaboration can make possible things out
of reach for the individual constituents, even when the
constituents are pretty remarkable in the first place. Jim
O'Rourke has made a lot of very interesting music over
the years (as a producer and as a member of Sonic Youth,
especially), but it seems to me he did his best work here.
And Grubbs, who really is a punk (cf. Squirrel Bait and
Bastro for confirmation), the old-fashioned hardcore
kind, benefits from the tonal colours that O'Rourke
brings as an arranger. Grubbs is a great and enigmatic
lyricist, and his shambolic tenor, especially at the top
end, has a forlorn, yearning quality which suits quieter
and more experimental music. All in all, this was one of
the essential bands of the nineties. Though others who
operated in the same general milieu (Tortoise, Trans Am,
etc.) got more attention, this is where there was unal-
loyed genius.

4 The Felice Brothers

I heard them when, recently, I appeared on the radio
show of the last great free-form FM DJ in New York, Vin
Scelsa. In the course of the show he played me this song,
'The Ballad of Lou the Welterweight', by some very
obscure upstate band. Where does Vin find this stuff?
And even though the singer (Ian Felice), sure aped mid-

sixties Dylan, the song as I experienced it was sly, funny, moving, beautiful. The rest of the record, *Through These Reigns and Gone*, is just as great. The Felice Brothers do have a drummer (Simone Felice), but I don't think he sings and plays well at the same time, because when he sings lead they don't bother to have drums at all. And he has the most beautiful voice of the three so he sings lead pretty often. I have seen video of the Felice Brothers performing in which Simone seems to be on crutches, which ensures that no drumming whatever can take place. This doesn't seem to affect the sound at all. The Felice Brothers play old folk music with a desperate down-on-its-luck quality, as if these guys really live the lives that Tom Waits is always singing about from his mansion in LA. All the other so-called roots-music bands should take note. If you haven't yet heard the recent Felice Brothers recording yet, you will soon.

3 The Kronos Quartet

Supposedly, this is a classical outfit, and it's one that a lot of classical-music aficionados like to dislike. But I think they are really a rock band that just reads music very well. The hit on their first album was the Jimi Hendrix cover 'Purple Haze', and they've recorded the best version of 'Marquee Moon', by Tom Verlaine. They recently released a single composed by Sigur Ros. I've seen Kronos live many times, and they are better live, like Bob Dylan, or The Who, or Guided by Voices, than in the studio. In a live setting, the two violins are more uncannily yoked together than they are on the recordings, and they often play the really dramatic material live. Starter album for neophytes: *Early Music* – an album suffused with melancholy, but which still manages to include a piece by Moondog. You know Moondog, right? The street musician?

2 The Cocteau Twins

This group of musicians relied completely on a drum machine. But in a way the drum machine in the Cocteau Twins' oeuvre was no more a drummer than Mo Tucker was a drummer in the Velvets. What was of interest was what was happening elsewhere, in the relationship between Elizabeth Fraser's lovely, incoherent warbling and the accompaniments concocted by Robin Guthrie and Simon Raymonde, her co-conspirators. The Cocteau Twins were all about melody, which is why the band were able, without much difficulty, to drift into the inoffensiveness of ambience later on. During the period when they seemed most revolutionary – on *The Pink Opaque*, for example – they were one of the few British bands that I was willing to listen to between Hüsker Dü and Minutemen releases. They were numinous and indelible, and the drum machine was just a click track.

1 World Saxophone Quartet

I'm a recent convert. Obviously, there are many other saxophone quartets. But this is one of the longest lasting, and their lack of generic prejudice, their willingness to go far afield, as well as their storied history (which includes extremely challenging instrumental originals and pop arrangements), allows for vocals, or even the odd percussionist now and then. This makes them incredibly cool, according to my standards of cool. They don't have to prove jazz credentials. They have them. They are confident enough to record an entire album of Hendrix covers arranged for four saxophones! It contains some of the best Hendrix renditions ever. An equally good place to start is the recent *Political Blues*, which is noteworthy for a sublime reading of 'Mannish Boy', with vocals by James 'Blood' Ulmer.

Because I Don't Believe in Lists

And try these other examples of the form: the Meredith Monk Vocal Ensemble, especially on 'Dolmen Music'; the Books, whose *Lemon of Pink* is one of the most rewarding albums of the twenty-first century (acoustic guitar, cello and laptop samples); Mouse on Mars, the greatest of all electronic duos; Piano Circus; the Handsome Family; Mimi and Richard Fariña; the New City Ramblers. Big Black. The Holy Modal Rounders. And Huun-Huur-Tu.

Heavenly Pop Hits from the Airborne Convent: Ten Songs that Define Flying Nun's Dunedin Sound

ANDREW BENBOW

For a period in the early eighties, while the northern hemisphere was asleep, a beautiful and influential, lo-fi, melodious rock-pop noise was emanating from near the bottom of the world. Over a period of about ten years (c. 1981–91) this music was picked up through frequencies spreading over the adjoining South Island, across the Cook Strait and Tasman Sea and then further afield to the Mother Country and Europe, where it was registered by the critics and indie-club DJs, and then bounced across and over the collegiate airwaves of North America. The origin of this noise was pinpointed to an octagonal town centre: latitude: 45° 52' south; longitude: 170° 30' east.

The label 'Dunedin Sound' was coined, half dismissively, to describe the murky, sometimes melancholic, but always melodic sixties-inspired pop music made in the city in the first half of the decade. Made by a bunch of like-minded (some would say incestuous) young men and women who saw a creative and social outlet in writing songs to play to a largely student home-town audience starved of touring acts. When an affable Christchurch-based record-shop assistant decided to start his own independent label, Flying Nun, and release the sound, gaining the support of student radio stations and a responsive music press, small ripples became confident splashes in the New Zealand music charts.

The essence of the celebrated Dunedin Sound contains

several distinctive ingredients. The main influences on the sound came from the sixties: The Beatles, the Rolling Stones, the Beach Boys, the Byrds and Love, along with the drone rock of the Velvet Underground, early Pink Floyd, with a pinch of Dylan's sly wit, and Leonard Cohen's downbeat poetry. Under these influences the result was a mix of sometimes jangling, sometimes droning guitars married to catchy vocal melodies, often accompanied down the aisle by prominent bass lines and background waves of keyboard. The recording inspiration came largely from the punk-rock DIY aesthetic – primarily channelled through the 4-track engineering of Chris Knox, a key figure in developing the integral lo-fi sound of the label. The legacy of these songs was a sympathy and often inspiration felt by the UK indie scene, with the likes of the House of Love and the Wedding Present recording FN songs, and the late-eighties/nineties US Indie sound with tributes coming in from the likes of Guided by Voices, Pavement, Cat Power and Yo La Tengo. The scene has also been referenced in literary fiction by Jonathan Lethem and Shena Mackay.

10 'Anything Can Happen' – The Clean (1982)

The driven pop sound of the Clean set the tone for what would become the sound associated with the label, mixing two-string droning melodies with open-chord strumming. 'Anything Can Happen' highlights the anthemic aspect of the repertoire. The song is a perfect blend of the Velvet's 'What Goes On' mixed with 'Mr Tambourine Man'. In most music scenes there often comes along a pioneering band that makes everything seem simple, a band who just gets up there and achieves the perfect mix.

That the Clean are universally considered to be the most influential band to come from the Flying Nun label is partly down to the fact that they entered into the spirit of things with a pure sense of energetic joy in making music, inspired by punk. Brothers David and Hamish Kilgour and bassist Robert Scott just picked up their instruments with little fuss and played the kind of songs that had inspired them. The results were a series of underground pop gems giving the band a cult status, especially in the eyes of fellow musicians. In musical terms 'genius' is not a word that can be applied to the Clean but 'holy' certainly is.

9 'Pink Frost' – The Chills (1984)

'She won't move and I'm holding her head'

If there is a pop-writing genius in this scene it would certainly be Martin Phillips. Backed by an ever-changing line-up in the Chills, Phillips recorded enough pop classics to have made a luckier man, born on another continent, a very comfortable living. The sense of humanity that comes through Phillips's finest pop songs leads me to believe that if Brian Wilson had not been born earlier, thus allowing himself to be the one to write 'God Only Knows', the Chills' songwriter would have stumbled upon it first. 'Pink Frost' was a weird choice for a 7-inch single. With its haunting murky melody and recording tied to a macabre nightmarish lyric, detailing the death of a girlfriend, the sense of anxiety that enshrouds the song would not have many a record executive, or commercial DJ, clicking their figures and pronouncing a sure-fire hit. Thankfully, the record executive in question was Roger Shepherd, and the radio DJs were 'working' for supportive student radio stations, and were quick to recognise the fact that 'Pink Frost' had the rare quality of being a song that you want to play again immediately the needle has hit the run-off grooves. If there was ever one song to catch the ear of John Peel and launch the Dunedin Sound around the world, this was it.

8 'Death and the Maiden' – The Verlaines (1984)

The Dunedin scene sprang up largely due to the fact that Dunedin is a university town were drink and the distraction of music are always good escapes from study and an entry into sexually explosive social groups. The Verlaines were the perfect student rock band, splicing catchy pop tunes with literary, artistic and classical music references, delivered with a cultivated, youthful air of pretentious arrogance, projected with graceful charm. No song in the world could sum up the overblown tragedy of university relationships quite like the lyric to 'Death and the Maiden' – 'You're just too, too obscure for me' to 'You'll only end up like Rimbaud, be shot by Verlaine'. Such literary references in the wrong hands could prove ponderous, but with its waves of guitar and brilliant repetitive one-word chorus, this song had many an overcoated student dancing and singing along to the band's literary namesake. To gain extra music-geek points, the band's first LP was submitted as a piece of work for frontman Graeme Downes's music degree. The video for the song is populated by key figures of the scene.

7 'Nothing's Going to Happen' – Tall Dwarfs (1981)

It would be contentious to label Chris Knox's songwriting as an obvious example of the Dunedin Sound. Being such an individual, visionary and prolific writer, it is easier to see Chris Knox as a bizarre hybrid of Mark E. Smith and Daniel Johnston. Within the scene he was a kind of grumpy but benevolent 'John the Baptist' figure: both encouraging and critical. His main contribution to the sound was the tone of the sound itself, recording the Clean and many of the other FN bands on his 4-track tape machine. In stark contrast to the 24-track pristine, overproduced sound which most record labels would consider essential to producing radio-friendly songs, Knox gave the label its signature murky lo-fi quality.

From the band's *Three Songs* EP, 'Nothing's Going to Happen' makes this list as a fine display of Knox's wit, providing a counter-balance to the Clean's optimistic song title, above. With its back-and-forth chord progression and rhythm guitar being more percussive than melodic, the song forms a bridge between punk and pop. The track's video is a fine example of the stop animation and Len Lye inspired scratch techniques which would appear in about 80 per cent of Flying Nun videos of the following years.

6 'Throwing Stones' – Sneaky Feelings (1984)

'Must be easy with all your friends happy just to agree with you, you've certainly won over them'

Dunedin, with its name derived from the Gaelic for Edinburgh, is the most Scottish city outside the UK and there are definitely links between the Dunedin Sound and Scotland. Scottish labels such as Postcard and Creation released music with a similar pop sensibility to that of Flying Nun, and there is something about the distinctiveness of both countries' vocal styles that lends a sense of otherness to the pop music they create. Creation released music by the Chills and there had been talk of the two labels distributing each other's records in their respective home territories. Another direct link was the arrival, as a young man, of Sneaky Feelings singer/guitarist Matthew Bannister in Dunedin.

It has been said that the musical influences on Sneaky Feelings were different from and more diverse than those of the rest of the Dunedin bands, but it is likely that the band shared records and tastes similar to Martin Phillips and Graeme Downes, at least. There is no doubting that Sneaky Feelings was Flying Nun's awkward, uncool band (which in a scene of nerdy white-boy musicians is a great achievement). The difference with Sneaky Feelings is that they filtered their influences into a much more eclectic, and often 'too gentle' output. The sound of Sneaky Feelings is similar to that of the Pastels or, latterly, Belle and Sebastian. Yet, of all the songs to come out of Dunedin, nothing captures the sense of menacing cold-ness of the city's winters quite like the jangle and scrape of the guitars which support the nasty peer group queen chastising vocal of 'Throwing Stones'.

5 'The Other's Way' – DoubleHappys (1984)

Seven degrees of separation for the Dunedin Sound would most probably be reduced to one degree of sepa-ration, with nearly every band containing a member who had passed through a version of the Chills at some point. The closeness of the bands led to often successful musical chemistry experiments and DoubleHappys was definitely one of those. Wayne Elsey had earlier been in the Stones, who had provided a side to the *Dunedin Double*, which, with its other three contributions from the Chills, the Verlaines, and Sneaky Feelings, had set an early template for the sound of the scene. Shayne Carter had been playing in bands such as Bored Games from the age of fifteen. The combination of the two, along with drummer John Collie, formed a magical two-guitar (no bass) sound that added elements of Television to their disposable pop songs. The iconic cultural moment of this song arrived in Carter's sporting of the classic Kiwi footwear of the eighties – the 'Nomad', for the record sleeve's photo shoot. The tragic moment was the too early and abrupt death, by misadventure, of Elsey during a train journey while returning from an Auckland gig.

4 'Can't Find Water' – The Great Unwashed (1984)

It made perfect sense for the brothers Kilgour, former members of the Clean, to name their next incarnation the Great Unwashed, and the name suited the messier sound the band was to make. With Robert Scott off writing pop songs with the Bats, David and Hamish got together with Peter Gutteridge to explore the less restrained side of the Clean sound. The result was a mix of looping, sliding and droning instrumental bases held together with crisp stitch-like single-note picking, played with a sparseness building towards intensity. Over this were placed simple, cool, impressionistic lyrics, leading to the songs sounding not unlike the Clean.

The pride of place given to the presentation of Flying Nun vinyl was of prime importance to establishing a sense of the sound, and the double 7-inch single of *The Singles* which contained this track was the most beautiful vinyl artefact to have been produced by Flying Nun. The perverse beauty of the object lay in that, with its Pollock-inspired splattered plastic-sleeved cover, the vinyl had a tendency to become warped or mouldy – essentially being attacked by the thing designed to protect it.

3 'Circumspect Penelope' – Look Blue Go Purple (1985)

Any self-respecting scene which prides itself on its sixties influence deserves a girl group, and Look Blue Go Purple was it for the Dunedin scene. With a mix of guitars, keyboard, flute and female harmonies, Look Blue Go Purple produced songs ranging from the catchy 'Cactus Cat' and the spit-in-your-face, relationship-ending, perfect slice of indie-pop that is 'I Don't Want You Anyway', to this moody keyboard-driven ticking off for an Ancient Grecian wife deserter. Sadly, Look Blue Go Purple didn't stick around for much more than two EPs, but its members went on to become elements of other bands, most notably Denise Roughan in the 3Ds – perhaps the most successful Dunedin band to break the chains of the Dunedin Sound.

2 'Flex' – The Jean Paul Sartre Experience (1986)

'Flex thyself and muscle me in, like we're in this together and it's a comforting thing – but it's not'

With its loopy guitars and ominous bass line, this song from Christchurch beat combo JPSE proves that perhaps Dunedin is a disturbed state of mind. 'Flex' is the musical equivalent of a stalker creeping up on its victim. The second Flying Nun band to take inspiration in choosing a moniker from a French literary figure, JPSE contained the artiness of the Verlaines but, with their lyrical inventiveness and sense of performance, they were a whole different kettle of smeared fish and sheep's heads. There were other Flying Nun Dunedin moments from outside the city, including the Bird Nest Roys' beautiful tribute to confectionery and childhood – 'Jaffa Boy', the Abel Tasmans' Chills-like 'Sour Queen', and the pop strand of the Clean which Robert Scott took with him every time he went up to Christchurch to make music with the Bats, but 'Flex' is the song that best captures a sense of unease always lurking somewhere in the music, be it drone rock or pop.

1 'She Speeds' – Straitjacket Fits (1987)

'These eyes may be steady but my cigarette is shaking'

If Sneaky Feelings were the scene's uncool band then Straitjacket Fits were the leather-jacketed cool hipsters. Perhaps the last great record to capture the Dunedin Sound was the EP *Life in One Chord*. The Fits had been going for a while as a three-piece before Andrew Brough, previously of the Orange, added the extra element to the trio of ex-DoubleHappys Carter and Collie and bass player David Wood.

What Brough brought (apart from a talent for writing the type of yearning ballad that would eventually see him ejected from the band for musical differences) was a style of picking to complement the looser style of Carter's guitar work, and a strong higher voice which added a majestic support to the often swooping rock howls of Carter's choruses. While the EP contains two Carter gems and a distinctly Brough ballad, it is 'She Speeds', with its soaring guitars and harmonies, which gives the true taste delight of this great partnership.

Not in My Radio Booth: Ten Tunes for Captain Butty

PATRICK McCABE

Whether anyone in England knows this or not, Tommy O'Brien was a famous Irish broadcaster, now long since deceased I am sorry I have to report, who during the forties and fifties had the seats of Covent Garden opera houses worn away with his cavalry-twilled buttocks. What of Tommy? Suffice to say that this man was a totem who bestrode the landscape of post-Independence with a confidence and magisterial composure that made his counterpart in Rhodes seem like a sad little toy soldier with notions.

I don't know for sure what music Alf Garnett liked (though I suspect that the words 'Lambeth' and 'Walk' might never have been a long distance from his lips), but this much I do know: Tommy O'Brien liked Count John McCormack. And so do I. One of my all-time favourite tunes is:

10 'Song of the Seals' – Count John McCormack

Whenever I think of the burbling phonetics that go on on that track – eerie glistening rocks and the weirdest of fishy semaphoring going on, I am reminded of nothing so much as an episode of *Dr Who*, which is not a series with which, normally, I would readily have associated the internationally renowned tenor.

Prog rock has been getting a bad press lately. But not any more. Not in my radio booth, at any rate.

And as a means of consolidating my support for that genre and unequivocally setting in stone right here in public, coming right up next I have my two 'real gone rave-o' choices: yes, a pair of mouth-watering 'platters of vinyl', as up-to-the-minute trendsetters have been known to describe LP records, a brace of warm-beer, cricketing wonders which take us off to Canterbury by train and beyond.

Did you ever hear 'Golf Girl'? That's my No. 9:

9 'Golf Girl' – Caravan

For it makes my spine jiggle. Why, it's got to be the strangest pink wonder of a song ever written. It's as if Stanley Spencer had been discovered breaking into your house at night.

Another good one from that time is 'Return of the Giant Hogweed'. But I only have room for one progressive number, so out go Genesis and in comes:

8 'Ernie (The Fastest Milkman in the West)' – Benny Hill

Poor Benny: put out of work by smart-alec pretend-socialists who didn't mean a word of that auld anti-Thatcher blather, which they have since gone on to shamelessly prove.

So let's hear it for Benny – the only comedian in the world ever to make a small-town English western.

To this very day 'Ernie's ghostly milk cart' goes rattling through the deadly quiet of the suburban streets of my imagination, especially in that tremulous moment just before dawn, when – every inch the equal of Eli 'Tuco' Wallach – 'Two-ton Ted from Teddington' goes for his doughnut.

146

Aside from the flames coming out of the British Embassy and the ubiquitous dyslexia of Noddy's fake skinhead band Slade, one of the more interesting events to take place in Dublin in the year 1972 was Philip Lynott, the powerhouse behind Thin Lizzy, consummately snaring the zeitgeist of that city to perfection in his song 'Dublin'. 'We'd laugh and joke and smoke and later on the boat, I'd cry over you'. In Dublin.

What a masterpiece. And that's my No. 7:

7 'Dublin' – Thin Lizzy

And now may I announce my No. 6 selection, which is 'Visions of Johanna' by the *Chronicles* genius, Bob Dylan. An artist who, for my money, stands shoulder to shoulder with Spokeshave, which is what they used to call the Bard when I was growing up, and John Milton indeed or any other scribe you might bother to care to name, Mr Keats included. This tune reminds me of the time when I was seventeen at a dance in Cavan in a carnival marquee, that hot summer night when I had occasion to remark to my waltz partner, a lady of considerably marked rural mien, that I felt 'the ghost of electricity howled in the bones of her face', being promptly rewarded with the response: 'Do you know what it is, I'm as warm as an auld horse.' So that's it then. At No. 6:

6 'Visions of Johanna' – Bob Dylan

I was very fond of Soft Machine in my younger days – and still am. Which is the reason why Robert Wyatt goes

147

straight in at No. 5 with 'Shipbuilding', of course – or any other track of his that you might care to name.

5 'Shipbuilding' – Robert Wyatt

In my early adult years I was to find myself domiciled in Apartment 4G, in the town of Longford, County Longford, the Midlands, Ireland, Europe – accommodations which came fully fitted with an atomic-age television screen and a double bed which folded out of the wall as, simultaneously, a miniature stage swung into position in the lounge and a girl in a mini-dress covered in black squares clicked her fingers and began to sing 'pop'. All of the foregoing, I am sorry to have to say, is in fact a lie, for nothing of the sort took place in Longford town, back 'in the day' or any other time. My domicile in reality being little more than a shoebox beside a chicken house. But in one corner there reposed *Burt Bacharach's Greatest Hits*. Thus:

4 'The Look of Love'

3 'Alfie'

– both by Burt the old silver fox himself, of course.

I do not harbour the slightest doubt in my mind that when I contest that analogous to some of the greatest miscarriages of justice in history, such as the bombing of Dresden and the massacre at My Lai, is the persistent and quite disgraceful tendency to omit the great Gilbert O'Sullivan from ubiquitous 'lists' such as these. No sight nor sign do you ever see of the glistering gleaming nugget of pure gold that is 'Nothing Rhymed'. Or 'We Will'. This travesty now ends. As in goes Gilbert at No. 2:

2 'Nothing Rhymed' – Gilbert O' Sullivan

Now it's time for No. 1, which is a tune called 'Terry' in which the unfortunate youth with whom the singer Twinkle is besotted doesn't look where he is going and crashes his bike into a plate-glass window – I think. Or maybe he just crashed. But either way, he was to depart this earth tragically and in so doing give us this event-packed, heartbreakingly plaintive eulogy by his girl-friend:

1 'Terry' – Twinkle

Twinkle also recorded a much lesser-known gem entitled 'Golden Lights', and it is this which always has me blub-bering for 'lost decades' before the first bar is out. Thus I would describe 'Golden Lights' by Twinkle as a sort of three-minute *Day of the Locust*, a cautionary tale, a soap-bubble parable about the drawbacks of fame and the heartless arid core of Machiavellian consumer cap-italism.

So there you are, that's it – my Top 10. Good listening, folks – I hope my selection will be to your taste. But I really must extend my basest and most abject apologies to both Terry Dactyl and the Dinosaurs and Lieutenant Pigeon for 'Mouldy Old Dough'. Maybe next year, pop-pickers: that's if Joe Dolce's not hanging around.

WAXING LYRICAL

From short stories to liner notes

Stav Sherez / Tom McRae / John Kelly /
Jon Savage

Against a Hopper Sky: The Ten Greatest Short-story Songs

STAV SHEREZ

The best rock lyrics approach literature. They're not poetry, they're closer to the short story. A focus on the telling detail, a pervasive sense of atmosphere, a moment of great moral reckoning – these are the criteria here.

10 'Poor Old Tom' – Peter Case (*The Man with the Blue Post-modern Fragmented Neo-traditionalist Guitar*, 1989)

A young, naïve sailor on shore leave gets drunk and kisses a girl. He's arrested, misses his ship, and gets railroaded for thirty-five years on a morals charge. But that's only the beginning of his troubles. Suffering from depression, he is transfered to an institution where he's given regular ECT treatments. When that doesn't work, they wheel him into an operating theatre and perform a lobotomy. By the time we meet him he's an old, homeless man trying to put together the missing pieces of his life.

9 'Out of Control' – Dave Alvin (*Ashgrove*, 2004)

The flipside of the Californian dream. A man pimps out his girlfriend so they can buy crystal meth. He sits outside the motel room cradling a gun and thinking about his past. His father's death from lung cancer. His ex-wife, now a Jesus-freak working two jobs, living in a mobile home, and still getting high with him occasionally. His own failings and relapses. A sober-eyed view of what drives people to addiction and self-destruction.

8 'The Hole' – Townes Van Zandt (*No Deeper Blue*, 1994)

An existential fairy tale for bad boys and lost girls. Townes weaves a sinister gothic allegory against a rhythm track which sounds like the beating of skulls. Walking in the woods one day, he meets an old witch-like woman who invites him into her cave. Once inside, she tells him he'd better learn to call it home. He pleads with her. Asks, what about his lover? His family? She tells him he needs to forget them. He's alone and always will be. She tries to kiss him. He fights and manages to escape the cave but quickly realises that what went on in there will stay with him for ever. A prophecy of death? A bad dream? Or just a warning about not going too deep into yourself lest you find demons residing therein? You decide.

7 'Jesus Didn't Die [for Faggots Like You]' – Tom House (*Jesus Doesn't Live Here Anymore*, 2001)

An examination of cowardice and prejudice powerfully articulated in the tale of a wild night of drinking, driving and gay-bashing. Two buddies pick up a gay youth and drive him out to the woods. The narrator's insistence that he thought they were only going to rob him is drowned out by his friend's frenzy with a baseball bat and a coil of rope. They leave the kid barely breathing and drive deep into the mountains. The quiet, the falling snow, the hyperventilating friend slamming his fist against the dashboard – these details build up an unbearable tension as the narrator questions his own actions and the meas-ure of his cowardice. Oh, and the cruel taunting nursery-rhyme sing-song of the chorus will spin through your head like a bad dream you can't shake off.

6 'Settled Down' – Richard Buckner (*Bloomed*, 1994)

A roller-coaster ride of recrimination and regret told in hallucinatory clarity by the master of the broke-heart lyric. Against Raymond Carver's home-patch of Chico, Buckner recalls a relationship dissolving in tequila binges, back-seat affairs and betrayal. The details are all there: the motel room, the broken promise, the unguarded night, the temptation of a stranger's smile. Buckner's voice sounds brushed with smoke and years as he mourns a love affair disintegrating in the dimly lit bars and migrant towns of California's Central Valley.

5 'Medication' – Damien Jurado (*The Ghost of David*, 2000)

The narrator's deceptively gentle opening statement that he has many concerns doesn't prepare you for the anguish and perdition which follow. His lover and brother both need him, constantly calling him up, asking for love. But his lover's married to a cop 'with a keen sense of trouble' and his brother's a schizophrenic riding the last high before total collapse. He shows him photos of graves with their names inscribed on them. He's seeing bugs on the wall and angels in the woodwork. He pleads not to let them take him away. But, by the next verse, the narrator's watching his brother being strapped to a table while doctors prepare the electrodes. In a voice drenched in anguish and guilt, the narrator prays to God to take his brother's life.

4 'Highway Patrolman' – Bruce Springsteen (*Nebraska*, 1982)

The most cinematic storyteller in rock, Springsteen's

narratives tell of bad choices, unkept promises and hope souring into desperation. This one looks at the moral complexities occasioned by blood and loyalty. It's the story of Esau seen through the economic lens of 1980s America. Two brothers riven by war and love find themselves on either side of the law. The landscape is the frozen emptiness of the Midwest. A sense of stillness and isolation pervades Springsteen's delivery. The way the narrator's actions belie his sentiments in the chorus adds a level of moral ambivalence rarely found in rock lyrics. Sean Penn turned this story into his fine directorial debut, *The Indian Runner*.

3 'The Janitor' – Richmond Fontaine (*The Fitzgerald*, 2005)

No surprise that novelist Willy Vlautin's lyrics should be the most literate and haunting of our times. The story is boy meets girl. Except he's a lowly janitor in a hospital and she's recovering from a savage beating by her husband. They talk, the janitor buys her things, spruces up his appearance. They're broken pieces of a puzzle who somehow manage to fit together. A day before her scheduled release they make a run for it and end up in a dusty desert motel where she locks herself in the bathroom and begins coughing up blood. And yet, despite all this, it ends in one of the most singular moments of grace ever to be found in a rock song.

2 'Night Accident' – Robbie Fulks (*Let's Kill Saturday Night*, 1998)

This one's straight out of a 1940s rural noir. All dark cornfields and penitential rain. The buddy picture turned on its head. Two friends end up in a wreck, their car lodged on the rails of the Burlington Northern Express. It's night. There's rain and glass and blood. The narrator knows he's going to die. He confesses that he slept with his friend's wife. He asks him for forgiveness. Then they spot a man walking up ahead. The narrator pleads with his friend to sound the horn but he ignores him. When the man disappears, he turns and strangles the narrator to the roar of the oncoming train. A masterpiece of menace and guilt, played out as Greek tragedy against a Hopper sky.

1 'Rock Minuet' – Lou Reed (*Ecstasy*, 2000)

Possibly the most extreme and harrowing lyric in rock. This is everything you don't want your life to be. A vision of the inner psyche as Bosch's Hell. The elegiac melody and Reed's deadpan delivery belie the dark subject matter. Following an opening couplet which has to be heard to be believed, the protagonist drifts from hate-sex to drugs to sexual degradation in an attempt to come to terms with his past. He dreams of the murder of his father as homoerotic fantasy. He participates in the kidnapping and torture of a man, getting so excited he ejaculates. The escalation of kicks finds its zenith in the slaying of a man who tries to cruise him one night. With the warm blood on his hands, the narrator manages to find a strange kind of redemption.

This Woman's Work: Why Female Singer-songwriters Are Better than Their Male Equivalents

TOM McRAE

I picked female songwriters because ever since Kate Bush I've felt more of an affinity to them than many of their male counterparts. Perhaps it's my own high voice, or perhaps it's because they seem to be more genuinely emotional and more risk-taking. The male singer-songwriter is widely despised by the media – especially these days – but not so much the women. Having compiled this list, I think I see why.

10 'Top of the World' – Patty Griffin

Happy songs are rubbish. All of them. True happiness can only be experienced by small children, dogs and insane people. For the rest of us there are the songs of Patty Griffin. She understands.

9 'Love and Affection' – Joan Armatrading

'I got all the friends that I want', sang Joan Armatrading in 1976. I thought that was just showing off; I didn't seem to have any. My dad's job meant we kept moving house and just when I'd made friends it was time to leave again. It probably didn't help that we kept being taken on holiday to monasteries. Not many kids there, just monks. Although you do find the best reverb in monastic chapels. I have this theory that the religious experience is actually based on reverb – which is why outdoor weddings always seem weird. God isn't in the detail, he's in the echo.

8 'The Last Time I Saw Richard' – Joni Mitchell

I hated Joni Mitchell for the longest time, high voiced, whiny, too many words – then one day the clouds parted and I realised I'd been wrong all these years. My old art teacher told me that one day I'd like Joni Mitchell's music and that I'd come to realise Salvador Dali was an over-rated twat. I may be paraphrasing. She was right on both counts. *Blue* is an amazing record. *The Persistence of Memory* is a dull, dull painting.

7 'Untouchable Face' – Ani DiFranco

Not many songs can utilise the word 'fuck' convincingly, but this has to be one of the best. It's such a beautiful, lilt-ing song with such a vicious refrain. I've often pictured a celebrity death match between Ani DiFranco and the woman who ripped her off completely – Alanis Morissette. In the fight Alanis attempts to stun her oppo-nent into submission by reading unabridged extracts from her painfully embarrassing teenage diary (or just singing one of her tedious songs), before the deceptively tiny Miss DiFranco suddenly steps forward and guts her like a fish. That would be justice.

6 'Golden Boy' – Natalie Merchant

I like people whose voices change noticeably over time. The deeper, smoked-out Joni Mitchell contrasts with her high-voiced years, and with Natalie Merchant something seemed to change about the time of this album, *Motherland*. I'm clinging to the hope that my voice will one day get deeper, but I suspect I'll always be more June Carter-Cash than Johnny.

5 'I Dream a Highway' – Gillian Welch

The best songs are either 2 minutes 45 seconds long, or 14 minutes. Or somewhere in between. This is on the upper limit of how long one song can be before Peter Jackson tries to film it. Everything Gillian Welch does seems so effortless: you never hear the wheels turning. And none of the songs are happy. Ever. Perfection.

4 'Love Actually' – Girl Called Eddy

My attitude towards the British music and film industry is neatly summed up by this song. There was a film called *Love Actually* that needed a theme song. Erin (or Eddy) wrote this song for it. It's beautiful and has the same title. It would have been a huge hit, launched her career and been the only good thing about a bad film. They chose an old cover version by Ronan Keating. Cocksuckers.

3 'Jasmine Hoop' – Kathryn Williams

I've toured with Kathryn Williams. She found something to tell me off about every single night, but it doesn't stop me loving her. 'I'm gonna tell you half the story so you'll come back' should read, 'I'm going to find some reason to shout at you for half an hour after the gig' . . . this song reminds me of getting my first deal, and being played Kathryn's record over and over by my label boss who told me that's how I should sound. Thinking back, he may have been right.

2 'Mushaboom' – Feist

It's rare to find myself ahead of the curve, I'm usually the last to any musical party – it took Kurt killing himself for me to realise Nirvana were any good (although Morrissey could do it now and I'd still need convincing), but for once I saw this coming. Feist's voice and the production of her records are great, but really it's the dancing in the videos that makes it all irresistible. I've never had dancers in my videos. Just rain.

1 'Wuthering Heights' – Kate Bush

When I was seven there was a crack the size of my fist running all the way down our kitchen wall. A scar in the land had been gouged by an ancient glacier and was causing our house to subside. The kitchen was apparently staging a breakaway move from the rest of the vicarage, in much the same way as my dad, the vicar, was attempting to secede from the rest of the family. When my parents split up in 1978 the whole world, including the bricks and mortar of our house, could see it coming. I was young but I was prepared. I had taken steps to fill the vacuum of parental affection with love for a woman who took up residence in my heart and has yet to leave. That was the year I fell for Kate Bush. The Sex Pistols arrived at the same time, but Johnny Rotten never inhabited my dreams in quite the same way.

The Pecking Order: Ten Songs About Chickens

JOHN KELLY

I collect songs about chickens in much the same way that Hugh Fearnley-Whittingstall collects the actual birds. I tend to them just as he does, husbanding them properly and making sure they have a good life. In return I get all the happiness that only a good chicken song can bring. Mood enhancers every one, they cheer me up without fail. As songs about poultry, they have no other possible outcome. Sad, dark or nihilistic chicken songs simply do not exist. Each work in the genre (and it is a genre) is a comical one. Chickens are comical. Songs about chickens are comical too. It follows. It's physics.

Old-timey fiddle scrapers and banjo pickers, when they weren't impersonating locomotives, were forever mimicking chickens. It gave them a chance to showboat. When guitars went electric, dexterous fretmeisters couldn't help themselves either with all that clucking and pecking and squawk. But chicken songs are not just about virtuosic display. Nor are they merely about novelty, e.g. the Nervous Nervous number 'Does a Chinese Chicken Have a Pigtail?' Or Roy Acuff's 'Sixteen Chickens and a Tambourine'. Or indeed any of the hundreds of others I might mention given more space. I could go on and on. And sometimes I do.

In my view, the true power of the chicken song first emerged when artists began to explore the symbolism of the chicken itself. The Dominoes' 'Chicken Blues', for instance, with its lines 'If you don't like chicken / Leave that hen alone', suggests that chicken doesn't always necessarily mean chicken. And in my, admittedly heretical, opinion Dylan's 'Lay Lady Lay' is not what it seems either.

But these of course are crucial theories for another day. Suffice to say that the genre's capacity for both the novelty and the literary survives to this day. The Bees raided the henhouse for 'Chicken Payback' and Bondo do Role excelled themselves with 'Solta O Frango' – proving that chicken songs are a still a universal language. I really do believe in the power of the chicken song. And I believe because I know that, in moments of crisis and despair, a chicken song can do the work of any amount of expensive Swedish vodka from my freezer. That's a fact. And now here, plucked from a worryingly large database, is my Top 10.

10 'C-H-I-C-K-E-N' – Mississippi John Hurt

The great blues singer teaches us how to spell chicken. A good place to start. Spelling Mississippi isn't quite so easy.

9 'Chicken Blues' – Billy Ward and the Dominoes

Recorded by a pioneering R&B/doo-wop group which featured the extraordinary voices of future Drifter Clyde McPhatter and his eventual replacement Jackie Wilson. An impressive vocal pedigree, therefore, and much harmonic athleticism. On this one they keep up the lewd but somehow classy standard set by their best-known song – the admirably boastful 'Sixty Minute Man'.

8 'A Chicken Ain't Nothing but a Bird' – Cab Calloway

A song written by Babe Wallace and recorded by the likes of Nellie Lutcher, King Perry Louis Jordan (who also recorded 'Ain't Nobody Here but Us Chickens') and Cab

Calloway. Great lyrics. Could be Fearnley-Whittingstall, in fact. It recommends boiling, roasting and broiling (in a pan or a pot) and informs us that chicken was a favourite dish of Henry III – unreliable information but perfect to tee up the rhyme: 'But Columbus was smart, said, "You can't fool me / A chicken ain't nothin' but a bird".'

7 'Memphis, Women and Chicken' – Dan Penn

From Vernon, Alabama, Dan Penn is the gentle southern-soul man who wrote some of the great songs of our time – among them 'Do Right Woman' and 'Dark End of the Street'. Here he turns his attention to getting one's priorities right in Tennessee. In blues, soul and country soul there are so many songs about fried chicken – but then if you've ever been in the American South you'll know there's not a whole lot else to eat – unless you're partial to possum.

6 'Chicken Strut' – The Meters

New Orleans' finest released this hunk of free-range funk on an album called *Struttin'*. The lyrics are simple and direct with the invitation to 'keep on struttin'' repeated over and over again. But this is no ordinary funk work-out. With the whacking drums of a clucking Joseph 'Zigaboo' Modeliste laying down that heavy voodoo groove, it reminds us that Louisiana was never a good place to be chicken – certainly not at night.

5 'The Greasy Chicken' – Andre Williams

A follow up to 'Bacon Fat', this one is a typical oddity from this R&B showman and proto-rapper. Politically incorrect and full of dodgy accents, it has an infectiously dragging groove. Williams is not quite as salacious on 'The Greasy Chicken' as he is elsewhere on record, but even so.

4 'Best Dressed Chicken in Town' – Dr Alimantado

Namechecked by both Johnny Rotten and the Clash, Dr Alimantado was a toasting Jamaican DJ who made some very fine records indeed. 'Best Dressed Chicken in Town' was perhaps his finest moment. His next finest moment was the album sleeve itself – his fly is open and he doesn't give a damn.

3 'Falsehearted Chicken' – Samamidon

Samamidon hails from Vermont and the song comes from his album *But This Chicken Proved Falsehearted.* I imagine people chuckling when I play him on the radio because *amadan* is the Irish word for fool – but that's neither here nor there. This guy is a curious item indeed. And he knows the full poetic pull of a chicken.

2 'Chicken Rhythm' – Slim Gaillard

Playing this one on national radio was quite an achievement. Its chorus of 'Flocka, flocka, flockaaaaa!' eventually becomes, more or less, a relentless string of expletives. In fact this song has more 'fucks' than *The Big Lebowksi.* Slim made some great records, he invented his own language (*vauti orooni!*) and he appeared as himself in Kerouac's *On the Road.*

1 'The Funky Chicken' – Rufus Thomas

I interviewed Rufus a couple of times and the last time

was in Memphis just weeks before he died. He was a real pioneer and, although hugely important figure in soul music, he actually pre-dated all of it. He was, in truth, an old-fashioned song-and-dance man and 'The Funky Chicken' was his greatest ever song and dance.

The Kids of AD 2000: Ten Greats from the Golden Age of Sleeve Notes

JON SAVAGE

Predicated on the rise of the long-playing 33rpm record, the sleeve note flourished during the late fifties and the mid-sixties. Like a bonus disc with DVDs today, it was an extra inducement to buy this new format and also served to introduce the listener to new sounds and new ideas, as information began to become part of consumerism. Plus there was the fact that there were 144 square inches of space to fill.

So these choices are taken from this golden age. Psychedelic design made sleeve notes obsolete in the late sixties, and if they were used after then, it was either as pure information or a camp throwback. Certainly punk rock had no time for such fripperies. The rise of the video in the early eighties took over the sleeve-note function as product enhancement, while the onset of the 5-inch CD reduced typesize and space to the point of illegibility.

The sleeve note still persists, most often in beautifully produced compilations by companies like Ace Records (UK) and Rhino (US) and in the hands of a few new groups, like British Sea Power – see their new record *Do You Like Rock Music?* They remind the reader that the sleeve note can offer free communication as well as sheer hype: that they are, in fact, an ill-reckoned art-form. As David Bowie scrawled on the back of *Pin Ups*, 'Love-on ya!'

10 Harry Smith – *Anthology of American Folk Music* (various artists, 1952)

This three-volume compilation was the sacred text of the fifties and sixties American folk revival, and this is the great-grandaddy of the sleeve note: a cosmology of graphics, photos, asides, comments and quips – a whole book in twenty-eight crammed pages. Smith brought his genius as an artist, writer, film-maker, occultist and poly-math to bear on his brilliant summaries of the eighty-four songs included, for instance on the infamous 'Stackalee': 'Theft of Stetson hat causes deadly dispute. Victim identifies self as family man.'

For more, read the essays by Greil Marcus and Jon Pankake in the booklet for the six-CD Smithsonian Folkways reissue (1997). There are also personal testi-monies of the *Anthology*'s first-time impact by Peter Stampfel, Dave Van Ronk and John Fahey – who in par-ticular continued Smith's inspired ethnography on his own albums and definitive compilations such as *Screamin' and Hollerin' the Blues* (Charley Patton, 2003) and *American Primitives Vol. II* (various artists, 2005). For an example of Fahey's own cosmology, find the vinyl of *America* (1968), with its eighteen-page booklet.

9 Anonymous – *Taboo* (Arthur Lyman, 1958)

What's now called 'exotica' – essentially easy listening/make-out music as techno travelogue – was an important genre in the late fifties, going hand-in-hand with the intro-duction of stereo sound equipment and LP records. Lyman had played with bandleader Martin Denny – whose *Exotica* hit No. 1 in the US in July 1959: the first to do so in *Billboard*'s stereo chart – and helped to start the trend with *Taboo*, offering 'primitive superstitions of an island volcano, woven into eerie, lush, tropical sounds'.

Recording quality and stereo sound were an important part of the sales pitch, and this note gives pride of place to Henry J. Kaiser's Aluminium Dome ('unmistakably modern') as well as itemising just how the 'perfect sound production' was achieved: '3 AKG Austrian microphones, a custom built Ampex 3-track $^1/_2$" magnetic tape recorder'. Play *Taboo* late at night, stack the sofa, tinkle those ice cubes and I'm sure you would get the correct 'frequency response'.

8 Derek Taylor – *Beatles for Sale* (1964)

So new that they needed interpreting, The Beatles had had detailed sleeve notes from the off. Taylor took on the demanding job of Beatles PR for a few months during 1964 and during his tenure he delivered these fantastic notes for what was then the group's most lavish package: the fold-out sleeve for their fourth album. They contain jokes, facts, boasts, and warnings – 'but you can buy this album – you probably have, unless you're just browsing, in which case don't leave any dirty thumbprints on the sleeve!'

Taylor, who died in 1997, brought both sophistication and a depth of understanding that was prophetic: 'The kids of AD 2000 will draw from the music much the same sense of well being and warmth as we do today'; 'the magic of The Beatles is, I suspect, ageless and timeless'. He went on to write for the Byrds among others, as well as two essential memoirs, *As Times Goes By* and *Fifty Years Adrift*. Of all those surrounding The Beatles, he remains the most thoughtful and insightful commentator.

7 Andrew Loog Oldham – *Rolling Stones No. 2* (1965)

A pre-punk perplex 1: the sleeve note as shock tactic. An admirer of Anthony Burgess's *A Clockwork Orange* – there was talk in 1964 of the Rolling Stones being involved in a film version of the book – manager Andrew Loog Oldham delivered his own homage to the master on the flip of the Stones' second album: the one with the moody David Bailey photo that shows them spots and all.

References to 'malchicks' and the Stones' androgyny dispensed with ('You bods ain't mistahs, with hair like that'), Oldham decided to up the ante: 'This is THE STONES new disc within. Cast deep in your pockets for loot to buy this disc of groovies and fancy words. If you don't have bread, see that blind man, knock him in the head, steal his wallet and lo and behold you have the loot, if you put in the boot, good, another one sold!'

The furore was immediate: questions were asked in the House of Lords, and a DPP investigation urged. Oldham claimed that he had written the notes 'for fun, in the bath', but the Stones' record company deleted the offending paragraph after the first pressing. You won't find it on any CD either, as in their wisdom ABCKO have decided not to reissue *The Rolling Stones No. 2*.

Lost in all the fuss was Oldham's talent as a writer: his two books of autobiography, *Stoned* and *Stoned Too*, are highly recommended.

6 Bob Dylan – *Bringing It All Back Home* (Bob Dylan, 1965)

Dylan had been writing sleeve notes since *The Times They Are a-Changin'* in 1964; rather like John Lennon's two books, *In His Own Write* and *A Spaniard in the*

Works, they offered another avenue for expression as well as clues to his future direction. By the time of his fifth album, they read like unsung rock lyrics: 'My poems are written in a rhythm of unpoetic distortion'; 'A song is anything that can walk by itself.'

You can see Dylan percussively tapping and tapping in *Don't Look Back*, and the notes have this kind of almost automatic cadence – allusive, amphetamined, absurd – that would appear in his next two albums. They also indicated a wider talent: while 1967's 'novel', *Tarantula*, failed to sustain this mood over book length, Dylan's autobiography, *Chronicles, Volume One* (2004) was justly hailed as a masterwork.

5 Frank Smyth – *Face to Face* (The Kinks, 1966)

Face to Face was the album that came off the Kinks' huge summer hit, 'Sunny Afternoon', and Frank Smyth's notes brilliantly capture that song's mood of bilious, languid decadence: 'If this is not enough, fate flings its last custard pie. The taxman cometh. And you are left with the glass of ice-cold beer, the sun on the uplands with dappled shadows and all, which is much better, as the poet has it, than a poke up the nostril with a burnt stick.'

In his excellent autobiography, *X-Ray*, Ray Davies remembered when he first met Frank Smyth(e): 'I saw what I thought was a down-and-out tramp lying in the gutter.' Davies described him as 'a poet and a writer, with a huge robust physique that could have allowed him to be mistaken for Oliver Reed – depending on how many drinks the onlooker had consumed and how smoky and dark the drinking club was'. Here, the man matched the mood.

4 Tommy Hall – *The Psychedelic Sounds of the 13th Floor Elevators* (1966)

The 13th Floor Elevators were true pioneers. Forming in deep Texas late in 1965, they were among the very first groups to use the word 'psychedelic' in their promotional material. However, within weeks of forming and recording their classic single 'You're Gonna Miss Me' they had attracted the attentions of the local police: the first of many busts that followed the band over the next few years and that, along with their drug consumption, sent them mad.

From the police's point of view, their attentions were understandable. The Elevators were explicit in their acid evangelism. They aimed to play most of their shows on LSD, while the band's jug player and spiritual guru Tommy Hall gave the game away on the sleeve notes to their first album: 'Recently, it has become possible for man to chemically alter his mental state and thus alter his point of view.' After that, it was open season.

Released in November 1966, *The Psychedelic Sounds* matched Roky Erikson's eldritch screams with a genuinely colourful, unsettling cover and Hall's philosophical, mystical screed. For instance, the song 'You Don't Know' 'explains the difference between persons using the old and the new reasoning. The old reasoning, which involves a preoccupation with objects, appears to someone using the new reasoning as childishly unsane.'

3 Various – *The Velvet Underground and Nico* (1967)

A pre-punk perplex 2: whatever is the worst that they say about you, that's what you are. And wear it proudly.

Like the Elevators' album, this is a total artwork (or, as

the Germans called it, *Gesamtkunstwerke*), of music, mood and attitude, right from the infamous peelable banana and Warhol stamp to the great photos by Billy 'Name' Linich and Nat Finkelstein. As such it is part of a trilogy of Factory multimedia pop packages from 1966–7, along with the Warhol-curated issue of *Aspen* magazine (December 1966) and the *Andy Warhol's Index Book* (1967) – both of which came with VU-related flexi-discs.

In the double-page fold-out, the anonymous compiler has put together ten press reports on the 'Exploding Plastic Inevitable' shows played by the VU + Nico during 1966. They are not pretty: 'Berlin in the decadent 30s'; 'a three-ring psychosis'; 'not since the *Titanic* ran into the iceberg'; 'a secret marriage between Bob Dylan and the Marquis de Sade'; 'the flowers of evil are in full bloom'.

Today this would kick-start a career but, in 1967, this was not necessarily a good thing. For those who couldn't see the group live, however (which meant everybody in Europe), these notes conditioned the response and added to an already heady allure.

2 Anonymous (probably Terry Riley) – *A Rainbow in Curved Air* (Terry Riley, 1969)

Another great late-sixties *Gesamtkunstwerke*, this time optimistic and hopeful. The two long pieces – playful and deeply psychoactive – feature Riley at his zenith, and are perfectly mirrored in the pastoral cover art and the utopian notes: 'And then all wars ended . . . The Pentagon was turned on its side and painted purple, yellow & green / All boundaries were dissolved / The slaughter of animals was forbidden . . . World health was restored.' Right on!

173

1 Lenny Kaye – *Nuggets* (various artists, 1972)

Like Harry Smith's *Anthology*, this was a compilation as catalyst: a codification of a mood, a history and a taste that quickly became a canon. In the hard-rock desert of the early seventies – it was grim: you had to be there – Lenny Kaye's compilation came as a blast of earthy two-chord energy.

Containing classics by the Electric Prunes, the 13th Floor Elevators, the Seeds and twenty-four others, *Nuggets* mined that classic year, 1966, when garage bands drank deep at the Stones/Them/Yardbirds well and came up with their own compressed and distorted mutations. 'This is the story of a transition period in American rock 'n' roll,' Kaye wrote; 'of a changeling era which dashed by so fast that nobody knew much of what to make of it.'

Inside, there were detailed notes on each of the songs – a ground-breaking work of scholarship mixed with love and attitude. Like his contemporaries Lester Bangs and Greg Shaw, Kaye harked back to 'the berserk pleasure that comes with being onstage outrageous' and 'the relentless middle-finger drive' offered 'only by rock 'n' roll at its finest'. Sounds like a manifesto for the age that these three, among others, helped to bring into being. Just to help the process along, Kaye mentioned the name then current in writer/fan circles for this kind of relentless two-chord nonsense: 'punk-rock'.

SOUNDTRACKS

From revolutions to all-day drinking sessions

Hari Kunzru / Kathryn Williams / Angus Cargill / Alexandra Heminsley / Niall Griffiths

Yodo-Go a Go-Go! Ten Musical Moments in Revolution

HARI KUNZRU

10 Woody Guthrie grafs his guitar

Dustbowl balladeer Woody Guthrie is revered by millions as the man who rode the rails across America, following migrant workers, acting as a political organiser and inspiring a later generation of folk musicians. In recent years it appears that his most lasting legacy has been the message he wrote on his acoustic guitar. The phrase 'This machine kills fascists' turns up even now on the axes of punky posers whose idea of politics is wishing they'd played Live Aid. Woody is presumably turning in his grave.

9 Public Enemy fight the power

It's odd to remember the nervousness caused by Public Enemy's blend of reheated Black Panther rhetoric, Nation of Islam uniform fetishism and histrionic turntable trickery. Reminding white America that the power structure had produced 'nothing but rednecks for 400 years' and (horror!) that Elvis, far from being 'the king' was just a white boy who'd profited by stealing black music was enough, at the end of the eighties, to produce calls for their immediate incarceration. Add to this Professor Griff's anti-Semitic outbursts, Flavor Flav's oversized watch and Chuck D's genuine outrage at the injustices meted out to African Americans, and you had a serious threat to everything a great nation held dear – or

177

a reason for media commentators to run around like headless chickens. One of the two.

8 Wings consider colonialism

The Beatles made various forays into politics. John and Yoko gave money to Michael X and bankrolled all kinds of revolutionary causes. George Harrison favoured transcendental meditation and the Maharishi Mahesh Yogi. Looking for the definitive revolutionary Beatle work, we're offered a plethora of choices. Lennon's bitter ballad 'Working Class Hero'? Perhaps 'Imagine'? It is one of history's ironies that the only song which really got the authorities hot under the collar was written by Paul, the chirpy one. 'Give Ireland Back to the Irish' was a response to the events of Bloody Sunday in 1972 and proved so controversial upon release that not only was it banned by the BBC, but on *Pick of the Pops*, Alan 'Fluff' Freeman wasn't even allowed to say the title, and had to refer it as cryptically as 'a song by Wings'. The song is so gut-wrenchingly terrible that I'm personally convinced the reason the ban on playing it on the radio has held up for thirty-six years is not its controversial theme, but because the music-loving public is collectively relieved not to have to listen to the damn thing.

7 The Dead Kennedys refuse to go jogging

America is the land of the free. It is also, apparently, the home of the brave. And California is the place where freedom means the hippy dream of peace, love and healthy macrobiotic fun in the sun. So the mere suggestion that there's something fascist about the sunshine state sent waves of outrage from San Diego to Humboldt county. With their first single, 'California Uber Alles', the Dead Kennedys (itself not a name calculated to win friends in the US liberal establishment) depicted a near-future America where the then state governor, Jerry Brown, instituted a bizarre 'denim and suede' long-haired police state, in which kids were forced to meditate in school and uncool people were given flowers, then (organically) gassed. In 1979 punks already knew that the only good hippy is a dead one.

6 Serge Gainsbourg calls his countrymen to action

France! Birthplace of modernity, a nation forged in the flames of revolution. A country which reveres its radicals and adores its transgressors. Who would have thought that a chain-smoking singer with sticky-out ears and a weakness for little girls could almost bring the place to a halt by making a reggae version of the National Anthem? Yet so great was the furore around Serge Gainsbourg's 1979 'Aux Armes et Caetera' that the singer was attacked onstage by angry Algerian War veterans. By drawling bits of the 'Marseillaise' (a spectacularly blood-thirsty song), in a tone which suggests he'd much rather be making sexual suggestions to Whitney Houston, Gainsbourg managed to suggest that the national 'jour de gloire' had long gone.

5 Red Krayola fight the phallocracy

The Red Krayola rival the Rolling Stones in longevity, having been in continual operation since 1966. While most everyone else in the late-sixties music scene was try-ing to make their guitar sound like a sitar, Krayola were miking up baking foil and writing songs that sounded like eighties post-punk, complete with discursive lyrics about the shortcomings of capitalism. When the 1980s finally came around, there was a brief moment when they sounded trendy. As far as it's possible to decipher the yodelling lyrics, their 1981 single 'Born in Flames' is a song about sisterhood, struggle, the birth of a new sub-jectivity, and other topics not covered by the Gallagher brothers. It came to the attention of film director Lizzie Borden, who'd named herself after the famous nine-teenth-century murderess, familiar to generations of American children through the sinister schoolyard rhyme:

Lizzie Borden, with an axe
Gave her mother forty whacks
When she saw what she had done
She gave her father forty-one.

This is a clue to the politics of Borden's sci-fi epic *Born in Flames*, which takes place in a post-revolutionary United States where women are expected to wait for their emancipation until the project of socialism is completed. The Women's Army will have no truck with this kind of half-way nonsense. Nor will various pirate radio DJs, feminist street activists or the badass avengers of the anti-rapist bike patrol. Red Krayola is their inspiration.

4 Caetano Veloso gets deported

Military dictatorships are not known for their sense of fun, or their support for underground culture. So the Tropicalismo movement which swept Brazil in the mid-sixties was closely monitored by the authorities. Tropicalismo was a new wave of art, theatre, poetry and music, which celebrated *antropofagia*, the cannibalism of all cultural forms, a highly charged idea for the mixed society of Brazil. Singer-songwriter Caetano Veloso was associated with the socialist left, and his new style of music outraged pretty much everyone – rightists who disliked his politics, leftists who disliked his incorporation of 'non-national' styles like rock 'n' roll as well as the mass of conservative bossa-nova fans, who wanted sugary love songs rather than weird new folk-rock hybridity. At the 1967 Música Popular Brasileira festival, Veloso was greeted with howls of protest as he harangued the audience, telling them 'E proibido proibir' – It's forbidden to forbid. No surprise that by 1968 he was in jail, and then had to spend several years in exile in London, a quarter of a century before the first caipirinha hit these shores.

3 Amon Düül are autonomous

Of all the communes in operation in 1960s Germany, Munich had one of the hairiest. The autonomes of Amon Düül believed in the freedom of workers from the state, political parties and other top-down structures. They obviously believed a lot of other esoteric stuff, since they decided to name themselves after an Egyptian god and a word they claimed was Turkish for 'moon'. The big question, other than who would do the washing up, was whether music or politics should take precedence, and in 1969 this caused a split. Amon Düül I believed in experimental living and 'anti-music', made primarily as an expression of their autonomous subjectivity. Amon Düül II wanted to be proper musicians. Predictably enough, the second group became successful, released a series of increasingly absurd prog-rock albums and by about 1975 had disappeared entirely up their own arses. The first lot released four albums, three of which consist of excerpts from a single acid-fuelled forty-eight-hour jam, conducted in 1968. By 1970 the politics of the far left and groups like the Red Army Faction had taken over from primitive tribal drumming, and they disappeared without trace.

2 Cornelius Cardew loses his sense of fun

Cardew's life is a cautionary tale about what happens when politics starts to dictate to aesthetics. The English composer began as Stockhausen's assistant, but junked serialism for an open and playful style of music, influenced by American avant-gardists like LaMonte Young and John Cage. In 1966 he joined free-improvising supergroup AMM and in 1968 founded Scratch Orchestra, a loose group of about fifty people, part radical musical ensemble, part experiment in living. A constitution was written and activities ('concerts' would be a misleadingly narrow word) were programmed according to a principle of 'reverse seniority' – the youngest member deciding on the first programme, then the next youngest, and so on. The Scratch Orchestra made some joyous noises, some of which survive on recordings of Cardew's masterpiece *The Great Learning*. Unfortunately, the composer's interest in revolutionary politics led him down the rabbit-hole of hard-line Maoism and eventually he abandoned Scratch for the Communist Party of England (Marxist-Leninist) and an aesthetic theory which led him to reject anything remotely fun in favour of turgid piano settings of Chinese folk songs and prole-friendly vocal works with unintentionally comical lyrics.

Choice examples include 'Revolution is the Main Trend in the World Today', 'Smash the Social Contract' and 'There Is Only One Lie, There Is Only One Truth', with its show-stopping chorus, 'There is the lie of imperialism and reaction / And there is the truth of Marxist-Leninism . . .' Cardew died in 1981, the victim of a hit-and-run accident outside his home, a tragic event whose only upside is that it spared him most of the Thatcherite eighties, which he wouldn't have enjoyed.

1 Les Rallizes Dénudés fly the friendly skies

By 1970 Japan's city centres were filled with so-called *futen*, long-haired youth intent on transgressing the strict social rules of their country. Among their idols was a mysterious band called Les Rallizes Dénudés, who specialised in twenty-minute drone epics and professed a belief, on the rare occasions when journalists could get them to answer a question, in 'total cultural assault'. Their style was that of the Foku Gerira (folk guerrillas), black-clad radicals who borrowed a lot of attitude (and fashion sense) from the Black Panthers. Les Rallizes made the authorities nervous – with good reason. On 31 March 1970 their bass player Moriaki Wakabayashi (along with eight other members of the Japanese Red Army, the oldest of whom was twenty-one), hijacked the Yodo-Go flight 351 from Tokyo to Fukuoka. After a three-day stand-off the hijackers ended up in North Korea, which was something of a bummer for them, as they really wanted to go to Cuba. Kim Il Sung wouldn't let them leave, and they have lived there ever since, masterminding various international plots and bizarre kidnappings. The band got another bassist.

183

A Big Green Highlighter Pen Machine: Ten Songs that Have Underlined Key Moments in My Life

KATHRYN WILLIAMS

These in no way represent my record collection, what I listen to now or what I want other people to associate me with, but it just happens that these songs found me and clung on when big things happened.

10 'Tiger Feet' – Mud

I was born to the sound of 'Tiger Feet'. Well, I like to think I was. It was No. 1 when I was born and I have always imagined sliding into the world to the sound of Mud.

9 'Wind of My Soul' – Cat Stevens

My first crush was Cat Stevens when I was ten. I had *Teaser and the Firecat* next to my bed and I kissed his beardy face every night. I bought the record for 20p at a jumble sale. I also remember having a sip of someone's coffee in the kitchen and thinking I would go to hell for it.

8 'Cry Baby' – Janis Joplin

I used to listen to this song on my mum and dad's record player every day before school so it would give me the courage to go to school when I was being bullied. They had big brown huge headphones that would block out the world.

7 'Lay Lady Lay' – Bob Dylan

This was on a cassette I played over and over when I was at my art foundation course. The first feelings of independence, freedom, uncertainty. I worked in a bar called the Pilgrim and I would put 'Lay Lady Lay' on and just sit there before anyone came in, imagining I was in a film and something was just about to happen.

6 'So Long Marianne'/ 'Suzanne'/ 'Sisters of Mercy' – Leonard Cohen

All played in my bedsit in Newcastle while playing scrabble and trying to keep warm in four pairs of socks. When my dole cheque came I would go halvers on a bottle of wine with my friend Bex and we would light candles and lie on the floor while Leonard Cohen softened our evening.

5 'Into My Arms' – Nick Cave

This is what I walked down the aisle to. My shoe fell off and I puked in my mouth.

4 'Feeling Good' – Nina Simone

Walking out after the ceremony. The giddy feeling in my head. I had jumped in, with both feet. I remember walking in time to the song. It was perfect in a stormy October one-shoed kind of way.

3 'Mr Bojangles' – Nina Simone

First dance as a married woman. This a lovely waltzing song. And it was strange being on the dance floor just me and my him. But this song is incredibly long, and I felt a growing sense of not wanting to be watched or be dancing any more. Strange because if I hear it come on, it makes me smile and think of the day and then slowly as it goes on I remember how long the song is.

2 'Carbon Glaciers' – Laura Veirs; 'Trouble' – Ray LaMontagne

My son came into the world when these were playing. I had gone through four canisters of gas and air at home, so it sounded like an echoing swirly Motorhead played through a water amp, but I'm sure my son liked it.

1 'Louie Louie' – The Kingsmen

The song my son first danced to. It's great seeing a person who just feels the music and moves naturally without feeling constrained by being watched. It's not really dancing. It's jerking and bending and it looks really fun.

What a completely fucking slushie list. I could have gone the other way and gone all 'oh the chord progression on this song', but I don't know if the songs you choose are the ones that stay. It's odd little things that come on in a room when you first meet someone. That's why it's so nice to get played on the radio and think of all the places where people are soaking in a song that you've written. Maybe while they are falling in love . . . or filling a meat pie in a factory.

Compilation Tape Classics! Or So I Thought: Ten Songs Used on More than One Occasion

ANGUS CARGILL

The mix tape is a thing of the past, the digital age has consigned the cassette to the annals of history. Today it's all too easy to burn a compilation in seconds, you don't have to listen through the tracks in real time (if at all). Back in the day though, filling a C90 tape took hours of thought and preparation, as you shaped and ordered each forty-five-minute side. You had to be careful not to run over and cut a song short, while equally not leaving any kind of gap at either end. And that was all before you started trying to fit the track listing on to the sleeve without smudging the ink.

There's barely enough here to fill one side, but the following were tunes that often figured on the many mixes I made through the twin-tape-deck years.

10 'Being Around' – The Lemonheads

In the mid-1990s Evan Dando was popular with the ladies. As a result, his band the Lemonheads were often derided as bubblegum or grunge lite, as though lacking the seriousness of Eddie Vedder, Chris Cornell or Kurt Cobain himself was a bad thing. Of course, they didn't really bear much relation to those bands at all – on their two classic albums, *It's a Shame About Ray* and *Come on Feel . . .* , they were just a great pop band with a bit of country thrown in (with Julianna Hatfield the Emmylou Harris to Evan's Gram Parsons). I could pick any of a dozen of their songs, but this was maybe the one I used the most, a great lyric – bouncy yet sad, bitter-sweet but funny.

9 'Just Like Heaven' – The Cure

My other favourite band from the grunge years was Dinosaur Jr, led by the ultimate monosyllabic intervie-wee, J. Mascis. Listening to them led me to Neil Young, but also, through their manic cover of this song, to the Cure, who up until then I'd always dismissed as miser-able goths. Sweet and catchy, this is in fact a great exam-ple of the perfect pop songs that Robert Smith sometimes wrote.

8 'Take Me I'm Yours' – Squeeze

From Dulwich's answer to Lennon and McCartney, this opens with some weird synth, classic new wave drums and a great lead-guitar line. It's also a perfect example of Chris Difford's kitchen-sink lyrics. I later ended up work-ing in a pub in Greenwich with his daughter, who in my mind at least was always the little girl from 'Up the Junction'.

7 'Get Me Away from Here I'm Dying' – Belle and Sebastian

Around 1997 Belle and Sebastian were an indie fan's wet dream. Literate bedsit lyrics: Check. Rarely play live: Check. Don't do interviews: Check. Art-school aesthetic: Check. Short stories in their liner notes: Check. This would all have been really annoying if they were crap, but those first two records and early EPs were full of bril-liant songs and, while they may not have lived up to their early promise, they were, at least, a more interesting alternative to Menswear or Heavy Stereo. This song, a classic sad-lyric/upbeat-tune combination, was a great introduction to their sound.

6 'Heaven Knows I'm Miserable Now' – The Smiths

Keeping with the indie theme here, this is one of Morrissey's funniest and most knowing lyrics, backed by Marr's genius guitar. And you thought it was just whiny, bedsit angst.

5 'Move On Up' – Curtis Mayfield

This, however, is one of those songs that you can play to anyone, anywhere, and they'll love it. So, a sure-fire mix-tape hit, which often worked well as the opener to side B.

4 'Do Right Woman, Do Right Man' – Aretha Franklin

Every girl in the world loves Aretha Franklin. Fact. So she always seemed like a good bet, especially for a romantically minded compilation (not, it should be said, that they ever worked). That it is also one of the most perfectly expressed sentiments of romantic equality was, I figured, a bonus. 'Take me to heart / And I'll always love you . . .'

3 'The Emperor of Wyoming' – Neil Young

In 1969 Neil Young decided to open his long-awaited solo album in typically contrary fashion, with an instrumental – this gorgeous country waltz – and all good compilations need an instrumental thrown in somewhere mid-way through a side. With horns, strings and pedal-steel this sounds like the theme tune to a great lost western, before all the bad stuff happens.

2 'Maggie May' – Rod Stewart

No one veers from the sublime to the ridiculous quite like Rod, but at his best he was *the* great blue-eyed soul singer, and this is a good track for any compilation. Although it's a sad lyric of lost innocence, it's also a naughty one, and a nod's as good as a wink, as they say. It's also one of the best uses of mandolin in a pop song. If I had ten wishes granted to me today, one of them would be to be able to tell Rod Stewart to buck his ideas up, musically I mean. It's time someone did. And he could start by stealing Ron Wood back from the Stones.

1 'Suicide is Painless' (Theme from *M*A*S*H*) – Mike Altman and Johnny Mandel

And so to my all-time favourite, and most used, compilation number. It was covered as a single by the Manic Street Preachers in 1992, but the version to go for is the original, a brilliantly evocative melody, beautifully played and recorded. I found it on 7-inch somewhere, and used it repeatedly as the Side A opening track (an accidental bonus being the authentic crackle and sound of the needle dropping to kick things off). Today I don't know what I was thinking – it's a song about suicide – but back then it seemed like a great statement of intent. This isn't going to be your average mix of recent hits, but a carefully selected and impeccably sequenced selection of great songs. And they're chosen just for you.

What Becomes of the Broken Hearted? Songs for the Dumped: A Step-by-step Guide

ALEXANDRA HEMINSLEY

There's no point in getting dumped if you can't use it as an excuse to listen to some truly execrable tunes. But it can't all be Céline and Rage Against the Machine – there comes a point when your record collection is going to have to help the process. Whether it be exorcising some of your very darkest thoughts in the safety of your bedroom, forcing out the tears you managed to hold back when you encountered your beloved with their new sweetheart, or getting you out of the house and leaping on to the dance floor to celebrate your regeneration, no break-up is worth its salt if it doesn't involve a few of these . . .

1 'Nothing Compares 2 U' – Sinéad O'Connor

An essential Step 1 for any fresh dumpee. Don't believe the 'purists' who claim to prefer the Prince original. They're just trying to cover their tracks after admitting to liking the song at all. Anyone who's really had their heart shredded knows that Sinéad's is the version that counts. Perfectly articulating the borderline psychotic conviction of the recent victim ('No noo noo, it's not being loved that I need, it's being loved by YOU'), it's definitely one for solitary listening.

2 'Back to Black' – Amy Winehouse

No matter what Amy Winehouse does for the rest of her career, it will always be a relevant fancy-dress option to

191

turn up as a 'Back to Black'-era Amy. The hair, the tats, the flailing references to her 'Blake Incarcerated' . . . All of which can detract from what a stunning piece of melancholy this is. From the sheer bleakness of the lyrics (which reference the appetite for drugs that followed the making of this album), to the gothic fantasy of the video, this adds glamour and musical oomph to what just sounds like hideous caterwauling from the rest of us. It's actually quite hard to listen to it from start to finish without feeling as if you have just had your heart ripped out.

3 'The Winner Takes It All' – Abba

Another member of the Horribly Real Lyrics Club. The unimaginable cruelty needed by Björn Ulvaeus in writing a song about his own marital strife and then – once separated but still in the same band as his ex – presenting it to her to perform, is almost admirable. No wonder Agnetha felt some time alone in a small hut was the only reasonable response to her time in Abba. As with Amy, this provides comfort of the 'At Least This Didn't Happen to Me' variety.

4 'Everybody Hurts' – REM

There comes a point in any break-up when listening to the self-indulgent gloom section of your collection must end. And this track represents it. Like you care that everyone else has felt pain! Yours was the worst! This small hint of feistiness signifies that it's time to move on to some more upbeat, revenge-themed numbers.

5 'Since U Been Gone' – Kelly Clarkson

Woo-hoo! Since your ex has been gone you've started to realise how wonderful your friends are, how strong you are, and how much you can yet achieve. Beloved of girls-with-hairbrushes-in-front-of-mirrors everywhere, this *American Idol* winner's break-out hit was an instant break-up classic. It has since only slightly been marred by the fact that Clarkson went on to release only break-up songs for another couple of albums. Either she had a massively draining and unrequited crush on manager Simon Cowell or her mother repeatedly listened to Alanis Morissette's *Jagged Little Pill* while expecting her.

6 'Irreplaceable' – Beyoncé

A further step on the road to recovery, as this track is as explicit about Miss B's agony at being cheated on as it is about her absolute conviction that her man is going to be the loser in the long term. This kind of self-respect (even if it is just the posturing of the heartbroken) is essential after too much time in your bedroom with Eric Carmen. It is also worth mentioning that the accompanying video is equally inspiring on account of being a design anomaly: Beyoncé is not wearing an asymmetrical and apparently highly flammable creation fresh from her mother's sewing machine, but is instead looking a little more casual.

7 'Heart of Glass' – Blondie

It's easy to be bedazzled by the icy New York coolness of Blondie-era Deborah Harry and not realise how poignant these lyrics are. The girl's crushed! The thought of anyone dumping this gorgeous and disdainfully hip blonde is frankly mystifying. The jauntiness of the tune, the majesty of the Harry and the sadness of the lyrics are a killer combination, giving hope to anyone who might doubt their ability to be heartbroken and fabulous concurrently.

8 'Dry Your Eyes' – The Streets

Mike Skinner deserves a knighthood for articulating male anguish so eloquently. While most blokes are divided on whether it's moving or cringe-inducing, a generation of women is grateful to know that men feel the agony of the dumped too. It's also good to know that guys have an outlet for their grief other than Grand Theft Auto or relentless, borderline-autistic repeating of Monty Python catchphrases.

9 'I Know It's Over' – The Smiths

The primary function of this track in any break-up is to cheer you up – because it's so bleak, so long, and sooo self-indulgent that by the time it (eventually) ends, the idea of having your heart stamped beneath the heel of a man in whose arms you'd hoped to die feels like a picnic in the park in comparison. Yes, yes, I know there's much to admire in the complexity of both the lyrics and the arrangement, but really, it's just unbearable. You could cope with anything after just one listen . . .

10 'Yes' – McAlmont & Butler

What would have been so violently inappropriate in the early days of a break-up suddenly takes on epic levels of joy once the healing is well under way. Contrary to what you might have believed in the Sinéad era, the wounds heal. What would once have sounded like malicious taunting from David and Bernard becomes a battle-cry for the victorious. Yes, you do feel better. And when you do, the lads are there for you.

Lilac Wine: The Ten Best Albums to Get Drunk Alone To

NIALL GRIFFITHS

Booze and music overlap in their effects on the human animal; the former can confer rhythm and melody upon the world's general noise, and the latter can inspire and intoxicate as much as any drug. Additionally, they share the qualities of being different each time they're experienced; there's always something new to be had from the best music and each moment of drunkenness. Both can banish what bores you and enhance what excites you. Rapture, heartbreak, contentment, strident self-confidence, puckering paranoia – all of these can be encountered and explored in one drinking spree with personalised musical accompaniment, especially when the only company is yourself, uncharted, largely, and unexplored; to be sure, booze and music and other people can make a wonderful combination too, but there are times when you don't want them around, times when their smells and shoes and haircuts and needy mewlings for attention distract you from your goal, which is not just to live but to live well, as if it's your last, or first, moment on the planet, brooding like a hawk with your face in your hands to This Mortal Coil's "Til I Gain Control Again' with the second bottle newly opened or bellowing on your knees with your arms outspread to Spiritualized's 'Lord Can You Hear Me?' with the third bottle now empty and cap-sized and catching the light from the low lamps on its fallen green sides (all solo drinking sprees need to be underlit). You're entertaining God when you do this; and when, with the wailing desolation of Mississippi John

Hurt's 'Angels Laid Him Away' offering a soundtrack to your dragging yourself off to bed, you at last accept the darkness of His/Her plan, you can be sure S/He gives an approving little nod.

I don't live alone any more, but I did, for years, in several cities across the UK. When I'd make arrangements to go out, I'd often start partying early and alone, giving myself a couple of hours' solo drinking time before the doorbell went or the car-horn honked outside the window. And oftentimes, gurning and sweating in a club some hours later or grinding my teeth in an after-hours bar somewhere, I'd look back on those fleeting couple of hours on my own before I went out, the vodka vanishing, each song remaining my – my – choice, and I'd think: I should've stayed in. I really should've stayed in.

Of course, a steady and useful and enjoyable drinking spree should last for longer than the average one-hour playing time of the albums on the following list; ideally, it should occupy most of an entire day, from early afternoon or late morning, say, through till at least midnight. What follows, then, is the soundtrack to an all-day solo session, from the sun arcing across the sky to the bloom of purple and red of sunset to the silver strobing of the stars, and you under them, musically boozed-up you. Somewhere outside your four walls, people are pretending to have fun, but within them, you truly are. You're living. You're a one-person bacchanal.

1 *Impromptus Op. 90 and Op. 142* – Franz Schubert

Start easy. Slide your way in. A smoky whisky, maybe, to smooth the day's edges, blunt them of anything sharp and jagged that might hurt. Track 3, here, the 'Andante in G flat major', will open your chest in the same way that the whisky is opening your pores, and make it responsive to what the day will bring and every day after that. It's the soundtrack to birth, minus the blood and screaming, of course. Everything trembles and tinkles and waits, agog, in a curious pale blue light.

2 *Complete Recorded Works Volume 2: Oct. 1924–March 1925* – Josie Miles

Something's now building, beginning to rumble towards you like thunder lumbering over the horizon. Modern music began with the blues and the blues began with the psalms, and that's all here in Josie's wailing: Why am I here? What do you want from me? What must I do to be loved? Where am I going? Josie encapsulates the fundamental yearning; it's the bass to the rhythm section of the tinkle and glug of the drink in your glass. If you harbour an anger, then 'Bad Mama's Blues' will articulate it: 'Give me gunpowder, give me dynamite / Yes, I'll wreck the city, wanna blow it up tonight'. You're going to win your war with the world without even leaving your home.

3 *Third/Sister Lovers* – Big Star

An album drenched in drink and scorched by sunshine – the sound of sixties California's dark side. You'll be sloshing enough by now to suspect that the song 'Jesus Christ' – with its odd fairground opening – might possibly be about you. 'Kangaroo' is the sound of a band and a mind collapsing with loss and longing, 'Stroke it Noel' the beautiful noise of tentative steps towards recovery. The new-issue CD contains as an extra track, a cover of 'Whole Lotta Shaking Going On', which you never knew referred to the DTs. At this point, you'll be loud and expansive and ready to receive joy. The world will be plodding on monotonously on the other side of your windowpane. Let it.

4 *Sandinista!* – The Clash

It might be tempting to go for the unflappable cool of *London Calling* over this, but *Sandinista!* better mirrors the thousand-sided jewel of near intoxication you'll have no doubt reached by now. Euphoria proper is still some way away, and without any other people around to drag your thoughts down the narrow alleys of their words, you'll be exploring the iceberg-clogged bays of emotion in your little alcohol kayak. Don't reach for the remote, don't give in to the temptation to skip; throw yourself completely into this unique experience and appreciate it for what it is – an uncontrolled and untrammelled burst of creativity. Allow it to batter you, smash and reconstruct you. 'Junco Partner' and 'Let's Go Crazy' will have you dancing; with 'Charlie Don't Surf', you'll be singing. And you'll be a kid again with the children's voices on side 6 and, regressed by the drink, might start sniffling with self-pity; I was once so young and innocent like them. Don't let this happen. Remember – this is fun.

5 *Up the Bracket* – The Libertines

Don't let the tabloids put you off – for an adrenalin rush, this can't be beaten. Appropriately, the peculiar effects of booze are amenable to being orchestrated by music, and this will slap you up into an exhilarating, seedy, somewhat grubby high. It is and you will be fast and frantic, dervishing until the closing track, 'I Get Along', threatens to spin you into a thousand pieces. The last sound on the album is a yelp from Docherty; part horror, part celebratory abandon. You'll know how he feels, by God.

6 *Orphans* – Tom Waits

Runs the drunken gamut; swagger, exuberance, confusion, sadness, despair. Personally, I'd intervene with the given order here and play the 'Bastards' disc between the 'Brawlers' and the 'Bawlers' – sooner exit Waits-world with the bitter-sweet bite of 'Young at Heart' than the stomping clang of 'On the Road', although you might need that after the tonnage of melancholy that the twenty tracks of 'Bawlers' will have shovelled on you. Plus you'll probably be a wee bit, well, lachrymose by now; not mawkish exactly, no, not that, rather let's say more receptive through booze than usual to an empathic appreciation of the woes of others. And, at 'Tell It to Me' and 'Never Let Go of Your Hand', you might be tempted to allow the leakage of one tiny tear. That's okay; let it go. No one's around to see you.

7 *The Very Best of the Beach Boys* – The Beach Boys

A welcome injection of happy junketing: salty, sunbathed, sea-stroked. Time for a few more sunbeams. 'Fun Fun Fun', 'Help Me Rhonda'; your half-pickled internal organs'll be frolicking about in your torso. 'Sloop John B' is the sound of defiant cheeriness, a determination to wrest the positive from the shitty situations daily life pilots you into. The gabble of voices on 'Barbara Ann' will be the invisible guests at your party of one, those that populate the inside of your skull, and they're all laughing and singing. At this stage of inebriation, you'll be able to harmonise with the best; astonishing how drink can immeasurably improve your singing voice. 'Do It Again' will have you doing exactly that.

8 *Original Dubliners, 1966–1969* – The Dubliners

Bit corny, this, I suppose, but then so is getting drunk on your own with a sense of starring in your own movie, and there's nothing wrong with corniness every now and again, and besides, at this point, you'll be needing a sing-song. Surrender to the corn, charge your glass, fill your lungs with smoky air and shout 'Weila Waila' to the darkening world outside the window. 'Black Velvet Band' will offer you a taste of the pain of exile, as will 'I Wish I Were Back in Liverpool', and this'll be authentic because that's what you are, here, surrounded by bottles, giving it laldy with your larynx and lungs – an exile from the world without, that place you're forced to live in which doesn't understand you and never has. But alone, here, in the place you feel safe, what you are makes perfect sense. Lose yourself completely in 'The Cork Hornpipe'. Close your eyes and you'll be madly capering in a Donegal barn, the forces of oppression kept at bay, forever unable to curtail such energy. Fond and foolish hope.

9 *After Hours* – Nina Simone

Winding down now. Mind and heart slowing, the booze shutting down parts of your brain, and there's no better accompaniment to this than Nina's soaring voice. Turn the volume right up on 'Lilac Wine', a shattered, heartbroken, and truly heartbreaking song but one which extols the unique power of alcohol to not simply evoke but gulp you in the might of illusion. Only booze and music can do this; break you and build you simultaneously. You're balladeering your own life here; Nina's keening your own personal loss, allowing you your fall yet insisting on dragging you out of it into a kind of razor-edged rapture. At this point, you know utterly that the world's scheme is as black as the night-time pressed up against your windows, as lonesome as your fingers steadying the neck of the bottle on the rim of the glass. And you wouldn't have it any other way. There's a level of acceptance at which everything makes sense in its pointlessness and its pain. If you haven't reached that level at this point, you soon will.

10 *Murder Ballads* – Nick Cave and the Bad Seeds

Such tar-black lullabies. Such a cracked coda of cradle-songs to close the feast day of yourself. You might be shredded by now, grog-groggy with a head full of roaring and wearing the need for sleep like a heavy overcoat, but allow yourself one last run on the roller-coaster. 'Stagger Lee's booming tribal drive and closing shriek of feedback will shock you back into some semblance of alertness, 'The Curse of Millhaven' might even chivvy you into a last spurt of reeling dancing before the fifteen-minute laughing nightmare of 'O'Malley's Bar' pins you back in your chair. 'Death Is Not the End' might close your eyes, but the hint in it of there being a kind of life after death which is just as fraught and desperate as this one before it might keep you awake and stewing. But what matter? You've lived and drunk away a day in delightful delirium and you're not dead yet. You've lived.

TAKE TWO

From dirty Dylan to bad influences

Jonathan Lethem / John Williams / Michel Faber / Simon Reynolds

Wiggle Like a Bowl of Soup: Ten Smutty Moments from Bob Dylan

JONATHAN LETHEM

Well, sure, he's no Prince. We're accustomed to thinking that Bob Dylan's great accomplishment, or one of them, was to liberate the pop music he inherited – the indigenous blues and R&B, as well as Elvis Presley and the rockers and crooners that emulated the Pelvis in his two modes – from an exclusive focus on below-the-belt matters. Dylan steered it north, to matters of the head (by his lyrical and conceptual brilliance) and the heart (by his convention-smashing stance of self-revelation). Certainly, one of the few places twentieth-century pop music *didn't* need a Dylan to lead it to was sex. And certainly Dylan abjured the obligatory teen-idol rituals that dragged even at geniuses like The Beatles (though millions found him sexy in spite or because of that abjuration). Yet under-sung in Dylan's arsenal of attitudes is the wink-wink-nudge-nudge, when he flaunts a taste for burlesque and cheesy double or even single entendres. Here's a quick roll call.

10 'V.D. Blues' (1961, bootleg only)

A Woody Guthrie composition, the 'V(eneral) D(isease) Blues' shows Dylan doing what he liked most to do in this stage of his formation: not explode the possibilities of popular song, but mark out a seemingly unbridgeable distance from them. Not to take anything away from the preternaturally crusty and time-lost quality that our young hero obtained in his voice and delivery, but one wonders how many people with the actual clap he'd met at this age.

9 'Spanish Harlem Incident' (*Another Side of Bob Dylan*, 1964)

Luscious poetic compression commemorating a night-time encounter – a less pensive one-night stand than the one depicted in 'Fourth Time Around' (she's not chewing gum, for one thing) – and explicit, if 'make my pale face fit into place, awww please' sounds as cunnilingual to you as it does to me. It's all in the delivery.

8 'If You Gotta Go, Go Now' (Or Else You Gotta Stay All Night) (1964; recorded 1965 and released as a European single in 1967)

Jubilantly splicing sex from sentiment, Dylan robs the trysting bed of any cover of bogus innocence: 'It ain't that I'm wanting anything you never gave before'. Sean Wilentz: 'Dylan was doing with words what Elvis had done with his pelvis.'

7 'Ballad of a Thin Man' (*Highway 61 Revisited*, 1966)

If Dylanology owes nothing else to the Todd Haynes' anti-biopic *I'm Not There*, it should be grateful for the stunning ten-minute set-piece that excavates what many listeners and critics have pussyfooted around in regards to this classic song: that it fuses a generalised tribunal against a vast universe of uptight, un-self-aware, received-knowledge-accepting *squares* (in the choruses, and the whole portentous atmosphere of the song) to an extremely intimate and uncomfortable portrait of a clos-

206

eted (but active) male *homosexual* (in the verses). Just listen: the song is full of hunky heart-throbs and guilty blow jobs. If I can face this truth, so can you, Missstaaah Joooones.

6 'Please Mrs. Henry' (*The Basement Tapes*, 1967; released 1974)

The whole basement affair (the basement of 'Big Pink', may I remind you) is peppered with smut, perhaps because of the locker-room atmosphere, and the presumption that these would remain informal, secret recordings. (Good luck with that.) Food and kitchenware in particular serves persistent double-duty as lewd metaphor throughout (those 'potatoes' that need to be 'mashed' in 'Million-Dollar Bash'), but so does furniture, like the easy chair Dylan's unready to vacate in 'You Ain't Goin' Nowhere'. The prize, I think, is carried by 'Please Mrs. Henry', partly for the horrendous 'If I walk too much farther / My crane's gonna leak', partly because the central implication, oral again, is brandished in the refrain: 'I'm down on my knees'. (But what's with 'I ain't got a dime'? – does the singer think the lady is a slot machine?)

5 'Lay, Lady, Lay' (*Nashville Skyline*, 1969)

Dylan as Teddy Pendergrass. Get a room! Oh, you've got one, with a bed in it, no less? Well, then, close the door.

4 'Tough Mama' (*Planet Waves*, 1974)

The meat-shaking-on-bones recalls *Highway 61 Revisited*, and the 'innocent flesh' that send's Galileo's math book

207

soaring. Dylan here conflates horniness with a renewed appetite for his career, on an album that announced his re-emergence: 'Must be time to carve another notch'. Rhymed, of course, with 'crotch'.

3 'New Pony' (*Street Legal*, 1978)

Dylan's cruellest lascivious song, with a celebration of his pony's flanks worthy of R. Crumb, and capturing the flavour of sexual rejuvenation souring into sexual revenge against 'Miss Ex'. There's also a hint of derangement in those backing singers incanting 'How much longer?', as Dylan locates an apocalyptic exhaustion with any hope of romantic love as a reply to the void.

2 'Dirty World' (*Traveling Wilburys, Volume 1*, 1988)

Ostensibly making affectionate fun of, yes, Prince, in his 'Little Red Corvette' mode of automotive-metaphors, this loose-jointed, wolf-whistling jape of a song comes across a lot more like Little Richard in the singing. Or Benny Hill.

1 'Cry a While' (*Love & Theft*, 2001)

Included just for 'late night booty-call'. Who does he think he is, Snoop Dogg?

I Don't Want to Go to Rehab: Ten Records by People Obviously in a Terrible State that Are Unfortunately Much Better than Anything They Made Once They Cleaned Up

JOHN WILLIAMS

10 *Death of a Ladies' Man* – Leonard Cohen

Phil Spector at his gun-toting maddest, Leonard Cohen at his Don Juan sleaziest. Just how much cocaine must there have been at these sessions? The result is a glorious, mad folly, and a record whose title tells you absolutely everything you need to know.

9 *Christy Moore* – Christy Moore

The seventies British folk scene was menaced more by Guinness than by cocaine. And among its heaviest boozers was County Kildare's Christy Moore, a feller who'd worked on English building sites before making it as a folk singer. This 1976 album remains his finest work. At a time when the stereotypes of the Irish revolved around construction work and the IRA, songs like 'Wave up to the Shore' and 'Little Musgrave' flew the flag for simple beauty. On his website Moore says of this period only that 'Looking back I was fortunate to come through these years intact. My work was poor.' The first part of that may well be true, the second part most certainly isn't.

8 *Slow Dazzle* – John Cale

This isn't the best John Cale record from his out-of-it

209

years. That's most likely the glacial *Music for a New Society*, with the *Hedda Gabler* EP and *Helen of Troy* next in line. Hell, it's probably not as good as the completely whacked-out *Sabotage* live album. However it's in this list because it's the first credible album I ever bought and the one that led me on to the Velvet Underground and in due course Patti Smith, punk rock, et al. It's a mixture of sinister rock 'n' roll songs and sinister ballads with a sinister monologue to close it out. Most arresting is the sinister cover of 'Heartbreak Hotel', most lasting the sinister ballad 'I'm Not the Loving Kind' and the sinister tribute to Brian Wilson, 'Mr Wilson'. Cale, at the time, was a brandy-and-coked-out loon, a Welsh Moon who thought it amusing to wear a Cambridge Rapist mask onstage and led a lurid private life in semi-public. To be honest *Slow Dazzle* is probably no better than the Cockney Rebel album I bought immediately before it, but still, it was a kind of year zero record for me.

7 *Rock and Roll Heart* – Lou Reed

Another mid-seventies meltdown who's turned into an irritating health fiend, and one whose current output is quite laughably bad (his musical adaptation of Poe's *The Raven* makes Rick Wakeman's *Six Wives of Henry the Eighth* look like Wagner). In the mid-seventies though, when he was an amphetamine-crazed wreck generally seen out and about in the company of a transvestite called Rachel, there was still some flickering of humanity, and an absence of the unbearable self-importance that renders his recent recordings unlistenable. It's a toss-up between *Coney Island Baby* and *Rock and Roll Heart* for the peak of his solo career. *Coney Island*'s title track is probably the most beautiful thing he ever wrote, but *Rock and Roll Heart* is more consistent. At the core of the album are the last three songs on side one: the Velvets-like 'You Wear It So Well', 'Ladies Pay', with its remarkable guitar playing, and the title track, with its cogent celebration of the dumb. He's never taken himself so lightly since.

6 *Gaughan* – Dick Gaughan

Dick Gaughan is the finest British guitarist and singer I've ever heard. And this, if maybe not quite his finest album, certainly contains his finest recorded moment, his epic version of 'Willie O'Winsbury'. Like Christy Moore, Gaughan wasn't spectacularly fucked-up on drugs at the time, he was just a seriously hard-drinking musician who'd been on the road too long, and was pushing himself too far. The same year he made *Gaughan*, his young daughter had a serious car accident, which made him start to re-evaluate his lifestyle, and the following year he had a breakdown, after which he quit the booze. His subsequent album, *A Handful of Earth*, is the one everyone will tell you is his masterpiece, and they're not far off. Since then, sadly, the sober Gaughan has replaced the booze with a dedication to desperately dull contemporary political songs (and an anal approach to computer programming much in evidence on his website). Approximately once per album, these days, he allows himself to wallow in beauty. Listen to *Gaughan* and you'll wonder why he ever wanted to do anything other than sing traditional folk songs and accompany himself on the guitar. With the possible exception of Ireland's Paul Brady, no one has done it better.

5 *Exit 0* – Steve Earle

Steve Earle's another one who's succumbed to an addiction harder to shake than heroin – self-righteous politics. Sterling Morrison once pointed out that anyone who needed Bob Dylan to tell them what was blowing in the wind in the early sixties had some serious problems, and much the same applies to the matter of Steve Earle and Dubya. Yes, Steve, we like totally agree, but could you go back to songs about cars and girls, pretty please? His second album, *Exit O*, recorded in his drinking, drugging and marrying-the-same-woman-twice days, majors on cars and girls – 'San Antonio Girl' and 'Sweet Little 66' etc. Best of all is 'I Ain't Ever Satisfied', with some of the best ooh-oohs in popular music – which is no small thing.

4 *Smile* – Laura Nyro

Now I could easily be completely wrong about this one on all grounds. She may have been completely straight and focused when writing and recording it (though in the next couple of years she was to split from her husband, have a baby with another man and find her life partner in the shape of another woman, so you'd suspect there was emotional turmoil, if nothing else), but it just reeks of cocaine to me. Domestic cocaine abuse at that: there's a line about coke and tuna fish as the essential groceries which kind of gives the game away. So why's it so good? Because, from her wonderful cover of the Moments' 'Sexy Mama' to 'Money' to 'Children of the Junks', this is one of those records, like Steely Dan's *Gaucho*, that captures a mood of decadent indolence and turns it into art.

3 *Young Americans* – David Bowie

Is there any entertainment world sight more depressing than the Mr Smiley David Bowie of recent years, all-round showbiz good sport? It's a mask far more terrifying than any previously adopted (apart from the Laughing Gnome, obviously). In fact the only time Bowie has seemed remotely real to me was on that seventies *Arena* documentary – called 'Cracked Actor', I think – on which he was this skeletal red-headed coke freak with absolutely no apparent redeeming qualities as a human being, and making the best, the riskiest music of his career. Only a coked-up egomaniac would have figured that recording with the best soul musicians in the business was going to be anything more than an exercise in bathos, but Bowie emerged triumphant. The conventional wisdom is to refer to *Young Americans* as 'plastic soul', but there's nothing plastic about it: it's Bowie's soul out there and so what if it's not a black is beautiful churchgoing Aretha Franklin soul, but a coked-up London boy on a death trip kind of soul? Just listen to the title track, listen especially to 'Win', and there's no mistaking it, there's just a little bit of heart here, the kind that gets revealed in the comedown after you've been up for a week. To be perfect *Young Americans* should really include 'Golden Years' from *Station to Station*, plus the clip of Dave performing it on *Soul Train*, but hey.

2 *Kill City* – Iggy Pop & James Williamson

The trouble with Iggy Pop is the same as the trouble with Bowie; the nagging sense that, underneath all the madness, there's a showbiz trooper with a ferocious work ethic and a willingness to do whatever it takes to get

213

noticed, no matter how crazeee. And, again, it's only in extremis that something like the real person makes an appearance. That's what seems to have happened to Iggy after the Stooges finally fell apart, following the failure of *Raw Power*. Now the orthodoxy is that, following the end of the Stooges, Iggy fell into a pit of madness and addiction before being rescued by Dave Bowie, taken to Berlin and helped to make the career-saving two-card trick that was *The Idiot* and *Lust for Life*. Somewhere in the midst of the lost weekend, though, came *Kill City*, a ragbag of demos recorded in Jimmy Webb's home studio with the Stooges' last guitarist, James Williamson, while the pair of them were down and out in Los Angeles, Iggy on day release from a sojourn in the Neuropsychiatric Ward of UCLA. *Kill City*'s an LA record through and through. The title track is as great a rock 'n' roll celebration of the City of Angels – 'where the debris meets the sea' – as has been recorded, more Rudy Wurlitzer than the Eagles. And then there are the power ballads, 'Sell Your Love' and 'Johanna': never before or since has Iggy flirted so lavishly with heartbreak.

1 *Rhythm and Romance* – Rosanne Cash

Mostly we hear the sound of addiction as a barely strummed acoustic and a cracked voice, or overloaded electric guitars and a wall of feedback – the sounds, if you like, of the terminally wired or the terminally smacked-out or both. But what about eighties cocaine addiction? How does that sound? Well, like this, I suspect: overproduced, full of crashing drums and intrusive synths, with a cover in which the woman who invented alt.country twenty years early is made over to look like one of the Bangles. Suffice to say it's a record that looks horrible, and in some ways sounds horrible, yet it's also one of the bleakest break-up records ever made. You see, up to this point Rosanne had been half of Rodney 'n' Rosanne, Nashville's young power couple: Johnny Cash's daughter and Emmylou's guitarist and songwriter, Rodney Crowell. Together they'd collaborated on a series of wonderfully bitter-sweet country records and now, in their coked-up hubris, they decided to cross over to modern rock, while at the same time their marriage started falling apart. So for every shiny pop 'Her Pink Bedroom' there's a heartbroken 'Second to No One' or 'Never Be You'. Likewise the seemingly upbeat rocker 'Halfway House', which manages to tie together in one brilliant image their pharmaceutical and marital troubles, is balanced by a touching song about Rosanne's old man called 'My Old Man'. And to top the whole thing off there's 'I Don't Know Why You Don't Want Me' – as sad a break-up song as has been written and, fittingly enough, written by Rodney and sung by Rosanne. Honest-to-God adult pain. What happened to Rosanne since? Well, the worst thing of all, judging by the evidence of this list: she got happy.

Lo, The Downcast Shall Be Exalted! Ten Reputedly Worthless Albums that Will One Day Be Recognised as Rather Nifty

MICHEL FABER

Over the last thirty-five years I've often found that albums which impressed me have been judged, by critical consensus, to be rubbish. Almost as often, everybody comes round to my opinion – many years later. Could it be that my ears are immune to the zeitgeist? Do I hear music out of time, undistorted by the filter of fashion? I could name fifty albums that I championed decades before some trendmonger told you they were cool. But here are ten which are still waiting for the world to wake up. Typically, they are mocked, apologised for, or omitted from discussion altogether. They can be found in bargain bins, cobwebbed corners of Amazon (if not deleted altogether), or even those snooty 'Worst Ever' polls compiled by smug journalists. Reading through this list, you will have the knee-jerk response that my taste sucks shit. Brethren, mistrust the jerks of your knees. They know not what they do.

10 *Thank You* – Duran Duran

This collection of cover versions earned notoriety when *Q* magazine voted it the worst album of all time – despite the fact that a remarkable proportion of the original artists were full of praise for it. Duran's take on Public Enemy's '911 Is a Joke' provoked critics to outrage at the sheer temerity of these middle-class white chaps covering a song that only black ghetto-dwellers could relate to.

(So, were these outraged critics black ghetto-dwellers, then? Er, no, middle-class white chaps, actually . . .) Overall, *Thank You* is a mixed bag, but 'Drive By' is a glorious piece of music by any standards, and the album stands a decent chance of being valued when the effete bleatings of Duran's supposed heyday (*Rio*, etc.) are long forgotten.

9 *drukQs* – Aphex Twin

The British have a strange habit. They viciously snub any artist who's been a Godlike Genius too long and who refuses to drop dead when the Next Big Thing appears on the journalistic horizon. *drukQs* was miles better than some of the earlier, worshipfully received Aphex Twin records. But it wasn't alt.country or whatever you were supposed to be listening to in 2001.

8 *Hooray for Boobies* – The Bloodhound Gang

Puerile smut for bored lads who've had a few drinks, right? Well, that might be true of the BG's other efforts, but this one was a little miracle of Lamarckian evolution. 'The Ballad of Chasey Lain' is the sharpest, most perceptive song about porn ever written. Indeed, virtually every track nails a social syndrome with exuberant wit.

7 *Songs from the Capeman* – Paul Simon

In the future, people will find *Bridge Over Troubled Water* unpalatably saccharine and will struggle to comprehend how an album as twee as *Simon & Garfunkel's Greatest Hits* managed to outsell everything else throughout the 1970s. But they will groove to this sassy

217

Broadway tale of Hispanic lowlife, in which Simon sings the memorable couplet 'Fucking Puerto Rican dope-dealing punk / Get your shit-brown ass out of here'.

6 *Tales from Topographic Oceans* – Yes

Still trotted out as Exhibit A in the pointless courtroom prosecution of prog rock. Even now that King Crimson and early Genesis have been rehabilitated by the Thought Police, this four-movement double album based on Shastric scriptures is decried as everything rock should never be. Can I tell you a bi-i-i-g secret? *Topographic Oceans* isn't trying to be *Raw Power*. It isn't trying to be *Born to Run*. Mind you, it's better than *Born To Run*. And arguably less pretentious.

5 *The Fall of the House Of Usher* – Peter Hammill

The ex-Van der Graaf Generator man recorded two different versions of this wonderfully gothic opera, the first in 1991 and the second (with eerie massed guitars replacing the drums) in 1999. Both times, the world sniggered in disdainful indifference. The awed respect that this album will one day command won't benefit Hammill when he's in the grave. But that's Poe for you.

4 *Ragga and the Jack Magic Orchestra* – Ragga and the Jack Magic Orchestra

Terrible name, I know. The thing is, the mass public never really liked or understood trip-hop. They only pretended to. Under duress, they were willing to own one Tricky album, one Portishead album and two Massive Attack albums (and they've since donated Portishead and

218

Tricky to their local Oxfam). Ragga and the JMO were imperious giants of trip-hop, but no amount of brilliance could save them from the junk bin. Their final single was titled, prophetically, 'Where Are They Now?' (See also *Salt Peter* by Ruby.)

3 *Their Satanic Majesties Request* – The Rolling Stones

Universally agreed to be the shambolic sound of a band that had lost its way. Which is true, I suppose, if you venerate rock 'n' roll. Me, I could never be bothered with Chuck Berry riffs and bad-boy posturing. The world has quite enough rock 'n' roll in it, but sadly only one *Satanic Majesties*. Mellotrons, bongos, Stockhausenesque collages – what's not to like?

2 *OVO* – Peter Gabriel

Detractors of New Labour's infamous Millennium Dome (for which this music was made) were withering in their contempt for *OVO*. Peter Gabriel's fan base was kinder, merely dismissing it as misconceived, overambitious and rather dull. There was general agreement that the songs might've worked better if Gabriel himself had sung them, rather than giving the spotlight to Richie Havens, the Blue Nile's Paul Buchanan, and Cocteau Twins' Liz Fraser. All three of whom deliver some of their most achingly beautiful performances ever, lifting this already fine album into the stratosphere. Gorgeous.

1 *Paris* – Malcolm McLaren

Recognised as a classic throughout mainland Europe, this immensely charming paean to La Paree is still regarded as *merde* by the Brits. Over here, McLaren will always be the Sex Pistols' ex-manager, the evil serpent in punk's Garden of Eden. And he can't sing! Ah, but neither can Catherine Deneuve, and their duet is one of the most touching, inspirational moments in pop music. Indeed, the whole album is a gem. A much more precious gift to history than the numbskulled *Never Mind the Bollocks*.

The Dirty Dozen: Twelve Great Artists Who Are Terrible Influences

SIMON REYNOLDS

There's an almost mathematical relationship between a band or singer's devastating originality and the number of copyists they spawn. Now, that's not always such a bad outcome: the legion of Stones clones include lots of thrillingly insolent sixties garage-punk outfits, plus Aerosmith. But sometimes the very best bands are the absolute worst influences. Here are a dozen rock 'n' pop visionaries whose largely impeccable recorded legacy trails behind it a tarnishing wake of travesty and lameness – the stains of being seminal.

12 The Byrds

Two major crimes here: creating the template for West Coast country rock (the Eagles etc.) with 1968's *Sweetheart of the Rodeo*, and being the major source for the jangled-guitar and pallid-vocalled sound that made eighties American alternative music such an unrocking wasteland.

11 Lou Reed

According to Lester Bangs (see below), 'The guy that gave dignity and poetry and rock 'n' roll to smack, speed, homosexuality, murder, misogyny, stumblebum passivity, and suicide.' Reed also opened the floodgates for 1001 non-singers sporting sunglasses after dark and peddling bogus street romanticism.

10 Syd Barrett

Inventor of psychedelia as regression-to-childhood on *The Piper at the Gates of Dawn* and rock's first major acid casualty, Barrett inspired a raft of wannabe lunatics on the grass such as Julian Cope and Robyn Hitchcock.

9 The Who

Blame them for Paul Weller, the late-seventies mod revival and the rock opera.

8 Van Morrison

Mystic visionary whose voice is the missing link between gargling phlegm and talking in tongues. Unfortunately the grumpy Ulsterman would inspire the 'raggle taggle'-era Dexys of 'Come on Eileen / Too-rye-aye' infamy, along with subsequent Celtic soul-stirrers like Hothouse Flowers.

7 David Bowie

The trouble with DB's constant artistic evolution and restlessly rapid procession through personae is that each of his myriad incarnations spawned its own set of mis-shapen progeny: Ziggy Stardust (Bauhaus and other goths, Sigue Sigue Sputnik), *Young Americans*-era plastic soul (ABC, Spandau Ballet), Thin White Duke/*Low* (Gary Numan, the New Romantic movement). Thankfully, the seed of Tin Machine has, so far, fallen on barren ground.

6 The New York Dolls

Okay, they (or rather Johnny Thunders) gave us Steve

222

Jones's glorious guitar sound, and the group stirred strange fancies in the heart of the young Steven Morrissey. But they also helped, via *Hanoi Rocks*, to sire the LA Sunset Strip hair-metal/glam scene of the eighties, from Motley Crüe to Guns N' Roses.

5 Lester Bangs

As historically potent a figure as all but a handful of bands, LB's proto-punk manifestos of the early seventies shaped a canon (Iggy, Velvets, garage punk) and coined an attitude (who-gives-a-fuck, noise annoys) that's been aped by countless dismal combos from the late seventies onwards, even though Bangs himself was far more open-minded taste-wise and emotionally sensitive than the bastardised cartoon version of his gospel.

4 Prince

The first postmodernist black superstar, he constructed himself from components of his ancestors (Hendrix + James Brown + Little Richard + Todd Rundgren + George Clinton) only to end up a genre himself: that breed of chameleon/musical magpie/pasticheur that includes Terence Trent D'Arby and Lenny Kravitz.

3 The Smiths

Have they inspired a single decent band? Okay, the Sundays and Suede had their moments and that tATu cover was fun, but Housemartins, Easterhouse, Echobelly, Gene . . . Most recently the Smiths have pooled genetic material with the Cure and injected some UK miserabilism into America's emo genre.

2 Portishead

One fantastic album (*Dummy*) of trip-hop torch songs became the blueprint for a mid-nineties deluge of down-tempo mood muzak that provided chicly depressive ambience for a thousand boutiques, hair salons and designer bars.

1 Radiohead

A great and original group, but oh, the plague they've visited upon the house of noughties British music, in the form of numberless rock bands that don't actually rock and vocalists wheezily fixated on strained upper-register singing (most notably Coldplay's Chris Martin) as the true modern sound of feeling a bit shit about the state of the world and/or the state of yourself.

COME TOGETHER

From confluence to disaster

Ali Smith / Matt Thorne / Lavinia
Greenlaw / Jack Murphy / Kevin Cummins

Chance Meetings and Perfect Marriages: Ten Unexpected Moments of Musical Cross-fertilisation

ALI SMITH

10 'Bier Bier Bier Downtown' – People Like Us

People Like Us is a mix-maker beyond the usual conception of mix, a finder of very startling collages in both found-footage filmwork and found-sound songwork. This track from the album *Abridged Too Far* is a found-sound grafting-together of some Germans singing a tub-thumping beer-cellar song and a sweet female voice singing, in German, the Petula Clark hit 'Downtown', plus the lumberjack noise of logs being sawn in two; it makes for a whole new cultural understanding as well as what you might call a new take on female and male mid-century Eurosong.

9 Soundtrack for *Milou en Mai* – Stephane Grappelli and Louis Malle

Though it wasn't exactly all fun and games in the studio when Malle had Grappelli and assorted musicians in to record this – which might have been predictable given the free-spirited Grappelli's usual refusal to be pinned down to anything as defining as a click-track or any strict repetition of what he'd just played – this sweet piece of lightness is a youthful enhancer both of the film it soundtracks and the eighty-two-year-old musician who pulls it, pure and unburdened, out of the studio tears-before-bedtime.

227

8 *'Je t'attends depuis la nuit des temps'* – Jodie Foster

When I was fifteen or sixteen I had a pen pal called Debbie who lived in Blackpool and was a Jodie Foster aficionada. She sent me a cassette once which had a recording of Jodie Foster singing in French, two songs, one rather soulful and heartfelt, called *'Je t'attends depuis la nuit des temps'*, and another called *'La Vie c'est chouette'*, from a film, if I remember rightly, called *Moi, Fleur Bleu*. I haven't heard them for thirty years or ever been able to find them again. Do they exist or did I dream them? (I can't simply have dreamed them – I can sing them.)

7 'All God's Chillun' – Ivie Anderson and the Marx Brothers

Ivie Anderson was most famously soloist for Duke Ellington. Born in 1905 and orphaned as a small child, she was brought up by nuns, studied voice, worked her way through the clubs and was spotted by Ellington soloing for Earl Hines. When Harpo Marx sparks off a set of gospel songs by blowing his tin whistle through the African-American quarters of the town in *A Day at the Races* (1937), Anderson steals the show, even from Harpo, in a shining performance, all energy and aliveness, as the washergirl leading the company in a great performance of 'All God's Chillun Got Rhythm'. Anderson died young, aged only forty-four. *A Day at the Races* is an unexpected chance to see her in her prime.

6 'The Good Years' – Karine Polwart and Edwin Morgan

The Roddy Woomble project to bring writers and musi-

228

cians together and see what happened resulted in the 2007 release of an album called *Ballads of the Book* and this chance meeting of Polwart the singer with Morgan the poet, whose original poem, from *A Book of Lives*, Polwart arranged here, making a song that's haunting and rich in its harmonies and its simplicities.

5 'Beach Baby' – First Class and Sibelius

Did the writers of this 1974 boy next door/girl next door summer hit know they were going to use the theme from the third movement of Sibelius's 5th Symphony at the centre of their pop song before they wrote it? Did they begin with Sibelius and progress from there to the Chevrolet, ponytail and the beat-up sneakers or did the high-school hop lead to the symphony and to the Sibelian horns (which casually segue into the 'Let's Go to San Francisco' theme half a minute later)? When I was eleven it was the song I most wanted to hear on the car radio on our fortnight's holiday, on the drive from Inverness to Scarborough and back again. I had never heard of Sibelius. Thirty four years on, last week, I heard Sibelius's 5th Symphony and into my head came: summer, Whitby, my yellow T-shirt that said 'Lipsmackinthirstquenchin-acetastin', and, yes, 'Beach Baby'.

4 'Les Bicyclettes de Belsize' and *Les Bicyclettes de Belsize*

I mean both the song and the film. The song, written by Les Reed and Barry Mason, was a pan-Europe hit for lots of people in lots of languages, but the film, directed by Douglas Hickox and about twenty-five minutes long, is a sweet and English piece of innocent effervescence, a love

COME TOGETHER

story in songs, made around 1969, a full-songed, gorgeous mini-musical which tips its British hat to *Les Parapluies de Cherbourg* in the form of an elongated commercial for . . . Raleigh Bikes.

3 'Annie Laurie' – Maxine Sullivan and William Douglas

Traditional Scottish song meets Cotton Club, recorded in 1937 by Maxine Sullivan backed by Claude Thornhill and his Orchestra. Twenty-six-year-old Sullivan, a self-taught jazz singer, had sung her way to New York and was looking for work; when Thornhill heard her cool/warm enunciation and her clear, clean, articulated swing, he had the brainwave of matching her voice and his arrangements to unlikely songs from long ago and elsewhere, which resulted in some rich and strange Shakespeare-swing but also in gloriously unexpected versions of 'Loch Lomond', 'I Dream of Jeannie with the Light Brown Hair' and, especially, this sweet and witty upbeat take on William Douglas's song, framed at the start and the finish with a little 'Comin' Through the Rye' shimmy and pure shoulder-shrugging joy throughout.

2 'Wild Mountainside' – Eddi Reader

On Reader's classic album *Eddi Reader Sings the Songs of Robert Burns*, one of the songs isn't by Burns. It's by John Douglas of the Trashcan Sinatras, who's written some of the finest songs of this recent turn of the century. Only a really great song dare stand head and shoulders with the likes of 'Ae Fond Kiss' and 'My Love Is Like a Red Red Rose', 'John Anderson My Jo' and 'Winter It Is Past'. 'The last mile is upon us / I'll carry you if you fall'.

'Wild Mountainside' is a travelling song that carries you with it, far-sighted and kind, the kind of rare, haunting, brand-new song that sounds like it has always been there.

1 *All My Life* – Ella Fitzgerald and Bruce Baillie

Is it Ella's song, recorded in 1936, that makes this Bruce Baillie short film made thirty years later one of the most beautiful moments of cinema I've ever seen, or is it Bruce Baillie's throwaway-seeming short film that makes its soundtrack, with the young Fitzgerald's voice full of hope and Teddy Wilson's warm swooning arrangement, so very powerful? The film is only two minutes thirty-odd seconds long, the exact duration of the song. It doesn't tell you what you're watching, or what its title is, until the final frames, when it simply announces the song, the singer, the band. All Baillie does, for the length of the song, is pan along a grassy, worn, gap-toothed garden fence; all he does is let the camera hit mundane, faded, cine-film reality at exactly the right places, in a vision of efflorescence, before he turns his camera skyward, lets it soar above the phone line into nothing but blue. *All My Life*. The perfect marriage.

Riding on a Bus with the Road Crew from Embrace: My Ten Favourite Examples of Bands Singing Songs about Other Singers or Bands

MATT THORNE

You'll notice some common themes among this list of songs, the most obvious being the distance between alternative and mainstream music. Usually when an artist names another artist or band in a song, they are looking for fame by association. It doesn't matter whether they're dissing the artist or praising them, it's a way of saying 'I'm better than them.' Or more honest. Or more real. Alternatively, it can be a way of giving props to another musician, acknowledging them as a contemporary. There are many examples in this list of indie artists mocking the more successful, or criticising the famous for lapsing into self-parody. Either way, it's a rich vein of songwriting, and there many other songs that could make this list. These ten, then, are my favourites.

10 'Prince Alone in the Studio' – Smog

Bill Callahan isn't the only musician to write about Prince (see also, for example, Hot Chip's 'Down with Prince'), but his song is easily the funniest and most pertinent. This song makes an explicit connection between the lo-fi musician toiling away in his home studio and Prince summoning his band to record all day and night in Paisley Park. What makes this song so funny are the details: while Prince has been recording, his dinner has burnt on the stove, and the women who came to the studio are wearing their 'special underwear'. But Prince ignores all this: his obsessive nature means the only thing that gives him pleasure is getting a guitar track right. I can't imagine what Prince would make of this song if he heard it, which is part of what makes it so much fun.

9 'Screaming Skull' – Sonic Youth

If, as Malkmus contends, singing about other bands is a weird thing to do, then this is Sonic Youth's oddest song, consisting mainly of a list of other bands and record labels. The artists seem chosen for no reason at all, although they are mainly mainstream indie bands (Lemonheads, Hüsker Dü). The song is from a weird, underrated Sonic Youth album, *Experimental Jet Set, Trash and No Star*, that showed the band retreating from the grunge inspired *Dirty* and trying to fit in with the lo-fi boom that had taken off around the time this album was recorded. It's a record that shows Sonic Youth observing and reacting to trends, particularly the rise of riot grrrl, and analysing the music industry. This song, like many on the record, feels completely throwaway, but at the same time, possesses the mystery and menace of their very best music.

8 'Highlands' – Bob Dylan

I've always been intrigued by the relationship between Neil Young and Bob Dylan. The impression I've got from various rock biographies of both artists is that Dylan is always slightly alarmed when Neil Young shows up, the boisterous energy of the latter threatening to wear him out. Dylan has confessed to being annoyed when he heard 'Heart of Gold' on the radio as he considered it too similar to his own music, but since then the two men seem to have become good friends, and reference each other in their music. In this song, Dylan is trying to play a Neil Young record but people are always telling him to turn it down. Is this a reference to the frustrated rocker in Dylan? Would he like to be backed by Crazy Horse? I once saw Neil Young play a few nights after Dylan and was struck at how much better Young's live version of 'All Along the Watchtower' was than Dylan's.

7 'The Old Matchbox Trick' – Lambchop

What I like most about this song is how Kurt Wagner manages to make poetry out of the most prosaic details of the rock life. The incongruity of this Americana band riding on a bus with the 'road crew from Embrace' makes this song, and is an explicit reminder that rock isn't something individual bands do alone. Even the most idiosyncratic artist will cross paths with all kinds of other musicians on the festival circuit, and other bands' idea of what makes good music may be very different from their own. The distance between Lambchop and Embrace couldn't be any greater, and there would be no reason of thinking of them together if it wasn't for this song. It reminds me of concert bills from old Reading Festivals where you can't quite believe these bands played together and how almost everyone aside from the headliners is largely forgotten.

6 'Musicology' – Prince

The title track from a so-so album, this song showed Prince acknowledging his musical tastes and influences, from his earliest loves (Sly and the Family Stone, James Brown, Earth, Wind and Fire) to the rappers he considers interesting (Chuck D, Jam Master Jay). This became a concert favourite, usually accompanied by another self-referential song ('Prince and the Band') and covers such as Wild Cherry's 'Play that Funky Music (White Boy)'. For some it marked the end of Prince's experimental period and the beginning of the time when he set himself up as a funk historian ('We got a PhD in advanced body movin"); for others it was the sign of a new maturity and the starting point from where he reinvented his career. Either way, it's a definite grower, simple stripped-down funk that gets more compelling with every listen.

5 'Range Life' – Pavement

Stephen Malkmus at his most gloriously snarky, in this stand-out track from Pavement's finest album, *Crooked Rain, Crooked Rain*. Sung from the perspective of 'someone who just doesn't get Smashing Pumpkins or where they come from', as Malkmus told defunct music magazine *Melody Maker*, the song also gets a dig in at Stone Temple Pilots, calling them 'elegant bachelors' and somehow making it sound like the worst insult in the world. Malkmus admitted that singing about other bands was a weird thing to do, but wanted something to talk about in interviews. Billy Corgan took it badly, and used his higher profile interviews to present himself as the underdog and suggest that Pavement were jocks, and also to suggest that there was elitist snobbery in there. It's not the only reference to other artists on the album, with 'Heaven is a Truck' offering a far more complimentary take on the excellent Royal Trux. Speaking of which . . .

4 'Death of a Heir of Sorrows' – Silver Jews

Stephen Malkmus wasn't the only one obsessed with

Royal Trux, among the most avant-garde and interesting of the mid-nineties indie rock bands. David Berman, the slightly loony lead singer of the Silver Jews, thought they were the best band of the nineties and wanted to be them. I once interviewed Berman and he claimed that his song about Royal Trux had countless layers, summing up how it felt to be a fan of a rock band, how it felt to have a serious drug habit, and also addressing his friendship with the band and the difference between his own attitude and the poise of Neil Hagerty and Jennifer Herrema, the couple in the band. Worrying about another band's success is something you rarely encounter in rock music, and the collegiate companionship of the bands on the American Drag City label is uniquely charming.

3 'Chelsea Hotel #2' – Leonard Cohen

This is an unusual one, in that everyone knows that the song is about Janis Joplin and she's the one giving Laughin' Len 'head on an unmade bed', but it's never announced in the song itself. It's actually the second version of a song Cohen didn't record but played live in concert, accompanied by a story that let the audience know Joplin was the woman in question. Later Cohen would regret his lack of gallantry, sending out an apology to Janis's ghost. I include it here as one of the most famous examples of sixties musicians getting together for sex; you could make a whole album of similar songs.

2 'Williamsburg Will Oldham Horror' – Jeffrey Lewis

There are lots of similarities between Will Oldham and Nick Cave – the question of how 'authentic' they are, the fluctuation between the gothic and the sensitive love songs, the question of whether they're really up there with Dylan, Cohen and Young – and Jeffrey Lewis does a similar deflation job on the alt.country idol in this poisonous track. Lewis plays on the Oldham of early albums, the man who sang about fucking mountains and sex with his sister, imagining the Palace man raping him in a deserted subway station. But behind the sick joke, there's a more serious question about levels of fame. Lewis knows he'll never be as successful as Oldham, and that Oldham will never be as successful as Neil Young. How many fans does an artist need to make a career worthwhile? Is it worth continuing anyway, and how seriously should one take the hipsters of Williamsburg?

1 'Nick Cave Dolls' – Bongwater

He's produced some of the best albums of the last twenty-five years, but there's still something inherently amusing about Nick Cave. Cave has said in interviews that he's always wanted to be funny in his music, and often is, but he's also funny as a concept. Ann Magnuson, one half of nineties band Bongwater, captured this brilliantly in her song 'Nick Cave Dolls'. In one of her trademark surreal vignettes, Magnuson imagines herself at a Spanish mansion where nude models are having a 'pose-athon'. Peeling off her girdle, she is sitting naked on a red vinyl ottoman when she's approached by Jeff, 'a famous balding actor'. Jeff tells her about how he's buried all his toys in the back yard so no one will play with them. He says his favourite toy is his Nick Cave doll, to which Magnuson coos, 'They have Nick Cave dolls now? I want one!' Who wouldn't?

Ten Songs Under Two Minutes (And Ten More Up to Ten Times as Long)

LAVINIA GREENLAW

In these impatient times we need songs that are over before we decide to press skip, songs which get down to business and never feel long enough, no matter how many times you play them.

1.59 'My Life's Alright Without You' – No Age (*Weirdo Rippers*)

1.57 'Let's Fall in Love' – Betty Carter (*Social Call*)

1.50 'Love You More' – The Buzzcocks (*Love Bites*)

1.46 'Mercedes Benz' – Janis Joplin (*Pearl*)

1.45 'Here Comes the Summer' – The Undertones (*The Undertones*)

1.41 'What Can I Do?' – Antony and the Johnsons (*I Am a Bird Now*)

1.21 'Till the Morning Comes' – Neil Young (*After the Goldrush*)

1.17 'Chick a Boom' – Tom Waits (*Real Gone*)

1.13 'Hymn' – Patti Smith (*Wave*)

0.44 'Why Hiphop Sucks in '96' – DJ Shadow (*Endtroducing . . .*)

We also need songs that go on so long we forget to do anything about them. They are arrogant and demanding, and know how to take their time, drawing us in and on, slowing the song (and us) right down while always accumulating.

8.04 'Il Pleure' – The Art of Noise (*Produced by Trevor Horn*)

8.39 'Movin'' – Brass Construction (*Greatest Hits: Movin' and Changin'*)

8.40 'Song for Sharon' – Joni Mitchell (*Hejira*)

9.15 'Safer' – Animal Collective (*Strawberry Jam*)

10.26 'Let's Be Still' – Yo La Tengo (*Summer Sun*)

11.20 'Sad Eyed Lady of the Lowlands' – Bob Dylan (*Blonde on Blonde*)

12.05 'Walk on By' – Isaac Hayes (*Greatest Hits*)

12.12 '"B" Movie' – Gil Scott-Heron (*Reflections*)

17.27 'Sister Ray' – The Velvet Underground (*White Light/White Heat*)

20.20 'Yoo Doo Right' – Can (*Monster Movie*)

Jane's Affliction: Ten Ailments/Accidents that Changed Pop Music History

JACK MURPHY

It's no surprise that there are a disproportionately small number of physically challenged people, either by incident or illness, who forge successful careers in the music industry. The road to stardom is notoriously arduous and those of weakened body, for whatever reason, are at a distinct disadvantage. What's more, it's a profession, perhaps more than any other bar fashion, obsessively and vacuously concerned with looks. For the people who hold the purse strings that usually means that anything remotely outside the norm is almost instantly doomed to a dismal lack of support, no matter how worthy. Survival of the fittest – in the sense meant by Darwin and in the sense meant by *Nuts* magazine – most definitely holds sway.

For these reasons it's well worth saluting those who have triumphed in the face of adversity and succeeded in a cut-throat world against unfairly stacked odds. This list has been compiled not in order of the seriousness of physical debility, or the level of tragedy involved in any accident, but instead considers how much each misfortune has permeated, influenced or twisted the musical contributions of these people into something unique.

10 Robert Wyatt

As drummer and singer for influential Canterbury beardy-weirdies the Soft Machine, Wyatt was at the centre of the English psychedelic movement that gave rise to Pink Floyd, among others. When the group disbanded he drifted through various projects without making much impact. Until 1973 that is, when, while at a party in Maida Vale, he fell from a third-floor window and was paralysed from the waist down. The force of this tragedy seemed to have the effect of focusing Wyatt's mind – he went on to release a series of acclaimed solo albums and even scored a few Top 40 hits, including a stunning version of Elvis Costello's 'Shipbuilding'. Astonishingly, he was once told by a *Top of the Pops* producer that it would be 'inappropriate' for him to appear on the show in a wheelchair, and an elaborate armchair was suggested for the performance instead. Wyatt refused.

9 Ray Charles

Unlike fellow blind prodigy Stevie Wonder, Ray Charles was born sighted but went blind after contracting glaucoma at seven years of age. Nevertheless, his immense gifts soon became apparent and when he was sixteen he hit the road, having already mastered saxophone, trumpet, clarinet, organ and, of course, piano. He went on to conquer R&B and sustained a stellar career over five decades, throughout which he continued to tour the world on an almost annual basis and apparently effortlessly produce albums in varying styles including jazz, soul and even country and western. Charles always gave the impression that overcoming sightlessness was the easy part, and his unprecedented crossover success in pre-Civil Rights Movement America was if anything a more impressive achievement. As if that wasn't enough, he threw in a few obstacles of his own, developing a seriously self-destructive philandering streak and a heroin addiction. In the end, though, as depicted in Jamie Foxx's Oscar-winning turn in the biopic, he bested all his demons, self-made or otherwise.

8 Rick Allen

In 1984 British rockers Def Leppard were already big news in America, where their *Pyromania* album had sold several million copies. On New Year's Eve of that year their drummer Rick Allen was jettisoned from his Corvette after he lost control on a bend of the A57 – also known as Snake Pass – outside Sheffield, seriously injuring his right arm and losing the left one completely. With the support of his bandmates and the help of a specially adapted kit, Allen spent a year and a half relearning his instrument and coming to terms with his disability, a process that culminated in a triumphant and emotional headlining performance at the 1986 Monsters of Rock festival in Donnington. The release of the Leppard's *Hysteria* album, which went on to sell millions of copies all over the world, followed shortly afterwards. 'That I could still play was my high point,' said Rick. 'My low point was discovering I couldn't wear a watch any more.'

7 John Martyn

John Martyn's journey from angel-voiced, baby-faced folk hero to enormous, guitar-slapping, one-legged minstrel has been a long and eventful one. Emerging in the late sixties, along with a whole generation of talented folk-rockers, Martyn immediately stood out for his pure singing, guitar technique and ability to assimilate other styles, most notably jazz, into the folk template. He's gone on to produce a body of work that, while erratic, has reached some lofty highs, and it's probably fair to say he still hasn't received the acclaim that's his due. This may in part be due to a long, well-documented wrestle with booze and drugs – in one incident Martyn was nailed under a carpet to the floorboards by his bassist Danny Thompson; in another he came onstage at a gig having just been bottled by his pal, Free's Paul Kossoff. For years his gigs were a lottery from which the punter could emerge having witnessed world-altering displays of soul-baring and guitar wizardry or alternatively a huge, growling bearded man stumbling grumpily around the stage. In such circumstances, it's a surprise that Martyn hasn't had to suffer more than the amputation of his right leg below the knee in 2003 after a cyst went septic – indeed, it's a wonder that he's still around at all, given that friends and peers like Nick Drake and Kossoff didn't survive the same treadmill. In spite of it all, he continues to tour and experiment.

6 Ian Dury

Art-punk geezer Ian Dury maintained he caught polio from a swimming pool in Southend in 1949. As a child he was frequently immobilised by the illness and suffered the lasting effects of it for the rest of his life. As a teenager and art student, he was inspired by Gene Vincent, and it was his death in 1971 that spurred Dury on to form his first band. By the time Ian Dury and the Blockheads released their classic debut *New Boots and Panties* in 1977, they'd perfected a winning combination of jaunty punk pop and Dury's witty, savvy lyrics. These qualities, allied to Dury's immense charisma and all-round likeability, gave the Blockheads a run of success that lasted until

Dury disbanded the group in 1981 and ultimately moved into acting. Before doing so, he received the ultimate accolade when the song 'Spasticus Autisticus', written to mark the international year of the disabled, was banned by the BBC, who found the unflinching lyrics a bit too close to the bone: 'I'm knobbled on the cobbles / 'Cos I hobble when I wobble / Swim!'

5 Curtis Mayfield

There wasn't much that Curtis Mayfield hadn't achieved by the late seventies. His career had taken in a series of hits with the Impressions, the redefinition of soul (with Sly Stone) to encompass black consciousness, and a clutch of classic soul-funk albums that are still being ripped off today. As well as this, Mayfield ran his own Curtom label (home to the Staple Singers and the young Chaka Khan, to name but two) and was a powerful civil rights campaigner. It's not surprising then that such an exceptional man was unbowed even after a lighting rig collapsed at a concert in Brooklyn, paralysing him from the neck down. He continued to work, recording the acclaimed *New World Order* album, for which the vocals had to be recorded while Mayfield was suspended face down in a harness. He died in his sleep in 1999.

4 Neil Young

Like Ian Dury, Young contracted polio as a young boy, as an epidemic swept Canada in 1951. His mother maintains that he was very close to death and the legacy of the experience has imbued Young's career with a unique and paradoxical combination of characteristics – vulnerability, recklessness, contrariness, pensiveness and, probably

244

most of all, determination. The most tangible proof of this is his work rate – he's recorded well over forty albums since the late sixties and put in enough years on the road to make the average loafing rocker blush. His closest parallel in this is probably the novelist and critic Anthony Burgess, whose prodigious output of over fifty books and countless reviews by the time of his death in 1993 was apparently instigated by being told he had an inoperable brain tumour in 1959. But more than that, Young's music itself has been directly affected by his experience of the illness, and at both ends of his impressive range, from the startling fragility of his pastoral acoustic work to the full-throated fatalism of the Crazy Horse rock-outs. Long may you run indeed.

3 David Bowie

It seems unlikely now, but in 1961 Brixton's finest, the fourteen-year-old David Jones, got into a scuffle with another boy, George Underwood, allegedly over a girl. Fairly unremarkable stuff except that George was wearing a ring and caught David with a good one to the left eye, leaving it permanently dilated and his vision impaired. While for many this might have been considered a high price to pay, for a future chameleon rock-god, it proved a palpable boon. The constant dilation of Bowie's left pupil means that from a distance in certain lights, it looks brown in colour, at clear variance with his other, very blue, right eye. This chimed perfectly with Bowie's constantly morphing persona of the seventies and the mysterious eye was the subject of much nonsensical rumour and speculation for a while, based mainly around the idea that David was indeed from another planet. In a freakish coincidence, Bowie also sustained an odd eye injury at a concert in Norway in 2004 when a lolly lobbed by a member of the crowd became lodged under his eyelid. After a volley of swearing and a twenty-minute hiatus, Bowie finished the gig like a true professional.

2 Tony Iommi

Struggling to make ends meet while trying to make the big time in late the 1960s, the members of Black Sabbath held down a variety of short-term dead-end jobs. Lead singer John Osbourne had a spell as an inept burglar which ended with a short stint inside (where he whiled away the hours crudely tattooing 'Ozzy' on his knuckles) after his fingerprints were traced. The cruel rumour was that he chose fingerless gloves for the job. However, as Sabbath gigs began to gain a loyal following, the four members were soon able to give up their day jobs. Disastrously, on Tony Iommi's last day as a cutter in a sheet-metal factory, he sliced the tops off two of the fingers on his right hand. This wouldn't have been too much of a problem for a right-handed guitarist, but being a southpaw meant that Iommi had to find a way of accommodating the injury in his fretting hand. At first he tried using thimbles but his fingertips were still highly sensitised, so to ease the pain Iommi decided to loosen the strings on his guitar, which in turn had the effect of lowering the pitch of the instrument and producing a slightly detuned sound. Once bassist Geezer Butler had fallen into line, the die was cast and a distinctive Black Country sound was born. It was as hard and heavy as a lump of pig iron and custom-built for the riffs Iommi was in the process of perfecting. Not only that, but it seemed an ideal match for the new direction the band was taking, led by Butler's burgeoning interest in the dark arts and the occult. A few months later Sabbath went into the studio and recorded their self-titled debut album in two days. The album was rubbished on its release but ultimately, with the Prince of Darkness onside, how could they fail?

1 Gene Vincent

It was while recovering from a traffic accident in 1955 that Gene Vincent began playing rock 'n' roll for a local radio station. Vincent had come off his motorcycle while cruising around his hometown of Norfolk, Virginia, on leave from the US Navy. While convalescing, he played guitar and paid a fellow patient twenty-five dollars for a song about a local stripper called 'Be Bop a Lula'. The accident had been serious enough for there to be the suggestion of Vincent losing his left leg, but he resisted and instead the leg was braced for a year, though it continued to trouble him for the rest of his life. When his career took off in 1956 Vincent began touring far and wide and, to ease the pain of performance, developed a stance that had him jutting out towards the audience, leaning on the mic stand with his right leg, while his weaker left leg trailed behind. This transformation of a vulnerability into an act of pure rock 'n' roll confrontation was entirely in keeping with the other accoutrements of Vincent's act – clad head to foot in black leather, possessing (probably to this day) the most blood-curdling scream in rock 'n' roll and with a face, as Les Dawson would say, like a bag of smashed crabs, Vincent was never likely to be taken to the bosom of middle America the way the likes of Presley ultimately had been. Nevertheless, his best work, backed by the Blue Caps (featuring in particular full-time plumber/part-time revolutionary rockabilly guitar virtuoso Cliff Gallup) is as thrilling as it gets. And of course, Vincent's invention of the leering, menacing frontman is one that has been assimilated by lead vocalists from Jagger to Strummer and beyond.

The Decisive Moment: Ten Photo Disasters

KEVIN CUMMINS

Working as a photographer for the music press in the eighties and nineties often involved being taken to exotic locations for several days by record companies. This was ostensibly to promote a band's new album or forthcoming tour, but it was often seen as a holiday on someone else's limitless expense account. Ninety-nine per cent of the time everything would run perfectly. However due to the personnel involved there was always the possibility of a major cock-up.

10 Public Enemy, Atlanta/New York City, July 1994

We met Chuck D in Atlanta and sat around waiting for Flavor Flav to turn up. Eventually Chuck asked us what we were waiting for and when we told him he said, 'Flavor is in New York. Why would he be here?'

After a hurried conference with the agitated PR, Chuck agreed to do a solo session there in Atlanta and then we'd fly up to New York to meet Flavor. Several hours later I'm jet-lagged and lying in bed in the Royalton Hotel in NYC when my phone rings at 3 a.m. 'Turn Channel 5 news on,' said John Harris, who was my writer for the trip. I tuned in just in time to see Flavor being handcuffed and led into a police station. He'd unfortunately been rear-ended by a rogue cab – doubly unfortunate because Flav was driving while disqualified. He was held in jail for two days and charged with approximately forty-seven motoring violations. He agreed to meet us a few hours before we were due to fly

249

back to London. We sat in his office all afternoon. No sign of him. Just as we were getting in the cab to go to JFK, he turned up and apologised for being late.

In John Harris's version of events I'm recorded as saying, 'How can you be so late when you've got a fucking big kitchen clock around your neck?'

9 Madonna at the Hacienda, February 1984

I shot two rolls of film of the relatively unknown Madonna dancing to a couple of her minor hits at the Hacienda. My assistant Rebecca was processing the film the following day when, inexplicably, she opened the darkroom door to answer the phone and realised she'd left the lid off the developing tank – thus fogging the film. There were only three shots left undamaged. 'Look on the bright side,' said Rebecca. 'It's only Madonna. Imagine if it'd been A Certain Ratio . . .'

8 Lloyd Cole, New York City, May 1989

Two weeks prior to this trip I had been in New York to photograph De La Soul. I met up with Lloyd socially and we spent that evening playing pool and drinking beer. Because I knew him reasonably well, Polydor (his label) sent me back out to New York to do the shoot without a PR. I turned up at the studio and we went for a beer next door.

'Who are you here to shoot this time?' he asked.

'You.'

'I told them I wanted to finish the album off and that you should come out next weekend. I'm not ready to do photos yet.'

There was no further discussion. We played pool and

drank more beer. I had a weekend break in NYC and flew home without taking my cameras out of the hotel room.

We eventually did the session three weeks later.

7 Dumptruck, London, May 1988

I shot this Australian band as a favour for their PR. We were taking photographs in St James's Park when the singer came over to me and whispered, 'Will you make sure you get the bass player on the edge of the shots, because we're sacking him at the end of this week and we'd like to use the photos for the rest of the year. We can just crop him off them.' Naturally the hapless bass player had no idea.

6 Duran Duran, New York City, January 1994

According to the band's manager, each member of Duran Duran was staying in a different hotel for 'security reasons'. The only time they were ever together was when they were onstage. Simon Le Bon, who was staying in the Four Seasons, refused to leave his room other than to go to the gig. He also refused to answer the phone. His manager had to fax him and Simon would respond twenty-four hours later. This made the task of getting a band shot quite laborious. A two-day trip turned into six days as we sat around waiting for the inevitable negative response for a photo request. Finally, I asked if I could just take a photo of Simon lying in his hotel bed. 'Great idea,' said his manager. 'I'll fax him.' Naturally, Simon said no. Well, he sent a fax sheet containing just that one small word. I never got a band shot. I was glad in a perverse way. They are the worst people I've ever had the misfortune to work with.

5 Black Grape, Havana, December 1995

A trip to Cuba organised by their American label as a way of enticing US magazines to cover the band. Bez missed the flight; Shaun fell asleep during all the interviews then told the journalists that he couldn't remember being in Happy Mondays.

Three days into the trip I finally got Shaun and Bez (who'd eventually found his way there via Frankfurt) to walk around Old Havana to do some photos. We took loads of pictures, then Shaun disappeared. I eventually found him in a barber's shop having his head shaved, thus negating the whole session. We had about ten minutes of daylight left. I managed to shoot half a roll of film of Shaun's new look. Fortunately I also got a shot of him having his hair cut to show my editor. This is now seen as the best shot from the whole trip. One frame. One picture. Five days in Havana.

4 Meatloaf, Manchester Apollo, June 1978

I was backstage with the journalist waiting for Mr Loaf to appear after his sound-check. Usually I prefer to shoot after the interview as the artist is more relaxed.

Meatloaf turned up, shook hands; the journalist turned his tape recorder on and said, 'So what's your trouble; is it glandular?'

He was physically thrown downstairs and I felt it wasn't the right moment to ask if a quick photo was out of the question.

3 Stevie Wonder, Lille, April 1989

We travelled from Paris with Stevie Wonder and his

252

entourage. He was sleeping all day and staying up all night. We were promised an interview and photos after the gig. I built a makeshift studio in a corner of a dressing room and waited, and waited. Finally, at 4.30 a.m., I was told Stevie was ready for me. I'd been briefed not to say 'look towards the camera' or 'look left' etc. I had to say 'please face left', 'face forward' and so on. He sat in the chair and I took a couple of Polaroids. Finally, I was ready and I asked him to face up. He ignored me. I asked again. Nothing. I left him sitting in the room on his own and went to get his manager. As he walked into the room with me he said, 'He's asleep.' He pushed Stevie Wonder's elbow off the armrest of the chair and he almost fell on the floor. A few seconds later, when I was ready to take a shot, he'd dozed off again. This carried on for the next hour and I had to be ready to take a photo each time his manager prodded him.

2 Sisters of Mercy, Leeds, November 1982

Not being a big goth fan, I didn't really know much about Andrew Eldritch and co. when I arranged to meet them at Eldritch's flat in Leeds.

It was only for an introductory piece on the band for the *NME* – probably half a page – so I didn't really want to spend too much time on it. We went into the cellar and I forced them all into a small space underneath a bare light bulb hanging from a rafter, which was my only light source. Just before I took the photo, one of the guys said, 'Why do you want me in the picture?' I told him it was a band shot and that I'd do some solo shots later. 'But I'm not in the band,' he said, 'I'm the journalist.'

JUST PLAIN NASTY

From bitchy Beatles to murder ballads

Richard Milward / Sam Delaney / John
Grindrod / Peter Patnaik

All You Need is Hate: Ten Nasty, Malicious Beatles Songs

RICHARD MILWARD

With songs such as 'All You Need is Love' and 'With a Little Help from My Friends', The Beatles helped me – and countless others the world over – to look on the bright, shiny side of life. Mixing clean-cut psychedelia with cherubic optimism, The Beatles seemed like the perfect boys to bring home to meet your parents. However, scratch through the chirpy, mop-topped exterior, and you will find jealousy, mockery, loathing, villainous walruses, and death!

10 'I Am the Walrus'

While John admired Bob Dylan, he felt he didn't half write some bollocks sometimes. Behold John's masterpiece of trippy piss-take. Also victim to John's psychedelic babble was 'semolina' Detective Sergeant Norman Pilcher – who apparently framed The Beatles for drug offences – and 'Eggman' Eric Burdon from the Animals, who used to enjoy cracking eggs over beautiful naked ladies. Goo Goo G'joob!

9 'Revolution 9'

While this might seem like your typical, everyday slice of musique concrete, be warned: this song will make you instigate lots of horrible murders. If you're Charles Manson, that is. Charlie, famous for living in caves and reciting the Bible's Revelation 9 to his 'Family', thought the Fab Four (with their 'faces of men and hair of women') were sending him secret messages regarding Helter Skelter – the race war that was about to hit America. However, instead of staying put round the campfire in Death Valley with his trusty Bible and Beatles records, Charlie decided to send his pals out on a manic killing spree, squirting Beatles lyrics and song titles in blood all over their victims' plush Californian apartments.

8 'She Said She Said'

She (later revealed to be male, and Peter Fonda) might know what it's like to be dead, but go to a party on acid and depress The Beatles and they're going to chuck you out. On one occasion in LA, John and George were tripping and enjoying a drinky with their good pals the Byrds. George began having a bad one. To his rescue came acid-enthusiast Peter Fonda, armed with the sterling advice: 'I know what it's like to be dead.' John felt like he'd never been born, and had Pete promptly removed.

7 'I'm a Loser'

Written in the heights of John's 'fat-Elvis' period, 'I'm a Loser' marks the onset of John's intense self-loathing. See also 'Help!' – not really intended to be the jolly singalong we all know and love, but one man's desperate cry for . . . Help!

6 'Jealous Guy'

Do what John tells you; he's just a jealous guy. Famous for his possessiveness, John knocked out many songs on the subject in his lifetime, culminating in his magnum opus

'Jealous Guy' – a beautiful, musical apology to Yoko Ono, after making her list all the men she'd ever shagged.

5 'Don't Bother Me'

In other words, George wants you to fuck off. Written in the heights of terrible influenza in a hotel room in 1963, George's first song written for The Beatles is a grand slice of self-pity. True to its gloomy sentiment, George later went on to disown the song, describing it as 'fairly crappy'.

4 'Run for Your Life'

John would 'rather see you dead' than to be with another man, little girl. More frightening, murderous jealousy.

3 'How Do You Sleep?'

Solo spite from John. Apparently, all Paul did was write 'Yesterday'. After The Beatles split up, John, Paul and George resorted to petty, schoolboy-ish name-calling. Numerous songs (for example Paul's 'Too Many People' and George's stomper 'Wah-wah') apparently set out to slurry each other's reputations. And 'How Do You Sleep?' is the most seething of the lot, climaxing with a very bad swear word and John's sardonic put-down: 'The sound you make is like Muzak to my ears.'

2 'Yer Blues'

Desperate self-loathing or a light-hearted parody of the British blues scene? While the prefix 'Yer' was meant to appear ironic, there's no denying the primal-scream passion in John's merry couplet: 'I'm lonely / Wanna die'.

259

1 'Maxwell's Silver Hammer'

The jauntiest song ever written about smashing someone's skull in. Totting up a body count to rival the Manson Family, Maxwell Edison is perhaps the most sadistic, emotionally detached character to appear in pop. However, John mocked Paul's 'granny-style' songwriting, and the other Beatles weren't too enthusiastic about it either. Just look at their sullen, emotionally detached faces on the *Let It Be* film. Mal Evans seems weirdly animated though, banging the hammer . . .

'Ooh, you bitch!' Ten Biting Lyrical Put-downs

SAM DELANEY

They reckon music is the food of love, but it can also be the rocket fuel of hate. For every song that says, 'You to me are everything, the sweetest song that I can sing' (the Real Thing) there's another that says, 'Sit down, bitch – if you move again, I'll beat the shit out of you' (Eminem). For some people music provides a refuge for rage. The fury they feel towards an ex lover, a hated peer or the whole damned unjust world we live in can be neatly verbalised in the cruel poetry of their favourite songwriters. But not me. As someone or other once sang, I hate hate. I typed the word into the search bar of my iTunes library and only 18 tracks out of the entire 6,275 contained the word 'hate' in the title (477 included the word 'love,' 49 included the word 'nice' and, for what it's worth, one contained the word 'superfunkycalifragisexy'). It's not that I don't feel the same despicable emotions as everyone else. It's just that I don't like to use music as a means of channelling them. Locking myself in the bedroom with Bob Dylan, Nick Cave or Leonard Cohen has never been my thing. Maybe I'm superficial, but I use music to cheer me up, not stoke the flames of anger and frustration that burn within me. This means that cruel lyrics have an extra big impact on me. I don't find them therapeutic – I find them shocking and disturbing. And certain lines of lyrical bile have had a lasting impact. I don't suppose you could objectively call them the cruellest lyrics of all time. Search around in the annals of death metal or hardcore hip hop and you'll find stuff that's much more upsetting, I'm sure. But here are the horrid words that

261

have made tiny scars on my delicate little soul.

10 'Run for Your Life' – The Beatles

I'd had this album on cassette since I was ten years old and must have listened to it a thousand times, thinking: 'Wasn't John Lennon a wonderful and peaceful man?' It took me until I was nineteen, driving along in my clapped out Citroën AX with *Rubber Soul* on the stereo, that the lyrics of its last track actually registered: 'I'd rather see you dead, little girl, than to see you with another man . . .' Huh? What are you saying, John? This doesn't seem to fit in with the spiritually enlightened world view you just outlined on *The Word* at all. 'You better run for your life if you can, little girl.' Crumbs! What a rotten sentiment to lace through such an upbeat melody. I felt so let down.

9 'All the Rage' – Elvis Costello

My eldest brother was nuts about Costello and tried to indoctrinate me with his music from the moment I was born. 'Oliver's Army? Watching the Detectives? What's it all mean, then?' I'd ask him. 'Nobody knows. It's just nonsense, mainly,' he'd claim all shiftily. But he knew all along about the miserable cynicism and cruelty that lurked behind every one of Costello's couplets. And it was only a matter of time before my slow-witted brain saw through the jangling frivolity of his melodies. 'He's so mean! Why do you like him so much?' I asked my big bro. 'I like him *because* he's so mean,' he muttered shamefacedly. That ain't an easy thing to hear from the mouth of your mentor and role model, I can tell you. I'm still getting to grips with it now, to be honest.

8 'Back Off Bitch' – Guns N' Roses

The song that nearly ruined my entire adolescence. 'You better back off, back off bitch.' 'Yeah! You tell 'em Axl Rose!' I thought. 'Goddam women suffocating you with their love. You gotta tell them to back the hell up before they start messing with all the fun you and your buddies are trying to have.' Only I wasn't Axl Rose, women were not suffocating me with their love and me and my buddies weren't having much fun at all. None the less, I was seduced by Rose's bullish approach to romantic entanglements and would adopt a similarly hostile attitude every time some poor ill-advised young lady showed the remotest bit of interest in me. Unlike Axl, I couldn't really afford to be choosy and my hard-to-get demeanour led to lengthy periods of romantic starvation. By the time I'd realised how preposterous these lyrics were, I'd have killed any sort of love, witch-like or otherwise.

7 'I Am the Resurrection' – The Stone Roses

The drought was eventually broken by a messy, awkward love affair played out in school playgrounds, tube stations and a bunker at the local pitch 'n' putt. Inevitably, it ended in a painful fiasco that Stone Roses frontman Ian Brown briefly encouraged me to channel into rage: 'You're a no one, nowhere, washed-up baby who'd be better dead!' he sang. For a few nights in the summer of 1990 these vitriolic words seemed like a perfectly rational response to my humiliation at the hands of a bike-shed temptress. Mercifully, it wasn't long before I went back to listening to Prince.

6 'Bob George' – Prince

At my school, listening to Prince seemed to double your chances with girls. So I listened to him a lot. So much that I grew to love him with all my heart. When my devotion to this ladies' favourite started to compromise my credibility among male friends who preferred NWA, I played them this berserk, rambling monologue from his banned 1988 *Black* album in which a psychotic pimp is interrogating one of his girls: 'U seeing that rich mother-fucker again . . . Prince?'

5 'Ya Mamma' – The Pharcyde

At primary school, if someone bad-mouthed your mum, you'd be more likely to cry than punch them. Then you started secondary school and, overnight, there was a complete amnesty on mum cussing. I stood agog in the playground on my first day in big school, listening to a constant exchange of wildly extravagant and brilliantly imaginative maternal insults. At first it upset me. But by day two I was getting my hands dirty on the front line of mum-abuse with the best of them. It was a sport and a global cult that eventually got its very own anthem courtesy of the Pharcyde, who ventured: 'Ya mama root 'n' toot and stole my loot and my suit . . . She's not pretty, oh what a pity, got the glass titty'.

4 'Mr Clean' – The Jam

The teenage Paul Weller was in a bar when he got it into his angry young head that some toff in a suit had craftily copped a feel of his girlfriend's boob. The cheek! The Modfather did what any real man would do in the face of such an affront: he scurried home to write a song about it. 'I hate you and your wife / And if I get the chance I'll fuck up your life'. Charming. In my late teens I shared not only the same haircut and shoes as the young Weller but also his scattergun nastiness and silly old inverted snobbery. I was always on the lookout for Mr Cleans to take against for some kind of perceived slight. Just goes to show – listen to too much of his early stuff and you can become a right unpleasant bore. These days I stick to his mid-eighties work – say what you like about the Style Council but 'Long Hot Summer' never made me want to go out and punch a stranger in the face.

3 'Can't Do Nuttin' for Ya Man' – Public Enemy

Flavor Flav was supposed to be Public Enemy's stooge. Sort of like Rodney Trotter to Chuck D's Del Boy. And yet here he was admonishing a scrounging friend with real eloquence and insight. 'Hey, maybe this guy is smarter than I thought?' I pondered. 'Maybe I could treat my own ludicrous array of degenerate pals with the same firm but fair approach?' Then, just as the song reached its final throes, Flav reverted to type, breaking into a fit of giggles and blurting: 'Kick that shit, homey! You've got a rip in your couch! Wash your butt!' Oh Flavor Flav, you've let me down – but most of all you've let yourself down.

2 'Frankly Mr Shankly' – The Smiths

There were two songs that rang around my brain as I struggled to adapt to the soul-corroding experience of grown-up working life. Michael Jackson's 'Off the Wall' taught me to suspend my misery until Friday night, when

I could 'leave that nine to five up on the shelf and just enjoy myself'. Or at least make the most of the three-for-one deals on alcopops available in most All Bar Ones in the late nineties. In bleaker moments, it was Morrissey's take on the daily grind that made the clearest sense. 'Frankly Mr Shankly, since you ask', he croons in a lyric aimed at Rough Trade record boss Geoff Travis. 'You are a flatulent pain in the arse.' 'Right on, Mozza!' I thought during my early days as an office drone. 'Let's throw off our chains of enslavement and start the revolution right now!' Then I got a pay rise and everything seemed much better.

1 'Bad Man' – The Cockney Rejects

One of my elder brothers was a skinhead. He liked the Cockney Rejects, who were a bunch of violent West Ham fans. This brother strong-armed me into an affiliation with both the band and the team. My relationship with West Ham flourished into a lifelong love affair but I always struggled with the Rejects' warped morality. Their first album, *Greatest Hits, Volume 1* documents their varied acts of football hooliganism. Then, on 'Bad Man', they've got nerve to self-righteously lecture a mate on a set of relatively trifling misdemeanours: 'One day you'll realise just wot you've done to me', lead singer Jeff Turner spat. 'Everyone they know that you never buy a round! YOU'RE A BAD MAN!'

Crazy in Love: Ten Terrifying Pop Psychodramas

JOHN GRINDROD

Broken hearts and obsessive love are the staple diet of pop. But every so often a song will go just that little bit too far, and not even know it. So this list is a celebration of the deranged world of unrequited love. I've tried not to include the obvious ones, like 'Psycho Killer' or 'Every Breath You Take', but here are ten songs which are clearly the products of diseased minds.

10 'I'm in Love with a German Film Star' – The Passions

Aw. How sweet. A crush on a film star she once saw in a movie. And then in a bar. But there's something unsettling going on here. The relentless bass, the sinister timbre, the vacant voice. And the insistent and strident 'I'm in Love!' over and over again at the end. This is not a well woman. This is, in fact, Kathy Bates in *Misery*. Similar in theme to the Carpenters' 'Superstar', where a tragic groupie weeps by her transistor, the Passions take the concept to a more chilling level, perhaps because of the lack of emotional engagement in the performance, or because Karen Carpenter had at least shagged the guy in her song.

9 'All Around the World' – Lisa Stansfield

So, okay. She's been around the world looking for her baby, she doesn't know why he's gone away, but she's going to find him. No, let's get this straight. She has actually been. Around. The. World. *The world!* You know, I think if this were a more sane or rational person they may have stopped at, I don't know, Epping. But not our Lisa. She's not really getting the message here. He's under witness protection and doesn't want to be found, love.

8 'It Must Be Him' – Vikki Carr

Lovely Vikki. She's waiting by the phone, bless her. But just as a watched pot never boils, the man at the centre of this drama refuses to call. She's trying to have a lot of fun, playing it cool like only a big-voiced showy madam can, perhaps flirting with croupiers from behind her cocktail. At one point she refers to herself as a chump. Now there's a word that needs a pop revival. And when the phone rings, 'Oh dear God! It must be him! But it's not him! And so I die!' She doesn't exactly take it on the chin, our plucky young showbiz pro, but she soldiers on to the next verse, pouring more drinks, hovering by the phone, presumably checking the line and dialling 1471 like Bridget Jones every five minutes. And then it rings again. But it's not him. And so she dies. And the song key keeps changing up and up, and the band gets more and more hysterical, and you begin to think the poor man may have a point.

7 'Make It Easy on Yourself' – The Walker Brothers

This is the most passive-aggressive song ever written. Oh yes, Scott's acting all magnanimous as his girl runs off with some other bloke, and he's trying to make the break-up go as gently as possible, for her sake, obviously, not his, he's bigger than all that. And when he says he's going to cry, he tops it with the beautifully pathetic 'and run to him before you start crying too, and make it easy on yourself'. Is this heavy sarcasm? Do I detect just a hint of Ben Folds's 'Song for the Dumped' ('Well fuck you too, give me my money back you bitch') behind the teary-eyed nobility? Just a tad, perhaps.

6 'Losing My Mind' – Liza Minnelli

Now Stephen Sondheim, there's a man who knows how to write a twisted lyric. And they don't get much more woman-on-the-verge-of-a-nervous-breakdown than 'Losing My Mind'. In *Follies* it's all lush piano and delicacy, in this Pet Shop Boys produced version it's more like *The Hours*: the sound of a housewife weeping into her gin as she tries to blot out the pain. Lines such as 'The coffee cup, I think about you' are brilliantly odd in isolation, and the song has a strangely fragmented quality to it. Perhaps she's in hospital after absent-mindedly driving her Datsun through a school playground. The way she sings 'You said you loved me, but were you just being kind' suggests she's waved bye-bye to reason and anything is possible.

5 'I (Who Have Nothing)' – Shirley Bassey

One line sums up the spirit of Dame Shirley's song. Her bloke's run off with some other woman (possibly Scott Walker's ex, who can tell?) and he's taking her to fancy restaurants and she's dripping with jewels, and as they eat their meal our heroine informs us that 'I can only watch you with my nose pressed up against the window pane!' Classy. I like to think of Shirley like a sequinned bag lady, with perhaps one boot like in Morecambe and Wise, and she's pressed against the glass of this restaurant window, her nose squished sideways, breath steaming the glass and one thickly eye-linered eye scanning the room for the sweet trolley and sneering at the new bird as she tucks into her tiramisu. There's no real sanity to this song. It is deeply, deeply disturbing.

4 'I Just Don't Know What to Do with Myself' – Dusty Springfield

As Dusty progressively loses it during this number I imagine her as that hysterical passenger in *Airplane!*, the one the other passengers are queuing up to slap/shoot/whack with baseball bats. It's Ravel's *Boléro* for lounge singers, the song builds up and up and up, and her performance by the end is staggering and immense. If going to a movie feels as bad as she makes it sound, then I really think she should stay in more, put her feet up and learn to crochet.

3 'Alone' – Heart

If one has to ask the question 'How do I get you alone?' then the answer is almost inevitably going to be 'Rohypnol', as the person in question clearly isn't all that interested. The way Ann Wilson screams 'I never really cared until I met you – *and now it chills me to the bone!*' probably isn't textbook rom-com material either. Crazier than the Dandy Warhols' stalker-fest 'I Love You' ('Although we've only known each other a bit / Already I can't sleep at night and I feel like shit'), this is the real deal. She has an axe, she's going to kill you, just run.

2 'I Know It's Over' – The Smiths

Poor Morrissey, his girlfriend has run off to marry someone else, and all he can do is sit there imagining being buried alive. And he loved her *so much*, right? Well, actually, as the song progresses it emerges they've never even so much as spoken to each other, and he's been stalking this poor woman for how long? This is well beyond the unhealthy end of the scale. Magnificent, appalling and extremely distressing all round.

1 'This Time I Know It's for Real' – Donna Summer

We are talking here about what is possibly the most intense stalker love song of all time: 'You'd be *amazed* how much I love you so, baby / When I get my hands on you I won't let go'. Now, this is one seriously worrying woman. And if following that logic that *this time* she knows it's for real, how many other poor suckers are lying dead in their motel showers on the path to true happiness? Later, after walking 'a tightrope way up high . . .' she exclaims that 'If I wait too long for you I might explode'. Like Peter Petrelli in *Heroes*, perhaps, with the white heat of her unrequited but stubbornly unwavering love. It is, in short, awesomely terrifying. *Cape Fear* with cowbells. Not so much 'Love's Unkind' as 'Love's Unhinged'. I often have little movies in my head when listening to songs. 'This Time I Know It's for Real' involves Donna Summer dragging a locked and bloodied trunk onstage and singing to it coquettishly. Fits perfectly.

I Don't Want to Hurt that Man, I Just Want to Kill Him Dead: Female Murder Ballads in the Pre-war Era

PETER PATNAIK

This list of songs is culled from the era before the Second World War, when these songs were pressed on to shellac, slapped into fungus-prone cardboard and sold as race records. These are singular songs – ones that didn't pass through the ages and become skiffle hits for British teens. These songs are the dark passions of the women singing them – and ones that only they could sing.

10 'Gravier Street Blues' – Laura Smith

Laura Smith was a very popular singer travelling up and down the Midwest – as far north as Chicago, though it is not reported that she ever toured the southern states, where her style of blues was not as popular. Smith's 'Gravier Street Blues' starts off as a typical blues 'I'm leaving you today' song – Smith is walking out on her man, leaving only blues and a letter in her wake. As the song unfolds, it is clear that the letter was not about leaving him but a note to the police stating what she had done – put him six feet under ground – and why she did it – because he had been seeing another woman. That reveal is punctuated by Clarence Williams's wonderful piano playing that mimics the beating/stabbing that Laura surely laid upon her man.

9 'Nobody Worries About Me' – Sadie Jackson

Sadie Jackson recorded only a handful of songs in her

career, which is a shame – her voice is clear and strong and does not fall into the vaudeville trappings of over-sings and harmonising on her songs. This side features Jackson bailing her trophy man out of jail for the last time, telling him not to worry about picking up his clothes because after all, she paid for those. She sits him down to talk, but talking isn't what's on her mind: her gun, from under the chair, fills him with lead. This is why nobody worried about her. This song has the same tune and pining tone as some versions of 'Nobody Knows the Troubles I've Seen' – a popular gospel song of the time – but Jackson brilliantly mixes it into a dark murder ballad explaining why nobody needs to worry about her: her revolver is the only friend she needs.

8 'Loud and Wrong' – Betty Gray

Betty Gray's 'Loud and Wrong', unlike a lot of female murder ballads, starts off as a murder ballad – the second like makes it clear: she can't stand her man. The crux of this relationship problem is that 'He's loud as the thunder, evil as a snake and he is always wrong at best'. This leads her to the conclusion that she could kill him with a baseball bat. The way Gray pauses between baseball and bat is sickening and wonderful. This is one of the best examples of phrasing and use of a pause in all pre-war blues.

7 'Don't Advertise Your Man' – Clara Smith

While most murder ballads are confessions or day-dreams, Clara Smith spins her tale of murder as a cautionary tale about 'talking up your man'. By 'talking up' she means telling your girlfriends about him buying you flowers, trips to the movies, anything. Keeping your man a secret is the best – because otherwise your girlfriends will try to steal your man away. She gives this advice, of course, after shooting her man down, the obvious solution to this trifling figure.

6 'Send Me to the 'Lectric Chair' – Bessie Smith

Bessie Smith's tale of murder is easily the most brutal account of spousal homicide I would care to hear. Here is the recounting of how this man died. Bessie enters the room and finds her man with another woman, a woman that Bessie has warned him about messing around with previously. She lets the woman leave, then draws her knife and 'goes insane'. After cutting him, she kicks him several times in the side and slits his throat. While the man is dying, she stands over him and laughs until he dies. Of course Bessie knows that she's going for hell for this, and doesn't want to wait around in jail for her trip, so she's pleading to the judge just to send her to the chair.

5 'Santa Claus Craze' – Elzadie Robinson

It's not often that a singer writes a song threatening Santa Claus's life, but here we are. Robinson's blues are that her man left her at the altar – something that she is blaming on Santa Claus, who delivered her husband to another girl's home. As her wish and for penance for breaking her heart, Santa has got to deliver her man back to her or, as she puts it, 'I'm going to break all the laws'.

4 'Satan Is Busy in Knoxville' – Leola Manning

Leola Manning's tale of murder is significantly different

from the other blues on this list as it doesn't detail her wishes or desires to murder her man or a triflin' woman. It details the true events of a serial killer who dispatched several people in Knoxville, Tennessee, in 1930. Manning details each killing with journalistic accuracy, each throat cutting is described in both location and detail. She doesn't pass judgement on the killer: the refrain is a simple 'Who murdered this man / Nobody knows / As the Good Book says, "They must reap just what they sow".'

3 'Hangman Blues' – Bertha 'Chippie' Hill

Bertha 'Chippie' Hill isn't really known as a great blues singer, as she stuck mostly to jazz and only dabbled in blues throughout her career. This side isn't a traditional murder ballad but it's a detailed description/imagining by Hill of her new career as a hang(wo)man. The first half of the side is Hill performing her duties and getting ready for her next client. The second half has a twist, as it is her triflin' man who is getting ready to be hanged. She's not remorseful of her task: she ends the song with 'Hangman blues I'm singing / Going to celebrate your death'.

2 'Two-by-four Blues' – Merline Johnson

'I got a two-by-four / And it just fits my hand / I'm going to stop all you woman / From running around with my man'. By that opening you know that the world that Merline Johnson lives in is about to see a lot of pain. Her first victim is her man, 'I don't want to hurt that man / Just kill him dead.' After his death she goes back to her previous man – two-by-four in hand – and warns him about his impeding doom because his other woman is stopping by his house while she is still there. I don't know if he'll be able to stop her two-by-four.

1 'Penitentiary' – Bessie Tucker

Most murder ballads are written from the murderer's standpoint – this one is written from the other woman's point of view. Leonard is cheating on his wife with Ms Tucker, who is fearful that his rampant running around will make her the victim of a well-placed two-by-four or pistol of some sort. Her response to this is to get to him first, and let the penitentiary be her new home.

COVERS

From country soul to recast spells

Jeb Loy Nichols / Steve McIntyre / DBC
Pierre / John Burnside

Country Goes Large: Ten Songs that Crossed the Border

JEB LOY NICHOLS

Let's face it, the border was never secure. What it was was an open border. The same churches on both sides, the same cotton fields, the same gravelled roads, the same cheap food. The journey from country to R&B was a short trip. It was a trip most southerners, black and white, made every day, usually via their radios. You couldn't, after all, segregate the airwaves.

My radio, a white plastic oblong with a green-flecked face, was a birthday present. It sat by my bed. My favourite stations were KOKO, a local country station, and KCMO, a station out of Kansas City that had a late-night R&B show called *Groovetime*. *Groovetime* was broken into three sections: from ten to eleven was the Go Show (uptempo songs and new hits), from eleven to midnight the Flow Show (mid-tempo songs and requests), and, from midnight until two, the Slow Show.

I listened under my blankets. The Flow Show and the Slow Show were my favourites. They were peppered with songs I knew, songs I'd heard on KOKO, country songs by Hank Williams and Merle Haggard and Waylon Jennings. Soul interpretations that made perfect sense to me; my bridge from one world to another.

Mine was the second generation of R&B radio listeners. The first generation were now making music of their own. Music with a foot in both camps, Nashville and Memphis, music that straddled the border.

10 'I'm so Lonesome I Could Cry' – Hank Williams and Al Green

I'm sitting with my father listening to 'I'm so Lonesome I Could Cry'. He tells me: listen to the words. I write them down and try to figure out how they do what they do. There are lonesome robins and midnight trains and purple stars; there's a man on the verge of tears. When I heard Al Green sing it for the first time I realised what I'd missed: the genius was in the choice of the word 'could'. Everything hangs in the balance, the world is poised. That one word creates a stillness at the heart of the song. The man might cry; awful things might happen. No singer has ever inhabited the border world like Al Green; every slipping word and fluid sound a reminder of how important one word can be.

9 'The Chokin' Kind' – Waylon Jennings and Joe Simon

Written by the great country writer Harlan Howard, 'The Chokin' Kind' was a perfect fit for both sides of the border. Waylon's version is straight southern soul, honky-tonk style. Joe's is stone country, southern-soul style. Both were recorded in Nashville within months of each other.

8 'Behind Closed Doors' – Charlie Rich and Bobby Womack

I first heard Charlie Rich sing 'Behind Closed Doors' while driving across the west with my family; it seemed to be played every ten minutes. It became a joke; not that song again. A song about the importance of secrecy, about the importance of keeping certain things separate.

It also, in my mind, became entangled in the behind-closed-doors dealings of Watergate. I remember looking at my family and thinking: everything is hidden. When I heard Womack's version it was an entirely different deal. Where Charlie Rich was a country charmer (what went on behind his doors was sure to involve roses and sweet talk), Womack had come to party. His was an open house, and his doors, when he chose to close them, hid who knows what kind of goings on.

7 'Stand by Your Man' – Tammy Wynette and Candi Staton

I remember being shocked on first hearing Candi Staton's version; it sounded too positive, too secure. Tammy Wynette had always been the queen of compromise, horribly aware of exactly what men were capable of. In her version, in good southern form, she did her duty: I suffer, therefore I am.

Candi knew: he's not for ever. What is? I'll stand by him today and let tomorrow look after itself.

6 'I Can't Help It if I'm Still in Love with You' – Hank Williams and Isaac Hayes

My favourite song of all time. Perfect in every way. Hank's version captures the always desperate inability to order your feelings. 'I Can't Help It' the great cry of the damaged lover. Isaac Hayes turns perfect art into melodrama. For Isaac the loss of love is the end of the world. For Hank it's something far more terrifying; it's the knowledge that life goes on, and you're stuck with a feeling you can't escape, and every time you pass her on the street the pain will be as impossible to bear as it was the first time.

5 'Don't You Ever Get Tired (of Hurting Me?)' – Merle Haggard and Bettye Swann

When Merle asks the question 'Don't you ever get tired of hurting me?', he knows the answer. Life is full of questions to which we don't want to hear the reply. Bettye's version is all front. While Merle waits around for the awful truth, Bettye asks the question and then, quick as a snake, skips town.

4 'Midnight Train to Georgia' – Jim Weatherly and Gladys Knight and the Pips

Not exactly country, not exactly southern soul. It started life, by Jim, as 'Midnight Plane to Houston'. Somewhere along the way both the transport and the destination changed. Gladys understood two things: first, going to Georgia, the heart of the south, was in all ways superior to going to a hell hole like Houston. She also understood that trains, especially at midnight, are in all ways superior to planes.

3 'I Hate You' – Dan Penn and Bobby Bland

Dan Penn, a white soul boy and writer of numerous southern-soul hits, tried on this track to go country. Not stone country, not Hee-haw country, just barely country enough to be called country. Bobby Bland, one of Dan's heroes, treated it like the deep blues it was. When I asked Dan how he felt about it he smiled and said, 'Bobby Bland singing a Dan Penn song? Hell, what in the world could be better than that?'

2 'Life Turned Her that Way' – George Jones and James Carr

My father once asked me what it was I listened to all night on the radio. I told him soul music. He thought about for a minute and said, 'Ah, like George Jones.' I couldn't disagree.

George was, to me, the greatest singer of country songs who ever lived. James Carr, one of the great southern soul singers, was nearly his equal. On this track, another Harlan Howard song, they go head to head. It's like a tournament of the abject: each version trying to be bleaker and more despairing than the other.

1 'Funny How Time Slips Away' – Willie Nelson and Joe Tex

Here's Willie in late-night blues mode, a country lounge song full of regret and resignation. It's a highly measured performance, sung by a laconic survivor. Joe Tex, on the other hand, seems to be in the middle of a full-blown psychotic breakdown. His vocal is very nearly out of control, the rhythm track is full of unexpected stops and starts, and there's a second Joe (drenched in reverb) commenting on the mistakes of Joe number one.

Willie, in his world-weary way, accepts that time changes things; he has his memories, his version of what was. Joe though, has been caught unaware, time has pulled the rug from beneath his feet; he's left with nothing.

Circling Back: Ten Covers that Helped Me Discover Great Songwriters

STEVE McINTYRE

I've always been curious about music. When a band or an artist I like covers somebody else's song I try to find out about the original. And that's how I was introduced to some of the great songwriters.

In the early 1980s I worked as a disc jockey at a college radio station. The place had been in operation since the early 1970s and had a wide selection of obscure music that I had a great time exploring. I discovered many covers and many original artists while browsing the stacks there. I also broke several state and federal laws at the station, but those are stories for another time.

10 'Ballad of Immoral Earnings' – Cristina (Kurt Weill)

I was working at the radio station when Cristina's album came out. I didn't pay much attention to it until one of the other disc jockeys played this song while I was listening. I was blown away and when I discovered that it was a cover I tracked down a copy of the *Threepenny Opera*.

9 'Son of Your Father' – Spooky Tooth (Elton John and Bernie Taupin)

By the time I really began getting interested in music, Elton John had already turned into some awful Liberace-like parody of himself. There's just something about a man wearing feathers that keeps me from taking him seriously. And for many years that kept me from enjoying Sir Elton's *Goodbye Yellow Brick Road*-era songcraft.

8 'Kiss' – Art of Noise featuring Tom Jones (Prince)

Prince's sexually ambiguous persona was difficult for a suburban adolescent to get around. So when he was at the peak of his popularity I did my best to ignore him. It's funny because when I was a pre-adolescent I was a huge Queen fan. I guess sexual ambiguity only bothered me when I was trying to establish my own sexual identity. It was only after Tom Jones's voice had grabbed me that I realised what a well-crafted pop song this is.

7 'Summertime' – Janis Joplin (George Gershwin)

I knew a woman in college who really, really liked Janis Joplin. If you spent any length of time with her you would end up listening to lots of Joplin's music. I never really liked Joplin, I found her voice to be annoying rather than 'gritty'. But this song interested me musically and started me searching out Gershwin's music.

6 'This Magic Moment' – Lou Reed (Doc Pomus)

This song actually got airplay on a radio station I listened to in my cube at work. The CD it was on was a tribute to Doc Pomus. I bought the CD for the Lou Reed song but the whole album was a revelation. There were little pop gems and heartfelt songs of love found and lost all sitting side by side. Not to mention big hits in such a wide variety of styles that I couldn't believe they were all written by the same guy.

5 'Don't Fence Me In' – David Byrne (Cole Porter)

Cole Porter's songs are so intimately woven into American culture that it's astoundingly easy to either take them for granted or ignore them all together. David Byrne's crazy rhythms made me look at Cole Porter as much more than sonic wallpaper.

4 'Poor Poor Pitiful Me' – Linda Ronstadt (Warren Zevon)

The Top 40 version of this song was pretty bouncy and happy. Little did I know she had left out the verse about sadomasochism. So I was completely unprepared when I checked out Zevon's work to find it filled with songs about junkies and other desperate lowlifes trying to find love and beauty among the wreckage of their lives. It really fundamentally changed the way I thought about music.

3 'Mama Told Me Not to Come' – Three Dog Night (Randy Newman)

Here's another frothy Top 40 tune that led me into a new and unexpected musical realm. When I checked out Randy Newman's work I was expecting to find more funny, wacky songs, but what I found were keenly drawn, blackly cynical portraits of an America that didn't appear too much in the music I was listening to. At first it was a little beyond my comprehension, although the songs still rattled around my head, even if I wasn't aware of it. I returned to those songs when I was a little older and a little more cynical and found that they really resonated with me. I realise that Mr Newman needs to eat, but it still makes me sad that he makes his living nowadays writing sappy songs for Disney movies.

2 'Spoonful' – Cream (Willie Dixon)

I grew up in Chicago and I'm a little ashamed to admit that I was introduced to many of the blues greats by pasty Englishmen. It's just a damn shame that in a city with such a strong history of the blues there is so little of it played on the radio. I just don't know how young people are supposed to learn about the blues these days unless somebody hits them over the head and drags them to a blues bar.

1 'Folsom Prison Blues' – The Red Rockers (Johnny Cash)

You've probably never heard of these guys. They had a minor college-radio hit with a song called 'China'. It was a terrible song from a terrible album that they released after selling their collective soul to the record-company suits and their focus groups. But their first album featured this little nugget of snarling cowpunk attitude. The singer sounds vicious and psychotic when he spits out the line 'I shot a bitch in Reno just to watch her die'.

Road Kill: Ten Musical Assaults that Didn't Turn Out so Bad

DBC PIERRE

At its sharpest, a cover version is a hit-and-run assault, smacking a song down, dragging it places it wasn't meant to go. The assailant might be somebody who thinks they can do better, or who thinks we'll believe it's a homage; or it could merely be the pop apparatus recycling itself, neither thinking, nor caring what we think. Either way, it's a forceful imposition of will upon a peaceful victim.

Putting this technical point behind us, let's now rejoice in a few that really got dragged into the bushes. Here I propose ten assaults that left their victims strangely better off.

10 'Moonlight Sonata' – Glenn Miller

In 1801, thirty-one-year-old Ludwig Van Beethoven allegedly dedicated the Piano Sonata No. 14 to his seventeen-year-old pupil, an Italian countess with whom he was in love.

History suggests the sonata, popularly titled 'Moonlight', didn't pull.

Its haunting melody wafted around unrequited for 140 years before somebody with an American sense of entitlement, namely big-band leader Glenn Miller, ripped down its flimsy pants and spanked it sore and glowing. Such an ambitious blasphemy came with a predictable cost, and Miller was duly cast into the sea in an aeroplane, never to be seen again. But if you hunt for it, his savagely passionate arrangement of the sonata is still around – much darker, fervent, with smoky sax, squeals of clarinet and screams of brass.

If Ludwig had arranged it this way, he would be on the eighteen-billionth position with the girl by now. A significant historical shame.

9 'La Quinta de Beethoven' – Cesta All Stars

While we're on Ludwig's love life, this is a fine accompaniment to musings of all he missed out on by being so serious. Here, a loosely assembled Salsa orchestra celebrates his Symphony No. 5 in the most tenuous way – in fact, this jolly nine-minute ramble challenges us to identify just which notes of the original symphony have been lifted – and the suspicion is, not a whole lot of them, given what happened to Miller. Still, lifting the title of a classical symphony and attaching it to such steamy tropical syncopations shows artistry, and, after listening for a while, you could swear it is in there somewhere – just in an infinitely less menacing way.

8 'New York, New York' – King

Frank Sinatra just wasn't famous enough to be let loose with such a chestnut, plus he dabbled in crime, and lived too long to be the true legend the song thinks it deserves. Thus, in another of history's deft corrections, the piece is here performed by Elvis Presley – or rather, by a Northern Irish postman called King who has been inhabited by Elvis. His mission on earth: to elevate this anthem to its rightful heights, and to tweak other songs by dead artists, including Kurt Cobain.

He finally lives!

7 'Quizás, Quizás, Quizás (Perhaps, Perhaps, Perhaps)' – Manny Valenz

Not to say anything about Doris Day's version, but here a harsh Latin predator sees fit to steal into the song that was supposed – after 'Que Sera Sera' didn't cut it – to add some continental edge to our girl-next-door. Manny Valenz gains entry with a high-octane Merengue band in a shameless hit-and-run assault, leaving it smeared with drumbeats and rude voice. The result can still make you think of Doris, but with an altogether different look on her face. And matted hair.

6 'James Bond' – Roland Alphonso

Something beautiful happened in the 1960s: Jamaicans, by then talented at piecing meals together from colonial masters' offal, set about pinching scraps of the masters' culture as well. I can even argue that from those early scraps, they went on to convert and possess the culture altogether.

Their vehicle: Ska, whose pilots tore great panels from the stately home of Anglo music, bashed the self-importance out of them and banged them back into languorous, clunking party structures. Needless to say, these are friendlier if dirtier tunes to inhabit. I could enter a dozen lists of pieces interfered with by Ska, from the soundtrack of *The Guns of Navarone* to 'Besame Mucho', but here offer just one example to speak for them all: the James Bond theme, suddenly alive in the absence of Bond himself.

While Anglos grew earnest scoffing the chicken's drumsticks, this is what Jamaica did with its feet. Respek.

5 'Don't Cry for Me Argentina' – Me First and the Gimme Gimmes

It's not often you find yourself cheering from the bleachers of a mugging, but this is one of those songs that really asked for it. Now a band of American rock conceptualists, including Foo Fighters guitarist Chris Shiflett, have nailed it to an alley wall where they thrash it blind in a high-speed punk-rock attack. Me First and the Gimme Gimmes are serial offenders in this respect, gleefully violating most popular songs that deserve it, and arguably a couple that don't.

Still, there's a dark appeal here, like the thought of taking a cattle prod round to your gran's.

4 'If You Leave Me Now' – Ive Mendes

Listening to men cry about abandonment just isn't sexy. It's one thing the boys who made up seventies band Chicago forgot when they wept the original. This isn't to poke sticks at issues of gender or sensitivity, or the status quo of any given time; it's just that men are pathetic wailers. Thus, despite its sweet melody and silken orchestration, the song had to wait thirty years for the right voice to take it behind a shed and smack it into context. Enter Ive Mendes, upholding the bossa nova tradition of whispering hot lullabies in a flat, husky tone, as if sung under the breath, without an audience.

Suddenly a breeze blows through it from Copacabana, and a voice you just couldn't leave.

3 'Wichita Lineman' – Jimmy Webb

An interesting cover in that it comes from an artist

snatching his own love-child back. Jimmy Webb original-ly wrote the piece for Glen Campbell, who made it famous back in the days when he sang tributes to every southern American state as if he were a native of each. Now Webb hauls it back like a mother finding her child in rehab, and rocks it in his arms. If you got anything at all out of the original, this feather-soft piano version with Webb's own voice will break your heart.

Suddenly the twang isn't power lines but heartstrings.

2 'Somewhere Over the Rainbow' – Israel Kamakawiwo'ole

We reach the category of shipwrecked icons awaiting res-cue. A teenage Judy Garland made this song her own in Louis B. Mayer's 1939 picture *The Wizard of Oz*. It went on to become her hymn, even as Hollywood oversaw her free fall through five marriages, several suicide attempts and a plague of addictions that cut her life tragically short. From its birthplace in bright, innocent longing, the song became a bitter cry from a mire of despair.

Then, in 1993, a half-naked, 340-kilogram Hawaiian with a ukulele found the thing washed up on history's beach and dragged it back up the hill. Often overlooked in music's mainstream, this rare resuscitation pumps the thing full of sincerity and innocence – perhaps, indeed, gives it the soul Hollywood never could.

Sadly, Israel himself quickly expired after this, though still a young man, due to simply being too massive. Still, we can say his work here was done. Ho'omaika'i 'ana, Israel.

1 'Send in the Clowns' – Mel Tormé

We've touched on the song for which Argentina has long since stopped crying, and probably even started laughing. Now we limp to the work whose listing demands I be clear in two vital respects: first, in separating the prodigious talent of its writer, Stephen Sondheim, from its subsequent kidnap by an infinity of aspirant sequin addicts who see the piece as a natural vehicle for Everything They Have to Give. And second, in making it utterly clear why the piece tops the list of justified, if not demanded, assaults, which is this: surely never, ever has more dire, self-pitying, bourgeois sentimentality issued from any species of organism. No sound, including my death sentence read aloud, could disperse my will to live with greater totality and speed than the first note of this tragic schmaltzfest.

I can therefore only marvel at the scale of the debt owed to Mel Tormé for wading in and blasting it with bass, rhythm and a truly bitching big-band arrangement. And I say:

You, misty-eyed, self-inflated karaoke victims: try doing the fucking thing now.

Love and Gunpowder: Ten Variants on the Screamin' Jay Hawkins Classic, 'I Put a Spell on You'

JOHN BURNSIDE

André Maurois, who knew a thing or two about both, once remarked that 'we owe to the Middle Ages the two worst inventions of humanity: romantic love and gunpowder'. I don't know which of these he thought the more dangerous, but the history of popular music is one long catalogue of stalker songs, voodoo spells and wild declarations of *amour fou* that even the Surrealists would have found disturbing, and this is the daddy of them all (as was Screamin' Jay himself, apparently: according to one report, Hawkins was 'pretty sure' that he had fathered fifty-seven children during his life; he just couldn't keep track of them all). A wild rant, complete with animal noises and saturated with unspecified menace, this great song was banned by several radio stations (for its 'cannibalistic' content), then covered by a wide range of artists before finally being inducted into the Rock and Roll Hall of Fame in the 1990s. Screamin' Jay, who composed the song in 1957 for a woman who'd walked out on him, originally performed it as a ballad, but that changed dramatically in the recording studio when, as Screamin' Jay tells it, the producer 'brought in ribs and chicken and got everybody drunk, and we came out with this weird version. I don't even remember making the record. Before, I was just a normal blues singer. I was just Jay Hawkins. It all sort of just fell in place. I found out I could do more destroying a song and screaming it to death.'

The reference to death is no accident. In spite of the gimmickry surrounding some of Hawkins's later performances and its eventual adoption as a Halloween favourite, 'I Put a Spell on You' is no mere novelty item, but a revealing glimpse into the true nature of romantic love – which, to be frank, is homicidal to the core. Some of those who have covered the song have admitted as much in their arrangements and vocals, some have tried to pretty it up, but the essential message is never far from the surface: be what I want you to be, or face the consequences. After all those silly love songs about 'waking in the park' and 'kissing in the dark', after the pleading tone of 'Love, love me do', and the masochistic whining of 'I would rather go blind, boy, than to see you walk away from me', it's refreshing when a large, rather plain man in a cape lays his cards on the table. Romantic love isn't about innocence and sweet nothings, it's about *possession*. 'You better stop the things that you do' (Watch out!) – and if you do try to get away, I'll probably come after you with a carving knife, some fava beans and a litre of duty-free Chianti . . .

Here are the ten best versions:

10 Natacha Atlas

This is the worst cover of *anything* I have ever heard – which is why it's here. Anything this bad just has to be celebrated.

9 Marilyn Manson

I put a spell on you, because you're mine – oh goth, get a life.

8 MC5

Weird and pious at the same time, as wonderful as it is dreadful, and check out the rambling, presumably political speech on the live recording, where Screamin' Jay is co-opted as a John Sinclair-style revolutionary. Far out, man.

7 Manfred Mann

They're British, you know . . .

6 Sherie Marshall

Cool jazz diva goes feminist on Jay's ass.

5 The Animals

Alan Price also did a version of this, which is probably as good, though perhaps a little too reverent.

4 Arthur Brown (and his Crazy World)

Surprisingly good.

3 Nina Simone

Classy and powerful as ever, with that extra whiff of masochist subtlety.

2 Creedence Clearwater Revival

Mad love in the swamp, this is the real Creedence, the jamming, slightly sinister, white voodoo boys from the dark interior. The audio equivalent of moonshine and pharmaceutical-grade drugs.

1 Screamin' Jay Hawkins

The original wild-eyed, finger-lickin', 57-varieties nut-job of pop, much lamented by music lovers everywhere, not to mention his innumerable grandchildren . . .

ENCORE

From a mass singalong to alternative Christmas classics

Friends of the editor / John Grindrod

Group Singalong: Ten Songs with no Particular Theme

FRIENDS OF THE EDITOR

Okay, I should explain, when putting this book together I had to do a music quiz and asked some friends to describe a favourite song of theirs (for whatever reason they wanted). The choices I got were so good I figured I should use them, and so here, sequenced by me, are ten tracks that would make a pretty fine mix. There's no hook or theme here, but think of it, if you like, as the list equivalent of the slightly embarrassing but secretly pleasurable encore when everyone groups round one mic to sing 'I Shall be Released', or 'The Weight' . . .

10 'Denis' – Blondie (Matthew De Ville)

The video of this gave me my first glimpse of Debbie Harry and while, aged only eight, I was too young to appreciate fully the pout, the hair and the New York cool, I knew then that Charlie's Angels were no longer number one.

9 'New Rose' – The Damned (Dave Watkins)

This was the first ever British punk single. It was also the song that I and my mates Tom and Ian decided would be perfect, performed instrumentally, as the cornerstone of our third-year high-school Music coursework. None of us went on to take Music GCSE.

8 'Fancy' – Bobbie Gentry (Jack Murphy)

A beautifully crafted (just) sixties funk-country classic that doubles as a heartfelt singalong number, this song has got the lot. Like any country song worth its salt, you'll laugh and you'll cry at the twists and turns of the tale, and of course there's a message to be gleaned as well. Sent out from their run-down New Orleans shack to work the streets by her desperate impoverished mother, it's not long before Fancy makes good and gets herself a sugar daddy. Even for C&W, the song's bizarre, ringing endorsement of self-improvement through prostitution is unsurpassed. Sadly, Fancy's career trajectory wasn't matched by Gentry herself, who, after huge initial success, nosedived until she retired from showbiz altogether in the late seventies. This song, though, continues to preach its message of heroic triumph over severe down-home, Deep South adversity: 'I might have been born just plain white trash, but Fancy was my name'.

7 'Oh Bondage, Up Yours' – X-Ray Spex (Jo Ellis)

I first heard this song when my cousin played it. I was about six and remember bouncing around the room. I didn't have a clue what Poly Styrene was singing, or what the song was about, but it stirred something primal and it still does. Barely decipherable lyrics, a saxophone that sounds suspiciously like a kazoo, the first line – 'Some people think little girls should be seen and not heard; but I think, Oh Bondage, Up Yours' – makes me want to fight . . .

300

6 'There are worse things I could do' – Rizzo's Song (Hannah Griffiths)

This is the heartfelt classic sung by Rizzo, the gobby, smoking Pink Lady and foil to everyone's favourite virgin, Sandy, in *Grease*. After defending her occasional sexual dalliances in the first verses, she moves towards a fleeting key shift into the major where she sings, 'I don't steal and I don't lie / But I can feel and I can cry', and it makes you remember that these are the qualities that really matter in a person; and then it goes 'And god I bet you never knew / That to cry in front of you / That's the worst thing I could do', and you realise that this was actually a love song to Kenickie and that she's really as vulnerable as Sandy, it's just she puts loads of front on. It's also the world's greatest karaoke song for ladeez.

5 'White Rabbit' – Jefferson Airplane (Will Atckinson)

Why? A strong woman's voice, plenty of drugs and no chorus. Genius.

4 'Where Do You Go To, My Lovely' – Peter Sarstedt (Andrew Benbow)

This is possibly the most kitsch, and certainly the most name-droppingest, song in the history of pop and yet there is something about it. A great mix of sixties cultural references and fairground melodies, it whips up the glamour of Paris (and an aside to the back streets of Naples), and as soon as it finishes you just want to play it again. This was recently used in *The Darjeeling Limited* in a way which suggests that, somewhere in the alchemy of melody and emotion, any scorn we feel for the song melts into nostalgic warmth.

3 'If I Was Your Girlfriend' – Prince (Lee Brackstone)

I heard it at a school disco. It made me feel very strange. I'd never heard a voice like it. Was it a man or a woman? As my David Bowie phase started to wane, a far unhealthier obsession with Prince began to take hold. It still sounds extraordinarily weird. Like the Reverend Al Green on helium.

2 'Outdoor Type' – The Lemonheads (Susan Holmes)

This is Evan Dando's brilliant, prolonged confession that he has lied about being the outdoor type in order to win the heart of a woman. In truth he's never spent a night in a tent, can't swim, can't even grow a beard. 'I can't go away with you on a rock-climbing weekend', he reasons, 'What if something's on TV and it's never shown again?' Here's a man who really needs a subscription to Sky Plus. But then there's the twist, as we find out he's not really invited after all. Whatever it is that Evan has done to try to convince her, in other words, has been to no avail and she has, presumably, gone instead with a bearded, Gore-tex clad hunk who owns his own crampons. Not just an anthem for indoor types everywhere, this is one for anyone who's ever found themselves doing something they hate in the name of love.

1 'Go Your Own Way' – Fleetwood Mac (Becky Thomas)

Lindsey Buckingham and Stevie Nicks of Fleetwood Mac break up acrimoniously. He writes a bitter love song about the demise of their relationship and then makes her sing lead vocals on it. She's effectively calling herself a cheating whore while making it sound like a redemptive, feminist anthem. And to top it off, she has a boy's name and he has a girl's name. Confusion and genius, all in three minutes of a simple pop song.

Follow that Star! Alternative Versions of Christmas Classics

JOHN GRINDROD

Since the days of Tin Pan Alley, an evergreen Christmas song with non-drop needles is something that most pop musicians aspire to produce. And if you can't manage your own then there's always a canon of seasonal greats to call upon. This Top 10 celebrates some of the best and worst versions of Christmas classics, while trying to avoid all the usual remarks you'd get on TMF about turkeys and crackers.

10 'Blue Christmas' – Elvis Presley (1957) and Low (1999)

This old American country standard was recorded by Elvis in his golden period in its most famous version. Like many of his early(ish) hits, it's a beautifully simple and driven arrangement, with the backing singers whistling like the wind through the verses while he laments his lost love in that gorgeously warm and sexy voice. It's such a definitive rendition that one might imagine that other performers would have been scared off; far from it. The list of covers includes those by Engelbert Humperdinck, Billy Idol and Shakin' Stevens. Remarkable though they are, my favourite has to be Low's pre-millennial version from their astonishing *Christmas* album, which seemed to arrive with instant nostalgia attached. This slower, more tremulous take is as delicate as newly fallen snow, Mimi Parker haunting the song like the ghost of Karen Carpenter.

9 'All I Want for Christmas Is You' – Mariah Carey (1994) and The Pipettes (2006)

It's taken me a long time to admit how much I love this song, and boy have I struggled with it. And I'm clearly not the only one, as Christmas 2007 saw it in the UK top ten alongside Wham's 'Last Christmas', entirely due to its popularity as a digital download. And I suspect it's the recent ability to buy the song by itself, while remaining untainted by the rest of Mariah's output, that has fuelled its ever-growing popularity. It seems to have made it as a proper Christmas standard, perhaps the most recent addition to the canon, in all of its Phil-Spector-via-the-*Red-Dwarf*-theme glory. And for me the breakthrough moment came at the Pipettes' Christmas show at the Roundhouse in 2006, when they finished their encores with a beautifully fluffy 'Lipstick on Your Collar'-style girl-group rendition while artificial snow fell from the ceiling. After that there was no way I could resist – lay your red carpet over me and cover me with scented tea-lights, Mariah, all I want for Christmas is you playing in Woolworth's while I queue to buy giant Toblerones and a hammer drill.

8 'Baby, It's Cold Outside' – Ella Fitzgerald and Louis Jordan (1949) and Margaret Whiting and Johnny Mercer (1949)

In the era when different record companies rushed to get competing versions of songs out, Frank Loesser's endearingly naughty duet 'Baby, It's Cold Outside' had seven competing versions released at the same time. Two of the most charming and enduring are by Ella and Louis (no, not *that* Louis, though she would sing a rambling and ludicrous version of it many years later with Louis Armstrong, when they both sounded like randy old folks in a home) and Margaret and Johnny (though you'll probably know this one as by Doris Day and Bing Crosby, to whom it's frequently misattributed). The first version goes for musicality – unsurprisingly, given the perfection of their voices. Ella's voice is lower than Louis's, which is quite sweet, and if the meaning of the song isn't communicated quite as theatrically as in some versions, the singing is heavenly, and the gentle swing of the production is as cosy as can be. Margaret Whiting and Johnny Mercer's version is surprisingly different, much saucier (the way she sings, 'Say, what's in this drink?' is rather more Rohypnol and swinging than you'd expect for the 1940s, and he sounds positively Machiavellian). It's a three-minute screwball battle of wills rather than a bit of gentle teasing, as it is between Ella and Louis. You can hear the world changing in this song – the post-war roles of frustrated women and cynical men who had seen a little too much overseas spilling over into sexy cocktail-party banter.

7 *The First Noël* (traditional) and *Carol Symphony* – Victor Hely Hutchinson (1927) reworked as the theme to *The Box of Delights* (1984)

Okay, so I'm going a little off-piste here, but *The Box of Delights* is about the most Christmassy thing I can think of, not least for the theme tune, a complex reworking of *The First Noël*. Yes, I could have done the old Greg Lake/Prokofiev thing here, but why not live a little? Hutchinson reworked this traditional carol as part of his Carol Symphony at about the same as Vaughn Williams was eating up these sort of things and spitting them out as Fantasias. It dances around *The First Noël* like a band of pagan sprites, and the TV theme version adds another layer of Radiophonic magic, as the orchestra gets sucked into a vortex of synthesised strangeness at the finale. After all that it'll make you want to hug an old Punch and Judy man.

6 'Christmas Wrapping' – The Waitresses (1981) and the Spice Girls (1998)

Every year without fail this song catches me unawares and makes me cry. 'Christmas Wrapping' is the song Frank Capra would have made had he been in a new wave band. From Patty Donahue's initial steeling, 'Christmas by myself this year' (bringing to mind Wendy Cope's assertion that 'the whole business is unbelievably dreadful if you're single') to the closing verse where she bumps into the guy she's been chasing all year while out buying those last-minute cranberries to accompany 'the world's smallest turkey'. This walks a tightrope of senti-mentality and cool in an almost impossible way and manages to be both at once. I have a lot of time for the Spice Girls – they never relied on covers, like their lazier boy-band brothers, and they had some great pop moments, but this particular number, a rare cover, wasn't one of them. It's a shouty mess, with none of the fragile bravado of the original, and adding references to Tesco and all-night garages in order to Britpop it up just makes it sound stupid. This is a fairy tale of New York. It loses something of that lovely Capraesque magic when you relocate it to Essex.

5 'White Christmas' – Bing Crosby (1942, 1947), Darlene Love (1963) and Michael Bolton (1996)

The most ubiquitous and covered Christmas pop song, Irving Berlin's classic number had its debut as a duet in *Holiday Inn* (the film, not the chain of inexpensive hotels), but the definitive Bing version was recorded five years later. It's a song all about mythologising Christmas, wanting it to be something it's unlikely to be ever again, something you may have misremembered from your childhood. Crosby's very grown-up vocal makes it a dignified resignation, passing on the baton to another for the hope of a white Christmas now that his own hopes seem so remote. Darlene Love's glorious Phil Spector version taps into the absurdity of the song as Berlin originally conceived it: 'There's never been such a day in old LA', she says of the sunny weather, making it not a lament but a joke at the expense of the myth itself and our expectations of it. Michael Bolton's cover is notable only because his frantic over-emoting makes the song sound like it's a desperate apology from a prisoner to a victim whose life he has somehow ruined, and for whom a white Christmas is the best they can now hope for ('May all your Christmases be white' has never sounded so desperate). A song for all seasons, surprisingly.

4 'Do They Know It's Christmas?' – Band Aid (1984), Band Aid II (1989) and Band Aid 20 (2004)

What is to be said? Not the best song in the world, but the three versions do tell us something about the evolution of pop in the last quarter-century. In 1984 British pop was on a world-beating high, full of pretentiously romantic bands who thought nothing of recording some high-concept charity single, whatever their ulterior motives. Pop was important, it was taken as read. By the late eighties it had become a less ambitious and confident affair, with no claims of artiness or political posturing. And by the mid-noughties the place had been taken over by Radiohead's children, tasteful dinner-party *authentics*, investing every syllable with a meaningful snivel. The original still fascinates me, and I remember That Night, when the short film of the recording of this song was shown on the telly for the first time, which left me thinking, 'But what can a *record* do?' Worth it for Bono singing 'Tonight thank God it's them instead of you', of course, which is presumably his position on the Irish tax-paying public.

3 'Sleigh Ride' – Ella Fitzgerald (1960) and The Ronettes (1963)

This is the pop troika (oh, okay, that's 'I Believe in Father Christmas', but even so . . .). Another one written in the war, like so many of these; sentimental escapist nostalgia for people kept apart by circumstances. Ella sounds like she's under a huge bearskin in her sleigh, about to drop off to sleep if only those bloody reindeer would avoid the bumps. The Ronettes, on the other hand, are standing up, cracking the whip and going at breakneck speed, thundering along in what could well be the single most brilliant piece of Christmassy production of all time.

2 'Santa Baby' – Eartha Kitt (1953) and Kylie Minogue (2000)

Such differing interpretations. In Kylie's version Santa

can expect a peck on the cheek and some warm milk. In Eartha Kitt's he will need Viagra and a safe word. Quite simply, Eartha sounds as if she will devour him in this delicious burlesque performance. I'm guessing Kylie is attempting to channel Eartha's cruel dominatrix, but she's a tabby next to a tiger. Some people are just too nice to play the bad guy convincingly. Kylie comes across as whingy and spoiled, whereas Eartha makes it all so debauched and dangerous. It's the world's most glamorous heist – *Reservoir Dogs* rewritten by Jackie Collins.

1 'Santa Claus Is Coming to Town' – The Crystals (1963) and Bruce Springsteen (1975)

Yes, more Phil Spector. Do you have a problem with that? The long chatty intro to this one, a xylophone-fuelled trip round the Milky Way, leads you to think it's going to be a slowie, but when the verse kicks in the wall of sound knocks you over with the sheer energy of it. The drumming is huge, the vocals electrifying. And Springsteen's raucous 1975 live version of it is a take, not so much of the song itself, which had been around since the thirties, but of the Crystals' cover. It's lovely because of the odd mix of machismo and playfulness. He gives the song a paternal slant, but you can't help thinking that a bit of him is imagining himself as a young black woman when he sings it, and that for me makes it all the more interesting.

Contributors

ROGER ARMSTRONG (p. 100) was social secretary at Queen's University Belfast from 1969 to 1972 and managed bands in Dublin and London from 1972 to 1974. He formed the pop/rock label Chiswick Records with two partners, Ted Carroll and Trevor Churchill, in 1975, which evolved into the reissue specialists Ace Records. He created GlobeStyle with Ben Mandelson in 1985 and chaired meetings founding World Music 1987. Still reissuing, he now has a new label, Chiku-Taku.

LAURA BARTON (p. 45) is a feature writer for the *Guardian*. She hails from Lancashire, lives in London, and her favourite song to drive to is 'Lazy Line Painter Jane' by Belle & Sebastian.

ANDREW BENBOW (p. 136) was born in Liverpool a couple of months after Paul McCartney left The Beatles. He has survived the amicable splits of several unreleased bands and is the proud owner of a Flying Nun Records rejection letter.

NEV BRADFORD (p. 87) is a singer and songwriter in the band Ray, whose LPs include *First Light*, *Deep Blue Happy*, *Daylight in the Darkroom* and *Death in Fiction*. He currently enjoys falling to sleep to the songs of Leonard Cohen.

JOHN BURNSIDE (p. 294) has published six novels, of which the most recent are *The Devil's Footprints* (2007) and *Glister* (2008). His memoir, *A Lie About My Father*, won the Saltire Scottish Book of the Year and the Scottish Arts Council's Non-fiction Book of the Year awards. He is currently working on a second autobiographical book, entitled *Waking up in Toytown*.

ANGUS CARGILL (pp. 40, 187) lives in south-east London and works in publishing. If push came to shove, he would pick Steve Earle's *Train a Comin'* as his all time favourite album, probably.

KEVIN CUMMINS (p. 249) was born in Manchester. He worked for the *New Musical Express* from 1977 to 1997 as well as freelancing for other major publications worldwide. His photographs are in the permanent collections of many galleries, including the National Portrait Gallery, the Museum of Film & Photography, the Museum of Fashion and the V&A Museum. A career retrospective: *Manchester: Looking for the Light Through the Pouring Rain*, will be published by Faber and Faber in 2009.

SAM DELANEY (pp. 10, 261) writes for the *Guardian* and is the author of *Get Smashed: The Men Who Made the Adverts that Changed Our Lives*. He has written and presented documentaries for the BBC, Channel 4 and Channel Five and also appears regularly on BBC Radio Five Live.

MICHEL FABER (p. 216) is the author of eight books, including the highly acclaimed *The Fahrenheit Twins* (2005), the international bestseller *The Crimson Petal and the White* (2002) and the Whitbread-shortlisted *Under the Skin* (2000), all published by Canongate. His

312

most recent publication was *The Fire Gospel* (Canongate, 2008), a reinterpretation of the myth of Prometheus.

LAVINIA GREENLAW (p. 238) has published three books of poems, most recently *Minsk* (Faber and Faber, 2003), and two novels: *Mary George of Allnorthover* (Flamingo, 2001) and *An Irresponsible Age* (Fourth Estate, 2006). Her memoir *The Importance of Music to Girls* was published by Faber and Faber in 2007. She has collaborated with artists and composers, and makes radio programmes. She lives in London and is Professor of Creative Writing at the University of East Anglia.

NIALL GRIFFITHS (p. 196) was born in Liverpool in 1966 and now lives in Wales. He is the author of six acclaimed novels: *Grits* (2000), *Sheepshagger* (2001), *Kelly + Victor* (2002), *Stump* (2003), *Wreckage* (2005) and *Runt* (2007), all published by Jonathan Cape.

JOHN GRINDROD (pp. 267, 304) is a karaoke fan. His top number is Michael Jackson's 'Earth Song'. 'Deceptacon' by Le Tigre makes him want to form a dance troupe and if he could be a member of any band it would be Althea and Donna (and John).

ALEXANDRA HEMINSLEY (p. 191) is the author of *Ex and the City: You're Nobody 'Til Somebody Dumps You* (Macmillan, 2007). She is a contributing editor at *Elle* magazine and writes regularly for the *Observer* and *Time Out*. She is books editor for BBC Radio 2's arts show *The Weekender*.

313

WILL HODGKINSON (p. 67) is a writer, amateur guitarist and lifelong garage-punk loser. He is the author of *Guitar Man: A Six-string Odyssey* (Bloomsbury, 2006) and *Song Man: A Melodic Adventure, or My Single-minded Approach to Songwriting* (Bloomsbury, 2007) and writes on music and culture for the *Guardian*, *The Times*, *Vogue* and *Mojo*. He first heard garage bands as a teenager and continues to annoy his family by playing 'I Never Loved Her' by the Starfires first thing on a Saturday morning.

JOHN KELLY (p. 162) once presented a three-hour-long special of chicken songs on national radio in Ireland. In spite of it, he still works as a writer and broadcaster and presents arts, music and travel programmes on RTE Television. He is the author of several books including *The Little Hammer* (Jonathan Cape, 2000) and *Sophisticated Boom Boom* (Jonathan Cape, 2003), and he is currently working on a 'proper' novel.

RICHARD T. KELLY (p. 61) is the author of *Alan Clarke* (Faber and Faber, 1998), *The Name of This Book is Dogme 95* (Faber and Faber, 2000), *Sean Penn: His Life and Times* (2004) and the novel *Crusaders* (Faber and Faber, 2008). He also edited *Ten Bad Dates with De Niro* (Faber and Faber, 2007), this book's cinematic cousin.

NICK KENT (p. 77) is the author of the acclaimed collection *The Dark Stuff* (Faber and Faber, 2007). He made his name as a contributor to the *New Musical Express* during the 1970s, and also enjoyed a career as a musician working with the Sex Pistols and his own group the Subterraneans. In 2002 he was presented with the

NME/Brats 'God-like genius' award for his thirty-year career as a rock writer, and he is currently a contributor to the *Guardian*, *Mojo* and France's *Libération*. He lives in Paris.

OWEN KING (p. 7) is the author of *We're All in This Together: A Novella and Stories* (Faber and Faber, 2006), and co-editor (with John McNally) of *Who Can Save Us Now? Brand-new Superheroes and Their Amazing (Short) Stories* (Free Press, 2008), an anthology of original literary fiction about modern superheroes. He lives in New York with his wife, the novelist Kelly Braffet.

RICHARD KING (p. 81) has worked for Domino Recording Co. throughout the label's history, from its formative years to its current position as the international home of Arctic Monkeys and Franz Ferdinand among others. His roles have included A&R, head of international and copywriter. He has also worked as a curator, concert promoter and publicist.

HARI KUNZRU (p. 177) is the author of the novels *The Impressionist* (2002), *Transmission* (2004) and *My Revolutions* (2007), all published by Hamish Hamilton. His work has been translated into twenty-one languages. In 2003 *Granta* named him one of its twenty best young British novelists. He is deputy president of English PEN.

JONATHAN LETHEM (p. 205) is the author of seven novels, including *The Fortress of Solitude* (Faber and Faber, 2003) and *Motherless Brooklyn* (Faber and Faber, 1999), which won the National Book Critics Circle Award among other awards. He has also written two story collections, a novella and a collection of essays, has edited *The Vintage Book of Amnesia* (Vintage, 2000), guest-edited *Da Capo Best Music Writing 2002* (Da Capo, 2002), and was the founding fiction editor of *Fence* magazine. His writings have appeared in the *New Yorker*, *Rolling Stone*, *McSweeney's* and many other periodicals. He lives in Brooklyn, New York.

GARY LIGHTBODY (p. 114) is best known as the frontman of the band Snow Patrol, whose multi-million-selling albums include *Final Straw* and *Eyes Open*. He also founded the Scottish collective the Reindeer Section, and has collaborated with Mogwai and Lisa Hannigan among others.

PATRICK McCABE (p. 145) was born in Ireland in 1955. His novels include *The Butcher Boy* (Picador, 1992) and *Breakfast on Pluto* (Picador, 1998), which were both made into acclaimed films, directed by Neil Jordan. His most recent novel, *Winterwood* (Bloomsbury, 2006), won the Hughes & Hughes Irish Novel of the Year in 2007.

STEVE McINTYRE (p. 284) is the proprietor of the music blog Cover Freak (www.coverfreak.com). He is obsessed with cover songs and Major League Baseball.

TOM McRAE (p. 158) is a British singer-songwriter. He has been nominated for both the Mercury Music Prize and a Brit Award. A survivor of the harrowing New Acoustic Movement, he now he divides his time between New York and London, when not on tour.

RICHARD MILWARD (p. 257) was born in Middlesbrough and is presently studying Fine Art at Central St Martin's College of Art & Design, London. His highly acclaimed debut novel, *Apples*, was published in 2007 by Faber & Faber.

RICK MOODY (p. 128) is the author of *The Omega Force* (2008), *The Diviners* (2006), *The Black Veil* (2004), *Demonology* (2000), all published by Faber & Faber, *Purple America* (Flamingo, 1998), *The Ring of Brightest Angels Around Heaven* (Abacus, 1998), *The Ice Storm* (Abacus, 1995, which was made into an acclaimed feature film by Ang Lee), and *Garden State* (Little, Brown, 1997). He has contributed fiction and essays to the *New Yorker*, *Esquire*, the *Paris Review*, *Harper's*, *Grand Street* and the *New York Times*. He lives in New York.

JACK MURPHY (p. 240) lives in London. The first LP he owned was *Shaky* by Shakin' Stevens.

PETER MURPHY (p. 91) is a senior writer for Dublin's *Hot Press* and a contributor to *Rolling Stone* and *Music Week*. He is also a regular guest on RTE's arts review show *The View*, and has contributed liner notes to the forthcoming remastered edition of the *Anthology of American Folk Music*. His debut novel *John the Revelator* will be published by Faber & Faber in spring 2009.

JEB LOY NICHOLS (p. 279) was born and grew up in the American Midwest. For the past twenty years he has lived in England and Wales, working as a musician and artist.

317

PETER PATNAIK (p. 272) grew up tall and strong in the great land of North Carolina. That is where he currently resides and attends to 'Honey Where You Been So Long?' – an mp3 blog documenting the pre-war era of blues music. It grew up tall and strong at www.prewarblues.-org.

DAVID PEACE (p. 74) was chosen as one of *Granta's* Best of Young British Novelists in 2003. He is the author of *The Red Riding Quartet* (Serpent's Tail, 1999–2002), *GB84* (Faber & Faber, 2004), which won the James Tait Black Memorial Prize, *The Damned Utd* (Faber & Faber, 2006) and *Tokyo Year Zero* (Faber and Faber, 2007). He has lived in Tokyo for thirteen years.

AMANDA PETRUSICH (p. 19) is a writer for Pitchforkmedia.com and a senior contributing editor at *Paste* magazine. Her work has appeared in *Spin*, the *Village Voice* and the *Oxford American*. She is the author of *Nick Drake: Pink Moon* (2007), part of Continuum's $33^{1}/_{3}$ series, and *It Still Moves: Lost Songs, Lost Highways and the Search for the Next American Music* (Faber and Faber, 2008).

DBC PIERRE (p. 288) is the author of two novels, *Ludmila's Broken English* (Faber and Faber, 2006) and *Vernon God Little* (Faber and Faber, 2003), which won the Man Booker Prize, the Whitbread First Novel Award, and the Bollinger Everyman Wodehouse Award for comic Writing in 2003.

SIMON REYNOLDS (pp. 21, 221) is the author of *Blissed Out: The Raptures of Rock* (Serpent's Tail, 1990), *The Sex Revolts: Gender, Rebellion and Rock and*

Roll (co-written with Joy Press; Serpent's Tail, 1995), *Energy Flash: A Journey through Rave Music and Dance Culture* (Picador, 1998), *Rip it Up and Start Again: Postpunk 1978–1984* (Faber, 2006) and *Bring the Noise: Twenty Years of Hip Hop and Hip Rock* (Faber and Faber, 2007).

JON SAVAGE (p. 167) is the author of *England's Dreaming: Sex Pistols and Punk Rock* (Faber and Faber, 1991) and *Teenage: The Creation of Youth, 1875–1945* (Chatto and Windus, 2007). He has written sleeve notes for Wire, St Etienne and the Pet Shop Boys, among others, and his compilations include *Meridian 1970* (Heavenly/EMI, 2005), *Queer Noises: From the Closet to the Charts 1961–1976* (Trikont, 2006) and *Dreams Come True: Classic Electro 1982–87* (Domino, 2008).

STAV SHEREZ (p. 153) is the author of *The Devil's Playground* (Penguin, 2006), shortlisted for the John Creasey CWA Dagger for best first novel. His short story 'God Box' appeared in *Perverted by Language* (Serpent's Tail, 2007). He is also a music critic and journalist. He has written for the *Daily Telegraph*, *Comes with a Smile* and *Zembla* amongst others. He is currently literary editor of the *Catholic Herald* (despite not being Catholic).

ALI SMITH (p. 227) was born in Inverness in 1962 and lives in Cambridge. Her books include *Free Love* (Virago, 1995), *Hotel World* (Hamish Hamilton, 2001), *The Accidental* (Hamish Hamilton, 2005) and, *Girl Meets Boy* (Canongate, 2007). Her work has been shortlisted for and won several awards.

MATT THORNE (p. 232) is the author of six novels, including *Eight Minutes Idle* (Sceptre, 1999, winner of an Encore Prize) and *Cherry* (Weidenfeld & Nicolson, 2004, longlisted for the Booker Prize). He also co-edited the anthologies *All Hail the New Puritans* (Fourth Estate, 2000) and *Croatian Nights* (Serpent's Tail, 2005).

MIRIAM TOEWS (p. 35) was born in Steinbach, Manitoba, and currently lives in Winnipeg with her family. She is the author of three novels: *A Boy of Good Breeding* (Stoddart, 1998), *A Complicated Kindness* (Faber and Faber, 2004), which won the Governor General's Award, and *The Flying Troutmans* (Knopf, 2008).

CATHI UNSWORTH (p. 105) has worked as a journalist for *Sounds*, *Melody Maker* and *Bizarre* magazine, and now works as a freelance editor. She is the author of the acclaimed novels *The Not Knowing* (2006) and *The Singer* (2007), as well as the editor of *London Noir: Capital Crime Fiction*, all published by Serpent's Tail.

WILLY VLAUTIN (p. 54) grew up in Reno, Nevada. He is the author of two acclaimed novels, *The Motel Life* (Faber and Faber, 2006) and *Northline* (Faber and Faber, 2008). He is also the songwriter and vocalist for the band Richmond Fontaine, whose albums include *Winnemucca* (2002), *Post to Wire* (2004), and *Thirteen Cities* (2006). He lives in Portland, Oregon.

JOHN WILLIAMS (pp. 123, 209) lives and works in Cardiff, where he has set several books including the imaginatively named *Cardiff Trilogy* (Bloomsbury,

2006). His latest book is *Michael X* (Century, 2007), a biography of the British black-power entrepreneur. He recently helped curate a tribute album called *Migrating Bird: The Songs of Lal Waterson* (Honest Jon's Records), which he earnestly encourages you all to check out.

KATHRYN WILLIAMS (p. 184) is a singer-songwriter from Liverpool living in Newcastle. She has made seven very good albums, the most recent of which is *Two*, with Neill MacColl. People like to tell her she was once nominated for a Mercury music prize. She knows. The award is very nice.